IN THE SOVIET HOUSE OF CULTURE

IN THE SOVIET HOUSE
OF CULTURE

A CENTURY OF PERESTROIKAS

Bruce Grant

PRINCETON UNIVERSITY PRESS   PRINCETON, NEW JERSEY

Library of Congress Cataloging-in-Publication Data

Grant, Bruce, 1964–
In the Soviet house of culture : a century of perestroikas / Bruce Grant.
p. cm.
Includes bibliographical references and index.
ISBN 0-691-03722-1 (cl : alk. paper).—ISBN 0-691-04432-5 (pa : alk. paper)
1. Gilyaks. 2. Ethnology—Russia (Federation)—Sakhalin.
3. Sakhalin (Russia)—Ethnic relations. I. Title.
DK759.G5G7   1995
305.8′009577—dc20   95–13063

This publication was prepared in part under a grant
from the Kennan Institute for Advanced Russian Studies
of the Woodrow Wilson Center for Scholars, Washington, D.C.
The statements and views expressed herein are those of the author
and not necessarily those of the Wilson Center.

Optimis parentibus

Contents

Illustrations

Maps

Photographs and Drawings

Preface _____

WALKING INTO any number of Moscow or St. Petersburg bookstores at the end of the Soviet period, I was always taken by the rows of books filed under "Soviet Cultural Construction," volumes dedicated to the production of an expressly Soviet way of life to bring together the vast state. The idea that culture is something to be produced, invented, constructed, or reconstructed underlined so much of the USSR's social vision, and its stunning reach was perhaps nowhere more strikingly seen than in the ways it transformed the lives of the peoples living along its furthest borders.

This book charts the cultural history of an indigenous people of the Russian Far East, the Nivkhi of Sakhalin Island, over the course of the twentieth century. Their collective trajectories over the late imperial and then Soviet periods speak to a process of modernization undertaken at remarkably great speed, and to a stunning roller coaster of shifts in state policy toward them. The very disdain in which they were held by Russian Orthodox missionaries, and the "lack of culture" which was presumed of them by European travelers, in turn made them ideal candidates for reformation under the new Soviet government, blank slates onto which a new Soviet way of life could be inscribed. Whereas tsarist officials hounded Nivkhi for their pagan ways, early bolshevik officials praised them, establishing hospitals and native-language schools in remote areas, a certain degree of local autonomy, and an array of cultural freedoms. Stalin, in turn, routed them, Khrushchev gave respite, Brezhnev paid as little attention as possible, and Gorbachev announced he would set them free. But who were these people after seventy years of Soviet rule? What transpired along the way?

The book therefore is part ethnography and part history, the product of my having set out to do a portrait of Nivkh lives in 1990, at the very moment when, with the disintegration of the state around them, nearly everyone I came to know was wrapped in an almost hypnotic gaze on the past. Had I arrived on North Sakhalin at almost any other time, say, in 1989 when the optimism brought on by elections to a new Soviet congress seized the country, or in 1991 when popular disillusion with all political avenues seemed to lead to a gritty nihilism, the book might have been a very different one. But the fascination with looking back was something I quickly grew to share, and the result is a story, in effect, that keenly challenged my own expectations at almost every juncture.

Three arguments underscore the chapters ahead. The first foregrounds and challenges the lens of timeless exotica through which we so often view indigenous peoples. Although Nivkhi I knew were aggravated by the remains of the Soviet period, by the gradual diminution of their own language, and by the routine discrimination exerted by others, they were far from passive or tragic figures at the hands of the Soviet state. From World War II on, Nivkhi considered themselves active participants in the design and implementation of state policy, and many of the nascent activists speaking out against the state in 1990 had been its most ardent supporters only decades earlier. A spirit of loss and mourning pervades the narratives here, but for Nivkhi the close of the Soviet period brought a bitter *double* irony, marking the loss of a distinctly Nivkh cultural tradition few could even know firsthand and the loss of the Soviet icons and symbols they had traded theirs in for. The Nivkh experience over the twentieth century was a tumultuous one, and over the course of six political generations, from Nicholas II to Gorbachev, Nivkh schoolchildren have been taught, in effect, that native life and language was to be forgotten, remembered, forgotten, remembered, forgotten, and now remembered again. But how much can be remembered after seventy years of social reeducation? How does this make us rethink the very notion of tradition, when so many Nivkh traditions are, in effect, statist ones?

This spurs us then to a second set of questions, to ask how we might produce new readings of Soviet and post-Soviet nationality policies that recognize the very hybrid identities produced by the Soviet state. Without the specificity of the lived experience of nationality reforms on Sakhalin, standard narratives of policies imposed by a homogenous state on a resistant populace do little to help us recognize the many Nivkhi who ardently supported state efforts even during what are now considered to be the darkest periods. I want to argue here for the production of a pan-Soviet identity that was reasonably effective among Nivkhi, and that brings us closer to understanding some of the mechanisms of persuasion and control by which states exert hegemony over their constituents.

Third, I am interested in the very way we look at the state in the process of cultural construction. When we look for cultural identity, our loci are commonly "nations," "ethnic groups," and smaller, more discrete communities, but states too, the holders of the monopoly over legitimate violence, by Weber's spare definition, beg these limits. In contemporary anthropology, the growing attention that has been paid to the invention of culture, the invention of tradition, and the production of national ideologies brings us closer to the spirit of the literature on Soviet cultural construction. With examples all around us, increasingly we know that states too have nationalist agendas of their own, creating discourses of homogeneity out of heterogeneity, order out of disorder, and purity out of impurity.[1] What remains, though, is a popular sense that statist efforts at culture creation are diminished by their artificiality. As reconstructions imposed from above, they want for authenticity. Yet who make up authentic Nivkhi today?

That the close of the Soviet period should become known as "perestroika," or restructuring, was only one of the many ironies for Nivkhi in the Soviet order. To learn of their experience became a process of navigating people's memories and historical records constantly being reconstituted, and of realizing that this latest round of perestroika was, for Nivkhi and Russians alike, only another in a long series of reconstructions over the twentieth century.

Acknowledgments

RESEARCH for this project was conducted over the course of five stays in the former Soviet Union and Russia: in Moscow from January to May 1989, and from September 1989 to March 1990; on Sakhalin Island from April to October 1990; in Moscow and Leningrad in November 1990 and November 1991; on Sakhalin Island again, and in Tomsk, from June to August 1992; and finally in St. Petersburg in March 1994. I am grateful to the following institutions for their support: Sigma Xi, the Scientific Society; the Social Sciences and Humanities Research Council of Canada; the Association of Colleges and Universities of Canada; and the National Science Foundation. During the writing, I was greatly aided by the support of Rice University; the Social Science Research Council; the Harriman Institute at Columbia University; the Kennan Institute in Washington, D.C.; and the Faculty Research Program at Swarthmore College.

Although this is not an ethnography of traditional Nivkh life, I owe an enormous debt to the Russian and Soviet ethnographers on whose far more extensive researches into Nivkh life I was able to rely when my own investigations found little of the world they had so richly described. Over the course of my research in Moscow and St. Petersburg, I was given the support of many associates of the Miklukho-Maklai Institute of Ethnography (now the Institute of Ethnology and Anthropology), including Sergei Aleksandrovich Arutiunov, Anna Borodatova, Elena Novik, the late Sergei Serov, Anna Vasil'evna Smoliak, Chuner Mikhailovich Taksami, Valerii Aleksandrovich Tishkov, and many others. I am grateful also to Aidyn Jebrailov, Irina Monthéard, Sergey Mouraviev, Vladimir Zinov'evich Panfilov, Nikolai Pesochinskii, Aleksandr Pika, Vladimir Sangi, and Olga Vainshtein. I am particularly indebted to Galina Aleksandrovna Razumikova for allowing me to work with the personal archive of her husband, Erukhim Kreinovich.

A chance meeting with Zhargal Murmane in November 1989 led to my eventual permission to travel to Sakhalin for the first time; it was from this meeting on that I was inducted into the generosity of Nivkhi who granted me their time and hospitality far beyond anything I had anticipated. I am especially grateful to Zoia Ivanovna Iugain, Lidiia Dem'ianovna Kimova, Murman Kimov, Galina Dem'ianovna Lok, Antonina Iakovlevna Nachetkina, Galina Fedorovna Ialina, and Valerii Ialin, who so regularly welcomed me into their homes during my peregrinations back and forth across North Sakhalin.

Having arrived on Sakhalin in April 1990 after a laborious and labyrinthine visa process, to what was then a closed border zone, it is unlikely I would have been granted permission to remain without the immediate support of the Sakhalin Regional Museum, which became the sponsoring institution for both my Sakhalin stays. I am grateful to the director, Vladimir Mikhailovich Latyshev, and to the rare collective of congenial and productive scholars at the museum, including Kira Cherpakova, Marina Ishchenko, Gennadi Matiushkov, Valerii Pereslavtsev, Mikhail Prokof'ev, Tania Roon, Valerii Shubin, Olga Shubina, Sasha Solov'ev, Mikhail Vysokov (now of the Sakhalin Center for the Documentation of Modern History), and Lena Zlatogorskaia. I am also particularly grateful to the staff of the Sakhalin State Archive. The bulk of the archival documents used in this study, including those eventually obtained in Tomsk, would not have been available to me without the unflagging kindness of Galina Ivanovna Dudarets.

During both stays on Sakhalin I was treated with many generosities from Nivkhi and Russians, including Konstantin Agniun, Tatiana Agniun, Zoia Ivanovna Agniun, Dmitrii Baranov, Liudmila Belskaia, Gennadi Belskii, Raisa Ivanovna Chepikova, Petr Dzhunkovskii, Boris Ivanovich Iakovenko, Ilur, Misha Iugain, Oleg Iugain, Sasha Iugain, Kalrik, Vera Khein, Ivan Khein, Aleksandra Khuriun, Sergei Kokarev, Nadezhda Aleksandrovna Laigun, Zoia Ivanovna Liutova, Elizaveta Ermolaevna Merkulova, Sergei Mychenko, Lusia Mun, Pavel Nasin, Anatolii Ngavan, Olia Ngavan, Galina Otaina, Svetlana Filippovna Polet'eva, Valentina Poliakova, Lena Prussakova, Mariia Nikolaevna Pukhta, Zoia L'vovna Ronik, Olga Afanasevna Rezantseva, Antonina Shkaligina, Viktor Borisovich Sirenko, Alla Viktorovna Siskova, Nikolai Vasil'evich Solov'ev, Raisa Taigun, Kirill Taigun, Tatiana Uleta, and Andrei Zlatogorskii. Special thanks also go to the convivial collective of Aeroflot in Okha, who I hope will forgive the otherwise untoward attention I direct toward their parent institution in chapter 7.

At Swarthmore College many of my students read the manuscript in draft stages and offered what were among the liveliest critiques of the work in progress. I am grateful to Sarah Adams, Kenrick Cato, Megan Cunningham, Krister Johnson, and Zaineb Khan from my seminar on historiography; and to Karen Birdsall, Kate Ellsworth, Caitlin Murdock, Andy Perrin, Chris Pearson, Erik Rehl, Laura Starita, and Hong-An Tran from the course on Soviet culture.

Finally I would like to thank George Marcus, my original research director, as well as Marjorie Mandelstam Balzer and Natalya Sadomskaia, each of whom gave critical advice and warm support from the project's inception to the final stages of writing. Marjorie Mandelstam Balzer, Caroline Humphrey, and John Stephan each provided considered criticisms to Princeton University Press, which they generously shared with me. Each have set standards in their own work which I have long admired, though my efforts to take up their recommendations here may seem at best partial. Mary Murrell from Princeton University Press took an early interest in the manuscript and gave all that one might hope for in a model editor.

I am grateful to a final group of colleagues, many of whom have read the manuscript in various drafts or have helped by way of advice and example: David Anderson, Alice and Dennis Bartels, Melissa Cefkin, Lindsay DuBois, Michael Fischer, Douglas Holmes, Jamer Hunt, Karen Knop, Igor Krupnik, Kim Laughlin, George and Melissa Opryszko, Stefania Pandolfo, Alcida Ramos, Nancy Ries, Patricia Seed, Mariya Sevela, Corinna Snyder, Yuri Slezkine, Pamela Smart, Nikolai Ssorin-Chaikov, Julie Taylor, Stephen Tyler, Douglas Vogt, and Robin Wagner-Pacifici.

Note on Transliteration and Terminology _____

THE TRANSLITERATION of Russian words follows the Library of Congress system. Soft signs and hard signs from the Russian language are recognized with one and two apostrophes, respectively. I make general exceptions for accepted Western spellings of names such as *Yeltsin*, rather than *El'tsyn*.

Rendering the names of Siberian and Far Eastern indigenous groups has proved the greater challenge to consistency. The important distinction for most readers will be between *Nivkhi*, the Russian word most widely used by Nivkhi and non-Nivkhi alike to denote Nivkh individuals in the plural (such as Sakhalin Nivkhi), and *Nivkh*, used here as a singular noun or adjective (such as Nivkh fisherman or the Nivkh language). I have not followed the Nivkh-language plural variant of *Nivkhgu* given the infrequency with which the term is used among Nivkhi themselves on Sakhalin.

Through the nineteenth century to the late 1920s Nivkhi were known in the Russian administrative and ethnographic literature as *Giliaki*, or in English translations as *Giliaks*.

In formal lists of Siberian ethnic groups I have followed the standardized Russian plural forms (*Khanty, Mansi, Tofalary*) for reference purposes. In less formal instances throughout the text I have used anglicized plurals to render the groups in a more readable fashion (*Giliaks, Buriats, Yakuts*).

Abbreviations ————————————————————

Since the end of the Soviet period some of the Russian archives below have changed both names and referencing systems. Here and throughout the text I refer to the names in use at the time of my research.

AMNH   American Museum of Natural History, New York

GASO   *Gosudarstvennyi Arkhiv Sakhalinskoi Oblasti* (State Archive of the Sakhalin Oblast'), Iuzhno-Sakhalinsk

INION   *Institut Nauchnykh Informatsii po Obshchestvennym Naukam* (Institute of Scientific Information in the Social Sciences), Moscow

IRKISVA   *Isvestiia Russkogo Komiteta dlia Izucheniia Srednei i Vostochnoi Azii v Istoricheskom, Arkheologicheskom, Lingvisticheskom i Etnograficheskom Otnosheniiakh* (Bulletin of the Russian Committee for the Study of Central and East Asia—History, Archeology, Linguistics, and Ethnography), St. Petersburg

PF AAN RF   *Peterburgskii Filial Arkhiva Akademii Nauk Russkoi Federatsii* (Petersburg Branch of the Archive of the Academy of Sciences of the Russian Federation), St. Petersburg

SOKM   *Sakhalinskii Oblastnoi Kraevedcheskii Muzei* (Sakhalin Regional Museum), Iuzhno-Sakhalinsk

TsGADV   *Tsentral'nyi Gosudarstvennyi Arkhiv Dal'nego Vostoka* (Central State Archive of the Far East, now the *Russkii Gosudarstvennyi Arkhiv Dal'nego Vostoka (RGADV)*, Russian State Archive of the Far East), Tomsk

TsGAOR   *Tsentral'nyi Gosudarstvennyi Arkhiv Oktiabrskoi Revoliutsii* (Central State Archive of the October Revolution, now part of the *Gosudarstvennyi Arkhiv Russkoi Federatsii (GARF)*, State Archive of the Russian Federation), Moscow

ZPOIRGO   *Zapiski Priamurskogo Otdela Imperatorskogo Russkogo Geograficheskogo Obshchestva* (Bulletin of the Amur Region Branch of the Imperial Russian Geographic Society), Khabarovsk

IN THE SOVIET HOUSE OF CULTURE

One

Introduction

> The train was flying . . . Across the windows from
> left to right, swirls the obelisk: "Europe-Asia" . . .
> It is a senseless post. Now it is behind us. Does
> that mean we are in Asia? Curious! We are moving
> toward the East at a terrific speed and we carry the
> revolution with us. Never again shall we be Asia.
>   *(Valentin Petrovich Kataev*, Time, Forward!)[1]

FEW COUNTRIES threw themselves into the headlong rush of modernity
as did the Soviet Union earlier this century, and few have carried the
many faces of modernism to their furthest and most compelling extremes.
Poised after World War I on the heels of stunning change, the new USSR
announced a decisive break from the imperial past. But what would constitute the new Soviet character? From the 1840s on, much of public debate in Russia had labored over its direction for the future. Would it open
its doors to Europe and the West, cast at once as cosmopolitan and ruth-
lessly self-serving, or would it turn to an Asia it saw by turn as meditative,
mystical, and crude? Where lay the future of the empire, and what to
make of the dozens of nationalities that composed it?

"Time flew through us," Kataev continued, as the Siberian cement
workers of his folkloric 1933 novel, *Time, Forward!*, raced to surpass the
quotas set for them by the government. As Stalin, ascendant in Kataev's
text, had explained,

> This was the history of old Russia: it was continually beaten because of back-
> wardness. It was beaten by Mongol khans. It was beaten by Turkish beks. It
> was beaten by Swedish feudal lords. It was beaten by Polish and Lithuanian
> gentry. It was beaten by English and French capitalists. It was beaten by Japa-
> nese barons. It was beaten because of military backwardness, cultural back-
> wardness, agricultural backwardness. It was beaten because it was profitable to
> do so and because the beating went unpunished. That is why we cannot be
> backward anymore.[2]

The USSR set itself to overcome its legacy of backwardness through an
express charge into the modern. But by the time Stalin came to power,
the country had already seen at least two directions emerge from the

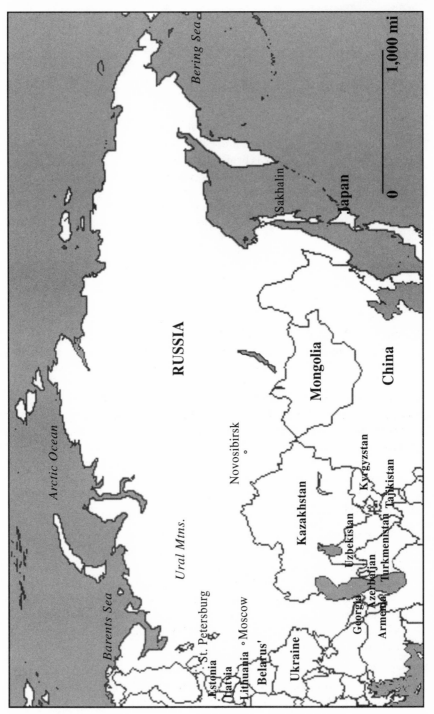

Map 1: Russia and the Former Soviet Union

modernizing gauntlet. The first was a remarkable flourishing in the arts and letters brought about by a sense of release from the past and the acmeism of the future. Experiments abounded. From conductorless orchestras in Moscow, to new utopian family communities, to the unlikely angles of Konstantin Mel'nikov's constructivist architecture, modernity challenged the very parameters of social thought. But at the same time, through the new channels of communication opened by technology, and the attendant shifts in economic and political life, modernization also set about a streamlining of the cultural sphere.[3]

The two emergent trends—one to diversity, the other to uniformity—point in turn to the early stages of Soviet nationality policy. The break from the tsarist credo of "Autocracy, Orthodoxy, and Nationality," set by Count Sergei Uvarov in the 1830s, signaled a clarion call to nationalities throughout the former Russian Empire to realize their independence freely under the banner of the socialist state. Lenin for his own part, as Frederick Starr has written, was eager to allow enough latitude to marshal support for the fledgling Union.[4] In theory, however, the textbook version went differently. Maintaining that ethnic tension was class-based, the bolsheviks held that the disappearance of class struggles under communism would in turn cause interethnic struggles (and perforce, ethnic identity) to atrophy. Free of oppression, Soviet peoples would flourish and come together as a new international ethnos.

The path of Soviet nationality policy throughout the Soviet period reverberated between these two mutual constructs. It was clear with time that the government was not looking to erase ethnic difference, but the competing politics of sameness and difference set the stage for a series of policy shifts, epochs unto themselves, throughout the country's tenure.

At the time of the October Revolution in 1917, sixty-five hundred kilometers to the east, some forty-five hundred Nivkhi lived on the northern half of Sakhalin Island and on the banks of the Amur River on the mainland, a territory widely considered their ancestral homeland. Russia had nominally governed their lands from the mid-nineteenth century, but the exigencies of distance had minimized the state's influence. Where Russian peasants across Siberia knew their relative independence in the maxim, "God is high in the sky and the tsar is far away," Nivkhi were still more decidedly in an Asian orbit. Fishermen and hunters with a complex language and an animist belief system, Nivkhi were active traders with their Asian neighbors, and many spoke a mix of Nivkh, Japanese, Chinese, and Russian to facilitate these ends. As an indigenous people once under the sway of Chinese Manchuria on the mainland, and on an enormous coastal island only fifty kilometers north of Japan, Nivkhi were part of an expressly Asian sphere that dominated the Sakhalin of that day. They were soon part of a country whose very vision of Asia would recast them, and whose very vision of time would transform them.

When I first began research on Siberian peoples in Moscow in 1989, perestroika was well under way, but access to field research for foreign researchers was, as it had been for decades, still considerably limited. With the prospect of not obtaining field access at all, I chose to study Nivkhi over other Siberian indigenous groups because of the enormous corpus of Russian-language literature devoted to them and the possibilities this presented as a project in reserve. Nivkhi, or Giliaks, as they were known before the October Revolution, are one of the five far eastern Siberian native peoples referred to as Paleoasiatics, largely because their language is so unique that it corresponds to no other linguistic group. In more popular nineteenth-century circles, Nivkhi figured in the Russian imagination as the notorious bounty hunters of fugitives on the run from Sakhalin's legendary prisons. The "Hades of Russia," Sakhalin was the most dreaded of exile posts at the turn of the century, and the most expert Nivkh hunters were rewarded for placing their talents in the service of the state. Indeed it was partly Sakhalin's dark history of exile suffering that has contributed to Nivkhi being one of the most studied of all Siberian indigenous peoples.[5]

Despite these scholarly riches, particularly those from the Soviet period, the materials that were not there often made more of an impression on me than those that were. With the exigencies of censorship both induced and imposed, the Soviet literature from the 1930s on gave us little sense of how Soviet policies, particularly those aimed at internationalizing the "small peoples" of Siberia and the Far East, the twenty-six numerically small groups delineated by the Soviet government in 1924, affected people's lives at the local level. There are few accounts where indigenous voices play a role, save for effusive testimonies to the success of Soviet government, which tell us mainly about the formulae of patriotic texts. We know a great deal, for example, about the prerevolutionary ways of life of Nivkhi *within* their own communities, such as kinship relations, belief systems, and material culture, yet we find little if anything on relations *between* Nivkhi and other groups. We know much about the early achievements of Sovietization, but learning how the Soviet vision was implemented and received in Nivkh communities requires a certain amount of piecing together.

Western literature on Soviet nationality policies is not readily helpful in providing answers, given the Western predilection for studies of Russians and the larger nationalities in the former non-Russian republics. Moreover, although Soviet scholarly works were largely approving of Soviet

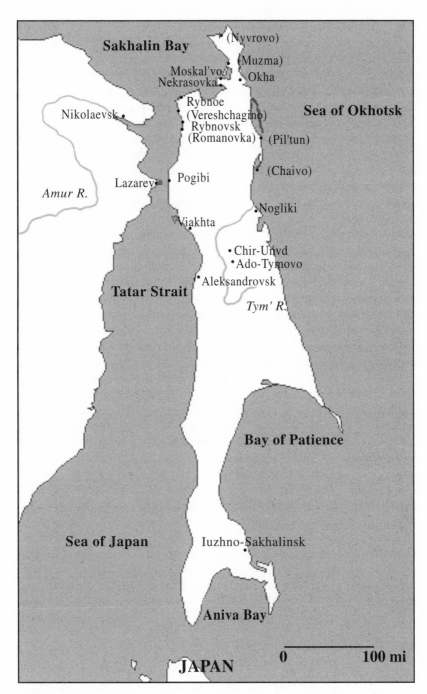

Map 2: Sakhalin Island

policy, Western scholarship often reflected an inverse tradition, denying the legitimacy of Soviet institutions altogether. The émigré scholar Alexander Shtromas once wrote, "Underneath the surface of almost total obedience to the powers-that-be, functions a society of almost total dissent,"[6] and one can see this approach written into numerous studies on former Soviet nationalities that emphasize the noble persistence of traditional culture in the face of the Soviet monolith. Soviet symbols and rituals are often dismissed because they were "imposed from above." Yet after several decades of Soviet rule, how distinct was "Nivkh" from "Soviet"? To what extent did Nivkhi see themselves as being not merely subject to but part of a Soviet Union?

As I grew more familiar with these literatures I realized that essentially two Siberias were being talked about, as well as two sets of native peoples inscribed there. The first is a vision of Siberia at its most malleable—a wild and untamed land which, for its simple, unforgiving climate and landscapes, has harbored within its boundaries both the true nature of the Russian soul and timeless, indigenous peoples. A testimony to the plasticity of representation, Siberia remains a mythical domain despite its enormous size, population, and modern achievements. Since its marginalization in the 1800s by Count Nesslerode, Nicholas I's foreign minister, as "a deep net" into which Russia could cast its social sins,[7] most of the literature on Siberia, as one European observed, dealt either with exile accounts or Siberian railway sketches.[8] Since then it would seem that not much has changed: in the twentieth century Valentin Pikul's *Katorga* (Labor Camp) has perhaps replaced George Kennan's *Siberia and the Exile System* in prominence, and the lore of BAM (the Baikal-Amur Mainline) has replaced tales of the Trans-Siberian Railway. Siberia has eternally been characterized as the place one retreats to, takes refuge in, or where one draws spiritual and material resources. It gained a special place in Soviet folklore when thousands of women and children were evacuated there during the German invasion in World War II, and it retains its appeal as the destination of millions more who, attracted by "a romantic desire to be closer to nature,"[9] signed up to forge their characters through work projects. Although Siberia has been distinguished throughout Russian and Soviet literature by its daunting distances, inaccessibility, and dark history of exile suffering, it must be noted that, as in many popular myths, "that which repulses is also that which attracts."[10]

> Siberia, now as through the centuries, means boldness combined with energy, daring, persistence and iron will of entire generations in carrying out plans and the ability to endure hardships—all those inner qualities which material incentives alone, no matter how strong, cannot arouse. There are few heroes in today's world who can measure up to the Siberians. These men and women

are the principals in the century's greatest epic drama. We shall see them locked in fierce struggle with limitless space and inhospitable natural conditions, conquering, day by day and hour by hour, obstacles which match Siberia's huge dimensions, the exceptional harshness of its climate and the incredible rigors of its natural conditions.[11]

Repeatedly Siberia is envisioned as symbolizing nature in contrast to the Russian center as symbolizing culture. This is the Siberia most of us in the West grew up with—visions of a snowy land imagined to be somewhere north of Moscow or Leningrad. Yet the Soviet vision has not always been that different. To speak to anyone in Moscow, St. Petersburg, or Novosibirsk is to appreciate the almost negligible role Siberian peoples have played in Russian popular consciousness, and to witness the history of state paternalism toward them, we are led back to visions of Siberian peoples as the children of nature that they were long presumed to be. Illustrated coffee table books of Sakhalin, for example, traditionally include sections entitled "Dark History" and "Our Modern Capital," followed by an article on "Nature's Heritage," which inevitably features natives in traditional dress gazing over pine boughs. Considered local color, indigenous peoples are frequently filed along with indigenous plants, as Catherine Lutz and Jane Collins found in their own readings of *National Geographic*.[12]

As a consequence of this vision of timeless primitives, one popular contention has been that Siberian native peoples have lived apart from the flow of events that affected their compatriots throughout the Soviet Union. As the Russian ethnographer Aleksandr Pika has asked,

> Over recent years we have come to know more of the tragic fates of Russian, Ukrainian, and Belorussian peasants at the end of the 1920s and through the 1930s. We have begun to understand more clearly how these events have influenced and continue to influence modern economic and cultural conditions, indeed, all spheres of our life. But what went on in places where there was no peasantry? For example, in the Far North, what became of the small nationalities and tribes of pastoral nomads, semi-sedentary hunters, and fishermen who, over the course of two or three years, were to have progressed from primitive communal society to socialism? . . . Northern peoples achieved socialism, and what of it?[13]

Cold, distant, and without history, these are the parameters by which much of Siberia is represented.

On the other hand, in a contrasting vision, we find Siberian indigenous peoples cast as the Soviet Union's truest moderns. Ever since the 1960s, when Soviet leaders began to announce that the formation of the Soviet nation had been achieved, Siberian indigenous peoples have been roundly

praised for their heroic leap from primitive-communal society to socialism. In contrast to their more populous counterparts around the Soviet
Union, Siberian peoples were considered to be less advanced along the
Marxist scale of historical progress, and their induction into modernity
meant the bypassing of the slave holding, feudal, and capitalist modes of
production. Numerous book titles herald this "stride across a thousand
years" where the early days of social reconstruction were "equal to centuries," and it became customary to preface studies of Siberian native culture with passages such as the following:

> The results of this gigantic undertaking [socialist construction] are readily visi-
> ble: the liquidation of illiteracy, the creation of written languages, the rise of
> native literary, musical, and dance ensembles, and, finally, the very existence of
> native intelligentsias—all this permits us to conclude that the cultures of
> [northern] native peoples have ceased to be "traditional" and have begun to be
> "historic," that is, developing.[14]

Through the cultural development of northern peoples, "a planned and
directed process,"[15] the Soviet government drew the indigenous population out from timelessness and brought them into history. Hence we see
the stride that Siberian indigenous peoples made to stay in step with their
new compatriots. "Without analogies in the history of humanity," Vladimir Boiko wrote in 1988, "peoples of the North, over a relatively short
period of time, all of one generation, made an enormous qualitative leap
from the most backward forms of social organization to modern socialist
forms."[16] Here we have the rhetoric of the child of nature moving in an
opposite direction, where the childlike qualities of the Siberian peoples
underlined "the remarkable receptiveness to all that is new and progressive."[17] Although David Anderson has pointed out in his studies of
Evenki that the five-stage schema designed by Marx in *Das Kapital*—
charting society's progress from primitivism to communism—was intended only with Western Europe in mind, this second vector of Marxist-
Leninist thought on Siberian native peoples returns us to the beacon of
Soviet uniformity offered in more familiar nationality debates.[18] As Boiko
concluded in the introduction to his 1988 study,

> The objective tendencies and laws of socialism lead to a deeper internationali-
> zation of all aspects of the social life of Soviet nations and nationalities, to the
> formation of a socially homogenous society, the development of the Soviet
> people as a purposefully social and international community, and to the univer-
> sal development of personality.[19]

What is so striking about this second image of thoroughly modern primitives is the very contrary direction it suggested for the more or less colonial policy taken by the Soviet state. In his path-breaking book, *Time and*

the Other, Johannes Fabian charted the ways in which colonial governments, and in turn the discipline of anthropology itself, kept their subjects at arm's length by denying their contemporaneity, or coevalness.
Rather than recognizing the interconnectedness of peoples in time and
space, governments and scholars used a range of narratives to suggest distance, and thus an inescapable alterity. The first narrative we see here—
that Siberian peoples were children of nature in remote locations—easily
resonates with Fabian's thesis. Lost in Siberia, a metaphor for distance
itself, and barely of the same social epoch, Nivkhi and other Siberian peoples could hardly be treated in the same manner as others. Yet by contrast, the "stride narrative," rather than denying coevalness, insisted on it.
With preexisting ties to communal life-styles, and with the remarkable
receptiveness of children at an early age, Nivkhi were slated to achieve
social parity, with alacrity, in a Soviet multinational state.[20]

We have, then, two dominant images of Siberian native peoples: one
that heralds their transition into the modern world and another that con-
signs them to the timeless world of yesteryear. Each relies on the rhetoric
of exotica, either through its cultivation or its forgetting, and each speaks
to the politics of representation. Most important, each of these positions
in turn informed the political cosmologies of successive Soviet planners:
If Nivkhi were children of nature, did they require special attention? If
Nivkhi were new moderns, should they be treated just like everyone else?

That Nivkhi were in effect assigned to both ends of the nature/culture
continuum at the same time is itself not unique. As John Comaroff has
reflected in his studies of British rule in Africa, "Colonial regimes seem
everywhere to encourage yet efface, to deny yet deepen, distinctions of
culture and color."[21] What *was* unique, if not stunning, was how these
two dominant approaches oscillated between political periods, leaving
Nivkh history in the twentieth century a revolving door of state policy
shifts. I want to ask then: How did the changing fortunes of each of these
ideal types influence the nationality policy of various periods? What were
the effects on the communities they were meant to define?

When I finally made my first visit to Sakhalin in April 1990 and stayed
there for six months, I realized the extent to which these polarized oppositions had governed my own expectations. When friends in Moscow
looked balefully on the prospect of half a year at a distant exile post, I
would reel off evidence of a populous island with many and varied modern conveniences. Somewhere in my mind, though, it was still Chekhov's
island of desolation I was expecting, and it took me some time to part
with my own romance of suffering when I arrived on this island of more
than 700,000 people, lush in the south with bamboo groves, beautiful in
the north with larch forests and deep blue seascapes.

So too was I expecting not so much Nivkh isolation but Nivkh separateness. Yet the stories told by Nivkhi with whom I lived and worked were very much in step with the turmoil around them. A great deal of what they talked about was new to all the accounts I had previously seen. Rather than a large prison colony at the cold edge of the world, the prerevolutionary Sakhalin of Nivkh accounts was a cosmopolitan island at the crossroads of the Pacific Rim and the North Asian mainland. Many Nivkhi were indeed illiterate and subject to the harsher effects of late-nineteenth-century colonization, as the redemptive theme in Soviet literature traditionally began, but many others shopped regularly at the Japanese, Chinese, and Korean stores that covered the island. That indigenous peoples were affected at all by Stalinist terror is not mentioned in Soviet literature, yet it was rare to meet a Nivkh who had not lost a family member during the 1930s or 1940s. In 1937–38 alone, a third of all Nivkh men were liquidated by the NKVD (the People's Committee on Internal Affairs, and predecessor to the KGB), according to one archival source. In more recent times what plagued many Nivkhi was a dramatic resettlement program introduced by Khrushchev in the late 1950s, when he attempted to streamline agricultural production by concentrating the country's rural population into agrocenters. On Sakhalin, between 1962 and 1986, more than 1,000 towns and villages were reduced in number to 329. Coastlines once lined with Nivkh villages every ten kilometers became littered with ghost towns. One wants to ask then: How did Nivkhi respond to these changes? What were the rationales for supplanting a Nivkh culture by a Soviet one? What did this process mean to Nivkhi, and how did they appropriate these new cultural forms?

After a year in Moscow I finally received permission for a six-month stay on North Sakhalin. My plan was to study forms of traditional life under the Soviet system. After a month of initial traveling and orientation on Sakhalin, I settled in the fishing village of Rybnoe on the island's northwestern shore. Home to some 250 residents, half of them Nivkhi and half Russians, Rybnoe housed the "Red Dawn" collective fishery where I worked for three months during the summer fish run. In the formal side to my research I conducted frequent and lengthy interviews with Nivkhi and Russians about the process of Soviet cultural construction and where it had led them. Topics usually ranged chronologically from stories of prerevolutionary life (either experienced or learned from parents), to the early Soviet reforms such as the institution of hospitals, to schools and special literacy campaigns organized out of "Culture Bases," to collectivization, to Stalinism, to 1960s resettlements, and finally to perestroika. In addition I made regular visits to other towns and villages on North Sakhalin where Nivkh communities were most concentrated, particularly

Romanovka, Rybnovsk, Liugi, Nekrasovka, Moskal'vo, Okha, Nogliki, and Chir-Unvd.

That my field research began during perestroika exerted a decisive influence. With the conjunctive elements of release, unease, and the considerable spirit of the absurd that Gorbachev's reconstruction evoked, Nivkhi I knew looked ruefully upon perestroika more as a source of collapse than for a promise of renewal. When I told the Nivkhi I met that I wanted to study Nivkh culture, most laughed and grew dark, looked gloomy and grew darker, or just looked at me darkly. Although perestroika had given some people cause for optimism, the dominant mood of most of the Nivkhi I knew in the summer of 1990 was one of tragedy and mourning. "You want to study our culture?" the responses would begin, "You're too late! It's gone! The Soviets ruined everything." And indeed these claims to desolation were not hard to believe. Less than 10 percent of Nivkhi today have any command of their native language; many are locked into degrading cycles of job and housing discrimination; and much of Sakhalin itself, despite its endowed natural beauty, is a landscape of man-made ruins. From poisoned lands and crumbling homes, it did not seem much of a step to ruined lives.

These tides of lament were at first so great that I began to wish I had not asked. Villagers I had expected to be retiring if not reluctant parties to my project badgered me to make note of their discontent. Yes . . . world going to hell in a handbasket . . . Soviets criminal, Nivkhi betrayed. This was a cathartic time and many Nivkhi seemed satisfied to have a foreign interloper about to record it. Yet it soon became evident that this new form of public therapy disgruntled local Russians who felt they were being left out of the equation. This added a further element of confusion: At this crossroads when Nivkhi were framing their selves through cathartic lament, the Russians around them were no longer professing hegemony. "You think *your* culture is dead?" Russian coworkers countered Nivkhi over endless rest periods at work, "At least you made some progress over seventy years. Our culture was once great! We were one of the most powerful empires in the world, and now look at us! We have a lot more to be sorry for than you do!" It is with no exaggeration that at least a dozen late nights ended in heated debates over whose culture was the most ruined, with myself the befuddled spectator.

However, it was in the less formal months that followed, when I began to run out of questions and when my hosts concluded that the baleful truth of their emptiness had been etched into my consciousness, that the narratives turned in different directions. Friends and coworkers regularly held forth with often lyrical nostalgia about the Soviet period, about impressive accomplishments under Stalin, and about the excitement of moving to new towns under Khrushchev. "Pro-perestroika" Nivkhi revealed

themselves to be most anti-perestroika in their opposition to political plu-
ralism, private property, and free speech. Radical anticommunist Nivkh
leaders turned out to be the very figures who engineered the closing of
native villages only ten years earlier.

The shifting allegiances between what constituted being Nivkh or Russian and what constituted being Soviet underlined for me the complexity
of the hybrid identities produced by the Soviet Union's efforts to interna-
tionalize its constituencies. It also laid to rest the David and Goliath angle
on which so many visions of Siberian indigenous peoples are based, that
these "small peoples" are down but not out, oppressed but still resistant.
As the historian Patricia Seed has noted,

> The belief that the standpoints of the subjugated are more "innocent posi-
> tions" until recently pervaded many of the histories written about peoples
> under colonial domination. In this genre, the lives of the colonized were
> conventionally cast as tales of resistance and accommodation. Histories of the
> independence of the formerly colonized were similarly narrated as straight-
> forward stories of liberation in which the formerly colonial powers were un-
> problematically villainous and the formerly colonized were equally evidently
> virtuous. Such studies narrowly constrained what could be said about both col-
> onized and colonizer. In particular these resistance and accommodation stories
> failed to achieve a vision of the emergence of a hybrid society formed by vari-
> ous accommodations and resistances among both conquerors and subjugated.
> The equally complex story of accommodation and the forging of a hybrid
> order was thus obscured in the strongly drawn story of subaltern cultural resis-
> tance and survival.[22]

Are we then, by privileging the concepts of tradition and modernity, and
by overstating the gulf between Soviet and Nivkh, missing out on the
very mechanisms that enabled the Soviet administration to recruit a patriotic Nivkh collective? How can we rethink our notions of the traditional
and the modern to account for these Soviet social forms?

The Nivkh insistence on "culturelessness" that so resounded throughout my initial stay may lead us to a further understanding of the hybridi-
ties that emerged from the Soviet period. In her 1953 monograph on
Makah Indians of the American Northwest coast, Elizabeth Colson re-
sponds to similar Makah contentions by distinguishing between notions
of "manifest traditional culture" and "latent culture."[23] More recently
Marilyn Strathern invoked this strategy in *The Gender of the Gift*, an ethnography of Mount Hageners in Papua New Guinea. Strathern is right-
fully uncomfortable with how readily many ethnographers ascribe Western categories of identity to their subjects of study. Through a strategy of
negation (the X or Y have "no society"), she calls attention to what are
essentially competing epistemologies in an ethnographic text, and shows

1. The northwest Sakhalin village of Rybnovsk, seen from the Tatar Strait, 1990.

how claims to culturelessness can be both acts of identity displacement and identity reformation.[24] This kind of "collective forgetting," Debbora Battaglia has added, "as a social mechanism of alienation, may generate not oblivion but an experience of sociality which takes the place of oblivion; that this productivity reveals, furthermore, a process of ideological inscription."[25]

That many Nivkhi I knew in 1990 chose to define themselves on the basis of loss is not hard to understand in the uneasy context of perestroika, when the dramatic turns left a vast number of Soviets feeling their lives had been spent in vain. Yet, to be sure, this negation could also be seen as "an extension of meaning," in Strathern's sense, or as its own process of "ideological inscription," in Battaglia's sense, as part of Nivkh efforts to redefine themselves in a context of enormous uncertainty and notable discrimination. Nivkh claims to culturelessness were rarely proffered without various degrees of blame ascribed to Russians qua Soviets. To this extent we see Nivkhi playing out their symbolic capital for their own negotiations of self and for assaulting, in a very conscious way, the Russian and Ukrainian holds on local resources.

In the course of my field research I seldom asked whether there was a

Nivkh definition of culture and what it might be. I presumed, like most people, that the Nivkhi I knew did not give these subjects much thought. Yet since then I have often been struck by the depth of Nivkh consciousness of themselves *as* a culture and the extent to which they have appropriated Marxist-Leninist concepts of collective identity. The senses of being in and *having* a culture (be it Soviet, Nivkh, or both) built on a shared knowledge of Marxist-Leninist theory from elementary school on. The regular and remarkably consistent message that Nivkhi were a backward people reformed by the Soviet state resonated from literacy units to Culture Bases, from ideology lectures at the fishery to home entertainment, from the produce of Soviet ethnographers to the imponderabilia of printed matchboxes. "Culture" meant having one's race stamped into the ubiquitous domestic passport.[26] "Culture" meant subscribing to official tenets of equality but having special access to goods and services on the basis of a continuing subordinate status rendered by structural discrimination. And strangely, "culture" came with belonging to a Soviet Union where, to at least my own surprise, it was rare to meet anyone of any apparent social group, anywhere, who did not know what ethnography was and what ethnographers do.

What emerged, which perhaps was most important, was the Nivkh sense of culture as an object. This came through often when Nivkhi talked of having "traded in" their culture for a pan-Soviet one. Like an automobile, culture appeared as a thing that could be repaired, upgraded, and, if necessary, exchanged. The idea of culture as a thing, subject to willful transformation, reminds us of what anthropologists Virginia Dominguez and Richard Handler have both referred to as "cultural objectification."[27] It also brings us closer, I think, to understanding the sense of loss brought about by the collapse of the Soviet state. With the Soviet vision of a utopian modernity now in rubble, there was little to suggest that the stride across a thousand years had been worth the effort, if it had been achieved at all. However, nor was it clear that Nivkhi had a tradition to reclaim. Lydia Black was indeed right when she suggested that little of the Nivkh world, as it was known to the earlier ethnographers Schrenk, Shternberg, Pil'sudskii, and Kreinovich, still remains.[28] This is, in short, the collapse of their visions of *both* tradition and modernity, leaving Nivkhi sorting through the remains of each of the different pasts to which they at one time subscribed.

What I explore, then, over the succeeding chapters is a story of cultural transformation through the lens of a very specific place and time, the lives of North Sakhalin Nivkhi primarily in 1990. I emphasize the temporal and the spatial locations precisely because, as I look back on how this book might have been written, a handful of other paths certainly could have been followed. What I might have taken further, for example, is a portrait of expressly Nivkh epistemologies and cosmologies in the modern day, particularly regarding ideas about the world of the unseen and the afterlife. Yet it seemed so apparent at the time of the research that to have focused on the traditional would have risked repeating the very cultural essentialisms from which Nivkhi so clearly wanted to diverge.

This is a study in retrospection then, retrospection by Nivkhi and Russians on the cultivation of Soviet identity on North Sakhalin Island. Through archival documents, travel accounts, and the copious literatures produced by officials and scholars, both tsarist and Soviet, the project creates a base to which extensive Nivkh narrative accounts respond. It is especially in the context of Nivkhi themselves sorting through the remains of the Soviet ethos they once subscribed to that I began to explore the reverberations of the dichotomous mythic constructions in which they have been cast. This is not a question of setting up the "myths" against "what really happened," but a mapping of the process of shifting and often contradictory interpretations brought about by our mutual attempts to re-create an elusive past.

While the accounts show that Nivkhi largely negotiated their identity over the last seventy years between the variously manifested dialectics of tradition and modernity, then perestroika, to borrow Walter Benjamin's phrase, represented these dialectics at a standstill. Yet, as in Trauerspiels, the baroque tragic dramas that Benjamin so admired, the narratives play with the very sense of loss itself as new definitions of self emerge.[29] Rather than meeting misfortune by turning inward, they provoke and challenge; they demand an audience. Rather than dwelling on shamans and mystics of romantic proportions, these professions of lament give us fishermen and native bureaucrats from a very real world, morally compromised by their pasts and haunted by uncertainty. How Nivkhi manage the past is essential for understanding what took place over the Soviet period, and for understanding rationales for current redefinition in the new geopolitical matrix of North Asia.

Two

Rybnoe Reconstructed

> In the ruin history has physically merged into the
> setting.
>   *(Walter Benjamin)*[1]

IN THE 1890s Grigorii Zotov was a St. Petersburg businessman who kept
an apartment on one of the city's most posh canal streets, the Fontanka.
He had extensive business interests in the Russian Far East. Through his
firm, G. I. Zotov and Company, he was among the first Russian businessmen to profit from the oil riches on Sakhalin Island, Russia's notorious
penal colony. And, from 1892 to 1902, he rented some of the best fishing grounds off Sakhalin's northwestern shore. He began with twelve
small fisheries which he administered out of the town of Rybnoe, the only
Russian settlement on the upper coast. At the fisheries or artels, as they
were known, Zotov employed more than 500 Russians, including 160
exiles. During the peak seasons, he employed up to an additional 60
Japanese men and more than 600 Giliaks, the largest of the island's
indigenous groups.[2] Fish from the area was sent to Japan, Australia,
Vladivostok, and Odessa.[3] When asked to prepare a report on the moral
codes of the indigenous peoples on Sakhalin in 1897, Zotov wrote that
Giliaks were reliable workers but, in contrast to the neighboring native
Oroks and Tungus, they had been largely resistant to Christianity, continuing to subscribe instead to their shamanic beliefs. "Of course, one
must take into account their isolated position and the almost complete
lack of interest on the part of the governing Russian population toward
their neighbors."[4]

One hundred years later in 1990, when the town of Rybnoe celebrated
its centennial, there was no mention of Grigorii Zotov or prerevolutionary riches. I had never heard of him, nor, when I asked some years later,
had many of the Nivkh or Russian residents of this small fishing town.
People knew that Rybnoe was one of the first Russian settlements on
the shore, set amid a cluster of smaller Nivkh villages. People knew that
Soviets then arrived, developed the area, and that the rest was a story of
gradual development and achievement. One could venture here that
Zotov's passage into oblivion was another casualty of the structural amnesia of Soviet historiography: As a private merchant and therefore an

exploiter, Zotov's main role would have been to demonize the past. But in 1990 this was a past too distant for most. The Nivkh men who worked in his fisheries, the most active and most educated of the Nivkh population, inevitably disappeared during Stalin's purges. Moreover, despite the fraying Soviet narratives of modernity and prosperity, who could imagine that this tiny, windswept village might once have been a hub of commerce?

Rybnoe in Profile

The Rybnoe of 1990 took its name not from a Russian rendition of a local precursor but from its main resource, fish. Loosely translated from the Russian as "Fishy," Rybnoe is located ten kilometers to the north of Rybnovsk (Fishtown), a town of seven hundred. In from the beach around a central square is the Rybnoe village soviet (or town council), a clubhouse, a general store, and a few dozen graying wooden clapboard houses from the 1930s, all standing at various degrees of incline. Fading political slogans ("We will catch up to and surpass America!") and rusty metal portraits of Lenin could be spotted through the taller pine brush alongside the public buildings. On cold days the wet sea air mixed with the strong smell of coal from the fishery's central boiler. A web of narrow, broken down boardwalks still connected the houses on the square to the *kolkhoz* or collective: Once meant to spare people from sinking into the sand and snow, they now added to the village's strangely collapsed look—part Lenin, part Stalin, part Dickens, part Solzhenitsyn.

Pitched on sand and overlooking the Tatar Strait across from the mouth of the Amur River, Rybnoe is home to a branch of the "Red Dawn" fishing collective, a set of wooden barns alongside the water for processing salmon and red caviar. Initially Rybnoe's long-standing independence from the kolkhoz system is what saved it from extinction during the rash of village closings in the 1960s. But in the mid-1980s flagging profits spurred the government to merge the village operation with the Rybnovsk and Nekrasovka offices of Red Dawn. A new sign had been made for the barracklike offices in Rybnoe, proclaiming the operation: "Rybobaza 'Rybnoe' Rybnovskogo Rybkominata Oblrybakkolkhozsoiuza" (Fish Base "Fishy" of the Fishtown Fishery, Regional Fishermen's Collective Union).

Along with Romanovka and Liugi, two towns closed in the 1960s but still inhabited by a handful of older Nivkhi, Rybnoe and Rybnovsk are collectively referred to as the Rybnovsk shore. Until 1964 they constituted their own *raion* or district administration, but following the concentration of rural settlements advocated by Khrushchev and Brezhnev, they are now administered through the oil town of Okha. Rybnovsk, being the larger of the two, has the greater fish-processing capacity, its own lighthouse, and a border patrol post to monitor sea traffic across the Tatar Strait. Despite the fact that Rybnovsk is being steadily reclaimed by the sea—water now covers what were once two central streets, washing onto a beached bank vault that was too heavy to move—and that local deforestation has rendered all of Rybnovsk almost two-feet deep in loose sand, it was Rybnoe, with its grassy knolls and low pine groves, rather than Rybnovsk, that the government declared to be "lacking in prospects" (*neperspektivnyi*) in 1982.[5] Rybnoe residents traditionally bore grudges against the Okha administration which had downscaled the shore's economy and left them without roads, running water, or natural gas. As in much of rural Russia, few roads link the shore to the surrounding population. Heavy transport trucks could traverse the two hundred kilometers of logging trails to Okha in roughly seven hours. The majority of residents on the shore traveled by Aeroflot helicopters, or more often by motorcycles with side cars, which were the main means of transportation within and between the villages.

Yet with the effects of food shortages brought on by the growing anarchy of perestroika, it was precisely Rybnoe's isolation that began to work in the residents' favor in the late 1980s. The store still received its allotted minimum of goods and had few passersby to pillage, in contrast to the larger towns and cities. Indeed, after a year of making my way through the gray warrens of Moscow streets and regularly doing battle in the stores of the capital, it was Rybnoe's general store that was by far the most luxurious I had seen. Television sets, irons, chandeliers, colored candles, tools, electric teapots, reasonable clothing, and extensive canned goods lined the shelves. Granted, meat and cheese were on the wane. Fruits and vegetables were rarities. But having heard so much of the proverbial days of plenty gone by, this was one place, it seemed, that offered a glimpse into eras passed.

That said, there was little else that spoke to a world out of time. Far from the calm I had anticipated in a small village on the edge of the Union, Rybnoe was in the same upheaval facing the rest of the country, distinguished further by a native resurgence in its most embryonic stages. That plans were under way to mark the village's century of existence lent an air of historicity to a year already turned upside down.

To understand the widespread discontent of the day was to understand the alienation of the entire economic system from the land and the absurdities on which much of that system was based. Until 1965 there were three fishing kolkhozes along the island's upper northwestern coast: "Freedom" in Romanovka, "Twenty-first Party Congress" in Liugi, and "Red Dawn" in Nekrasovka. Freedom and Twenty-first Party Congress

2. Cleaning caviar over a light table in the Red Dawn fishery,
Rybnoe, 1990.

were successful, wealthy, and populous, whereas Red Dawn, the weakest
of the three, had never met its plan in the more than thirty years it had
been in operation. Yet it was precisely the first two whose property was
transferred to the third after the 1960s relocation policy, and their corre-
sponding villages closed. The town of Nekrasovka remained the head-
quarters of the still unsuccessful Red Dawn, and it has become something
of an exhibition village for visitors as it is one of the few towns along the
upper five-hundred-kilometer stretch of the island with running water.
Relocations gave the once all-Russian Red Dawn the title "national kolkhoz," meaning Nivkh kolkhoz, and entitled the administration to special access to goods and services through specific nationality-based policies. But by 1990 most people agreed that Red Dawn's national status
had long been fictional. Of the 500 members of Red Dawn, some 150 of
whom are Russian administrators based in Nekrasovka, Nivkhi make up

73 percent of the unqualified labor ranks. In Rybnoe, what little work does exist is assigned by the Russian and Ukrainian transient supervisors to themselves. Inquiring as to the kolkhoz's history of misfortune, few visitors discover what is clear to anyone living on the shore: In the waters off Nekrasovka, there are almost no fish.

What the alienation leads to is a daunting pall of indifference. In the Rybnoe branch of Red Dawn where I worked during my stay, the policy was that the fish had to be cleaned, sorted, and salted within six hours of reaching the village pier. It was a rare occasion when this was accomplished in less than twelve hours, at a stage when it was difficult to work with the fish because of the advanced stages of rot. It made little difference to the workers whether the end product was of the highest sort (sent for export) or of the lowest (animal feed). The salary was more or less the same, and even the most retiring of senior citizens knew more readily than I that the fifty kopecks we earned each hour was roughly three cents at free exchange rates. A ton of processed pink salmon, which garnered from U.S.$4,000 to U.S.$8,000 at 1990 European market prices, earned Red Dawn thirty-five rubles, or roughly $1.75 at the most generous rates of exchange of the day.

The problem with the fishing collective ran deeper than the question of incentive or morale. At the heart of the matter was the disjuncture between natural calendrical cycles and the structure of the kolkhoz system. Off the coast of Rybnoe there are only two short fish runs. The summer run of pink and chum salmon traditionally begins shortly after the "Day of the Fisherman" on July 9 and continues for six weeks. In January, February, and March, there is a sporadic run of navaga. In times past, Nivkhi divided their spare time collecting other foodstuffs, hunting and fishing for whatever else was in season. In 1990 as kolkhozniks, they were obliged to be at work eight hours a day all year round regardless of the work load. This was an often deadening process, marked by sitting inside the kolkhoz buildings, listening silently to the sound of sand beating against the glass, and playing card games for weeks on end.

Good supervision also came at a premium that was evidently out of reach for the Rybnoe operation. The job of kolkhoz supervisor was normally held by a transient Russian or Ukrainian administrator who would come to the island on a two-year contract to make extra money and accelerate a pension through special government isolation allowances. The Rybnoe fishery had gone through seven heads in only the previous six years, and it surprised no one when the last supervisor quit his job to go where the real money was, in becoming a stock clerk at the general store and having priority access to deficit food items. Worker discipline was widely said to have suffered for the instability, and on the day following the formal start of the fish run in July, the current overseers

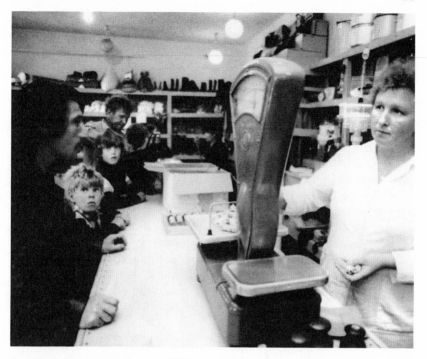

3. The Rybnoe general store, 1990.

posted a diffident note in the store announcing the imposition of a dry law on the village territory, prohibiting the sale of alcoholic beverages until the end of August, "in the interest of the sound processing of the national fish resources." "The bread's going to fall again," one of the Nivkh fisherwomen muttered ruefully when she saw the decree, and true to form, within one day of the announcement, Baba Talonova, the entrepreneurial village baker cum bootlegger, began plying mason jars of *brashka*, her special semifermented yeast drink, by night, and squat inedible loaves by day.

Drinking could not be called a special problem in Rybnoe. To my own eye it was practiced with the same regularity as in the capital, which is to say, widely, and could not be seen as a differentiated practice among Russians and Nivkhi. But it certainly played a regular role in the fishery, where monotonous work was frequently punctuated with convivial breaks. Work at the kolkhoz was divided into four main sectors. Boats bringing the fish for processing in the Rybnoe facilities arrived once a day or more at the village pier, where the fish would be weighed and sent along a graded water chute to the first of the kolkhoz buildings for processing. At its first stop, the cleaning section (or *razdelochnyi tsekh*), cutters would open the fish and remove the entrails, sending any caviar down special conveyors to a separate caviar workshop where the caviar would be washed, salted, and sorted over light tables before being refrigerated in barrels. After cutting, the fish would be passed down a ramp to washers, who would rinse out the gills and bellies with kitchen spoons protruding from water hoses, and pass the fish along a conveyor to the next building for salting (the *zasol'nyi tsekh*), packing into barrels (the *uborochnyi tsekh*), and refrigerated storage. Women predominated in the cleaning and packing sections; men held a monopoly in the salting and storage sections, but workers could be exchanged between sections on any given day as needed.

The salting section is the largest of all the buildings, a dank, dark series of six-foot deep concrete vats sunk into the ground and bridged by narrow concrete catwalks. The depth of the vats and the proximity of the adjacent icehouse keeps the salting section at a constant 10 degrees Celsius. The work was not significantly more difficult than in the other sections, but it involved some heavy lifting and therefore had taken on the folklore of an all-male domain. Generally the younger men on the kolkhoz worked there. They drank more heavily, cursed with abandon, and worked, albeit only occasionally, with vigor.

The day routinely began with the construction of the salting tables. False floors were laid over two or three vats to create a working area, and large tables with high ridges were filled with sacks of salt. Fish arrived on a conveyor belt and was cordoned off so as to arrive at the foot of the table. The fish, large three-kilogram pink salmon (*keta*) or the smaller two-kilogram chum salmon (*gorbushcha*), were stuffed through the insides with coarse salt and stacked on trays in one of the vats, along with layers of salt and crushed ice. A brigade leader in theory decided who went for the ice, who salted, and who was to be taking breaks. The fish remained in the vats for up to a week, and then continued on the conveyor belt through a narrow opening into another building where it would be washed, sorted, and packed. In the cleaning and packing sections, workers were paid through an averaging of time and the number of fish processed; in the salting section, the kolkhozniks were paid as a brigade for the sum of fish salted. On my first day in the salting section, however, it became clear that there were loopholes in the system.

One bleary Saturday morning in July, a heavy load of fish was being delivered at the pier, and workers were straggling in from their homes after a boisterous summer evening the night before. The salting brigade assembled at eleven, and we drank. Following a set consumption hierarchy that opened with the best first, two liters of vodka were quickly divided among the twenty salters and neatly consumed. At approximately twelve we set up the salting tables, a twenty-minute task, and drank again. One of the junior members was sent on a mission to steal caviar; bread was obtained. We drank a third time, thus concluding the vodka reserves.

The fish was not on schedule. The ladies in the cleaning sections were having their own problems staying vertical, hence the first conveyor belt did not roll in until approximately two, after what was two and a half hours of concerted resting. With the first fish, there was a lethargic twenty-minute display of worker honor, followed by a forty-five minute rest and the sampling of the atrocious Azerbaijani wine *Agdam*. We returned to work for thirty-five minutes, then rested for another thirty. This continued more or less until five, when we parted for an hour for dinner. On a more auspicious day the work would have been long completed.

By six o'clock the fish was on its eighth hour and indeed a great deal had accumulated over the course of the day. This began a somewhat stricter regime with more sporadic breaks, marked by the consumption of quantities of beer obtained over the dinner hour. By eleven the stalwart had graduated to the graver heavy-duty rot gut, *samogon*, and at 11:30 P.M. an upper-level supervisor from the cleaning section made her first belated appearance of the day to castigate the churlish, many of whom were by then contemplating the most extreme rung on the beverage totem, beer complemented by a judicious bug spray accent. By this time the better part of the still untreated fish had begun to sour in an unpleasant manner. A great post-midnight push concluded the task at 2:00 A.M., whereby the brigade retired to the bathhouse for our weekly washing in rusty orange hot water.

While the salters were easily the most engaging members of the kolkhoz collective, the salting section was also the least lucrative. Honor codes oblige every member of the brigade to stay until the job is done, thereby starting a process where everyone works a little at the start, followed by one person stealing away for a rest, leading others to feel they are being taken advantage of, leading to mass abandonment in short order. As the summer fish run wore on, Baba Talonova, boasting a brazen orange head scarf and dangly plastic earrings, could regularly be heard from across the village square, wailing into the telephone demanding more yeast from her suppliers. "How am I supposed to make decent bread, *elki-palki!*" she demanded with the conviction of a great film actress.

At a time when Sakhalin had recently elected a new governor, an intense-looking former economics professor who vaguely resembled a popular hypnotist who had been plying his trade on Soviet central television, many people on the northwestern shore took up the banner of privatization and economic reform within the kolkhoz system. Gorbachev had already introduced the system of independent cost accounting (*khoz-*

rashchet), which mainly served to redistribute budget burdens and aimed to reduce deficits, and for Red Dawn this meant slightly greater access to its own profits for the purpose of at least ostensibly negotiating reinvestment and selling to buyers other than the state.

More telling, however, were the limits on reform, introduced at almost any stage where entrepreneurs sought to appropriate kolkhoz property. In 1989 the fledgling Nivkh cooperative *Ykh-Mif* (Our Land, in Nivkh) proposed to sell fresh fish, berries, and fiddleheads to local stores, items that rarely got to state markets despite fish being the mainstay of the island. Resistance from all sides was marked. In the first months of its existence, an almost continuous round of Moscow commissions arrived to scrutinize and harangue the less than a dozen members of the fledgling collective, while Nivkh government representatives frowned on their local cousins for embodying open dissatisfaction with the existing state of affairs. The newly elected Red Dawn chairman, eager to be liked but more eager to prove himself as a manager for the new age, endorsed the workings of free enterprise only so far as they remained under his jurisdiction. One day when I pressed him on the new cooperatives trying to get started, he asked me quizzically, "How am I supposed to help someone else start a fishing business on my own property and meet my quotas at the same time?" His logic made enough sense within the realm of the system, but it was less clear to others why the property was his to mete out in the first place.

In Rybnoe, as the village soviet met monthly to decry the scourge of waste and idleness around them, large amounts of crude oil used for the generator were dumped regularly on the ground; as the garbage receptacles had evidently long been abandoned, refuse blew across the village square like tumbleweed. Never far from one's field of vision were the pastures of detritus: rusting metal wire, torn salting gloves, plastic bags, and pitched vodka bottles amid piles of orange radiators; these were punctuated by the more colossal ruins: beached steam boilers three meters tall, sinking into the shore, and piles of old rails that once trolleyed the fish on carts from the pier. Most disturbing perhaps was that in the Okha district of which Rybnoe was a part, 25 percent of the lumber felled and 15 percent of the fish caught annually went to waste because of a lack of processing facilities. Asked how this could happen, kolkhoz administrators pointed to a five-year plan for felling which is greater than the capacity for processing, and the need to collect one's salary.

After the closure of neighboring towns over the 1960s and 1970s, the Rybnoe village council remained known as the Liugi Council, despite Liugi no longer officially being in existence. During the same period, the role of the village soviet, once a watchdog of civic propriety wielding considerable influence over local affairs, had atrophied along with waning interest in official mores. With the flag of a hammer and sickle waving over its threshold, the soviet office still bore the markings of the schoolroom that was originally housed in the one long room under its roof. The walls were covered with portraits of Lenin and Gorbachev, as well as construction paper directives listing the progress of committees under the soviet's aegis. The soviet's main function was to organize the regular meetings of the elected executive committee, which in Rybnoe consisted of fifteen members, and to ensure that the laws of the state were implemented on the territory of the village. The soviet's immediate realm of administration incorporated the day care center as well as the local House of Culture, which in turn included a three-room clubhouse with an auditorium, a games room, and a small library. Representatives of the village soviet were to preside over the burning of books every quarter when the library received its list of volumes to be removed from the shelves. They also oversaw the annual and quarterly socialist competitions (*sotssorevnovaniia*) between the medical feldsher, the baker, the store, the House of Culture, and the post office. Socialist competitions were one of the main avenues of worker incentive dating from the 1920s. At the onset of each fiscal year, central planners in Okha issued production goals to which each of the village civic organs were to strive. The store resolved to sell more foods and wares, the feldsher resolved to conduct more physicals, the library resolved to lend more books, and the post office resolved to sell more magazine subscriptions. A red pennant was issued to the overall winner for each year's competition, and Lidiia Ivanovna, the Russian manager of the post office who had arrived from Western Siberia telling locals only that she wanted to escape her past, was certain that she would become this year's winner.

The role of the soviet was also to oversee the work of various civic committees to improve village life, of which there were many. The Voluntary Friendship Society, regarded by most villagers to be neither voluntary nor friendly, had been created only two years earlier in 1988 to monitor public order on holidays and to combat the growing habit of drinking on the job by conducting spontaneous raids. The problem was that few would cooperate on the raids into the kolkhoz and private homes, and the fact that the society's only active member was one of the village's two Communists was starting to give party-mindedness a bad name. The Women's Council was designed ostensibly to similarly ensure standards of propriety in the home and the day care center, although the woman registered as the head of the council claimed not to know of her having being named for the job nor to like the invasion of privacy that the council stood for. In a similar vein, the Comrade's Court, a local conflict resolution body, had also lost much of its luster. The idea of the court was that villagers accused of minor legal infractions could opt to go before a village tribunal rather than immediately being reported to the police. The most popular cases involved personal matters such as adultery, which routinely attracted neighbors and onlookers to the clubhouse as the details of the events were being replayed.

The activities of each of these bodies was duly recorded in the village registers, neatly typed out by the council secretary and resonant with phrases culled from political how-to manuals that lined the bookshelves of the council office. To examine the minutes of the meetings was to find the kind of complaints heard every day in the corridors of the kolkhoz or the general store. The local head of the kolkhoz bemoaned his constituents' dependence on the fishery office to conduct even the most minor repairs on kolkhoz housing; the day care center was tired of the central coal boiler breaking down; pensioners railed against the decrepit state of the boardwalks; the post office declared that the electrician should be ashamed of himself, and so on.[6] Still, the rich prose of the transcripts never quite matched the people to whom they were credited. For an entry on 19 April 1989 the chairman of the council was recorded having opened with three tightly spaced pages of a speech on voters' requests and the fundamental role that these played in the democratic process. Logical, fast-moving, and well-composed, with many historical notes, this was from the same fellow I knew to revile writing, public speaking, and the turgid turns of phrase that were the stuff of officialese. "Of course I didn't write it myself, what do you think?" he responded when I asked him. He grimaced as he toyed with a matchbox that read, "Twelfth Five-Year Plan: Goods to the People! Furniture in 1990, up 130 percent!" "Who on earth cares about those kinds of things?" And indeed, following the town meetings, the real work fell to the village secretary to produce documents suitably innocuous for inspection by the district authorities. Hence, in its first 1989 report to the district executive committee in Okha, the Liugi village soviet, named in honor of a neighboring village, which did not officially exist (but really did), announced that it was entering into a socialist competition with neighboring Rybnovsk (not actually conducted); that it had held a number of political enlightenment lectures at the House of Culture, with titles such as "Stories about Communists" and "The Rules of Etiquette" (not actually held); and that conditions were created favorable to perestroika, democracy, and the tenets of the decisions of the Twenty-seventh Communist Party Congress in Moscow.

For most Rybnoe residents these were the small absurdities of daily life that hardly merited attention. But while the ebb of disintegration and the toll of abnormality had perhaps become the norm over the last twenty years, the turn of the decade and the start of the 1990s had introduced extremes previously unknown. To open any newspaper was to find the headlines charged with discontent. The four-page issue of the province-wide newspaper *Soviet Sakhalin* on 8 June 1990 led with the following: "From Clouds over Land" (on controversial land reforms); "Sad Story" (on the lack of funds to continue running a children's scout camp); "Records Be Damned" (on whether the amount of street litter in Iuzhno-Sakhalinsk, the island center, would qualify to be included in the *Guinness World Book of Records*); "Why I Quit the Party"; "Why I'm Staying in the Party"; "How to Avoid an Economic Crash"; "Get Out Your Passports" (for food rationing); "The Market: For and Against"; "Humiliation" (on lineups for alcohol); and "Wait until September" (on striking elementary school teachers). The June 30 edition of *The Sakhalin Fisherman* was no less mindful of the surrounding turbulence: "We Are against the Market"; "Is there an Administration in Ramskoe?" (on anarchy in a farming town); "A Millionaire with No Millions" (on a failing kolkhoz); "Are All Our Fish Swimming Away to Japan?"; and a single nonpolitical piece, "Do Paranormals Really Help in Police Work?"

Nor was television any less charged. When not glued to the Czech soap opera "Suburban Hospital" or the command repeat screening of the Brazilian melodrama "Slave Girl Izaura" that had so riveted the country in 1989, Rybnoe was privy to the renovated, if ill-performed, television news show *Vremia*, where the fingers of Russian elders would point in every installment as to who should be ashamed of themselves, why, and what to do about it. In keeping with the times, *Vremia* revamped its opening credits early on in the summer: In place of the bold red star hovering over the globe to a trumpeted battlefield call came images of a sunset, the Kremlin, a space capsule landing in the sea, a satellite, a forest fire, tanks, singing dolphins, and surgeons at work. The Far Eastern evening news edition at 8:00 P.M. (noon Moscow time) acquired a new lead anchor, the boyish Viktor Stepanov, who looked regularly ready to burst into tears for love of his country and the truly miserable state into which it had fallen. New scriptwriting enabled him to insert brotherly monologues about the proverbial "cold, hunger, and devastation" (*kholod, golod, i razrukha*) besetting the nation, peppered with generally awkward interjections of "In my opinion" and "The way I see it."

The combination of live *Vremia* tapings and the nonsensical requirement for anchors to activate their own microphones, a simple but forgettable task that might best have been left to a studio technician, made the show's rating among Rybnoe residents shoot up. The July 5 edition was illustrative of *Vremia*'s new, if rather perverse, popularity when (1) Viktor Stepanov forgets to engage his microphone and mimes resolutely into the camera for half a minute; (2) studio hands mix film clips, transposing river pollution in Kiev for promised footage on the Communist Party Congress; (3) Stepanov neglects to engage his microphone a second time; (4)

4. In the Soviet House of Culture, Rybnoe, 1990.

the announced film clip on a model collective farm fails to appear, and Stepanov silently answers his Fisher-Price desk phone with such artifice that one finds it difficult to believe that anyone was speaking at the other end of the line, let alone that the phone might be connected. After a calculated delay he returns the phone to its carriage and announces the clip a second time. The footage appears without sound, then the sound appears without footage, and the resulting confusion is masked by a confident display of the (old) *Vremia* emblem; and (5) an early segue into the foreign news makes an attempt to pick up the slack but is interrupted by the full-screen sports graphics in the middle of a commentary on German reunification. In this spirit it was encouraging to see the next evening's installment, where the long-suffering Stepanov was replaced by the far snappier Tatiana Komarova, who managed such polished commentaries that it was possible to imagine she had written them herself.

It was clearly a season of experiments. For stimulation, central television offered up a smorgasbord of international programming, featuring

weekends of French, Italian, Belgian, and Norwegian imports. For consolation, there was the always popular Vladimir Molchanov, who opened
his Friday evening editions of "Before and After Midnight," as he did on
July 29, with avuncular therapy for the harangued viewer. "How are
you coping with this hot, hot summer?" he opened in sympathetic
tones. "You must be *very* tired." The Soviet Mr. Rogers for adults, in-
forming even the lumpiest of his guests that they had "expressive, beautiful eyes," he appeared to be at once the earnest state aesthete and his
own parodist.

But for all the lure of the new, it was also a time of disillusionment, of
people who saw the present being turned against the past, and who were
not happy with what they saw. "Market" by and large meant nothing but
rising prices; "perestroika" was the hypocrisy of promised renewal that
brought only collapse. In the age of *glasnost'*, the Russian word signifying
not merely "openness" but the revelation of what had previously been
concealed or private, many held that some things were better left as they
had been before.

The Drive for Independence

The grumblings of discontent held sway among the people I knew on
North Sakhalin in 1990, and these reached a new pitch when Boris
Yeltsin announced he would be visiting the island at the end of August,
not long after having been elected president of the then Russian Republic
(the Russian Soviet Federative Socialist Republic, or RSFSR). Geographic
isolation evidently figured in the political calculations behind the trip,
since in addition to Iuzhno-Sakhalinsk and Okha, he scheduled a visit to
the Rybnovsk shore, pronouncing it to be "the remotest destination" of
his tour around Russia. I was looking forward to his visit, since all of
Rybnoe and Rybnovsk did little in the days leading up to the event but
ready him for slaughter, snorting about price increases and plotting how
they would give him a piece of their collective mind. Yet when I arrived
in Rybnovsk late, missing the bearish scowling politician by some twenty
minutes, I found even the most hardened anti-Yeltsin Communists smiling and gurgling like children in his wake. Yeltsin's helicopter had set
down in Rybnovsk for all of fifteen minutes, in the true whistle-stop tradition of the West. But rather than kissing babies or pledging state largess,
Yeltsin mounted a small stand with a performance that could have se-
duced voters only in the era of late perestroika. "What a nightmare!" he
repeated several times as he winced for television cameras. He cast his arm
toward the town square half consumed by sand drifts. "This place is a
dump!" "Do you seriously live here?" "This is straight out of the seven-

teenth century! Places like this make me ashamed to be Russian!" Vastly insulting all those around him, Yeltsin wooed the crowds, and they loved it. Please, come and insult our town!

Precisely at the time when Yeltsin had come and gone, and the fish season had ended, Rybnoe became not quieter but more restless. Yeltsin and the island's governor, Fedorov, urged their new apostles to act, to break free from the fetters constraining them, and do business. In local parlance this was quickly translated into an antikolkhoz movement, and within two days of Yeltsin's visit, neighboring Rybnovsk had held a stormy worker's meeting and decided to separate from the supervisory town of Nekrasovka. The new name for their operation: "Freedom"! And so in their own way, along with Lithuania, Latvia, Estonia, Georgia, Moldova, and other progressive alienated bodies, Rybnovsk too found its own voice for the time.

It was another matter for Rybnoe. Fewer in number and somewhat less revolutionary in nature, residents of Rybnoe greeted the idea of separation more coolly than their counterparts in Rybnovsk. Moreover, Dzhunkovskii, the Russian kolkhoz chairman, was in Rybnoe at the time, and on Saturday morning I found the collective outside the gates of the kolkhoz office, gathered around the chairman in his naval regalia and epaulets. All seemed to be as usual: Dzhunkovskii asked for questions and stifled each in turn with an erudite smile and a promise to examine the matter in detail some other time. His charges asked questions about holidays and whether they would ever be able to see the much talked about Japanese import goods. They left out the more provocative issues: Why was X working and not Y? Why did the supervisors do no work? Why is half the work force drunk every weekend? Why does the head supervisor assign himself all the highest-paying jobs? Finally they came to the matter of separation. Dzhunkovskii urged all present to consider the matter "sanely and without emotion," whereby surely they would come to a prudent conclusion. Or as he later suggested, they could wait on a transition period of perhaps five years. Five years was a popular waiting period for separations, since Gorbachev had proposed the same to the Baltics. But five years also seemed a bit long when Misha Kolomyitsev, a Russian machinist some thirty years of age, lean and mangy in his bleached brown denim work jacket, shouted with the ring of a practiced incendiary, "Sure, think it through, and then decide!"

In good form it was decided by Dzhunkovskii to form a commission to examine the matter. Someone proposed Sonia Biktasheva, the dry, laconic Comrade Procurator, and she feverishly resisted. Sergei Nikolaevich, the slippery Ukrainian manager of Red Dawn's Rybnoe branch, proposed instead two of the senior kolkhoz supervisors, himself and

Kolomyitsev—that is, the same people who always formed such commissions—and the matter seemed sufficiently doused. By this time the rank and file were milling impatiently in the background. The meeting was declared closed and the leather-skinned, prematurely aged husband to the Comrade Procurator nudged the tractor driver (husband to the head of the Voluntary Friendship Society who organized the antialcohol raids) and said, "Let's drink!"

But that was Saturday. On Tuesday, news of Rybnovsk's final decision to separate reached Rybnoe, and people began to discuss it all again in earnest. The noble commission had studied the matter in traditional style and decided "they would see," but they were quickly superseded by waves of the less patient. Most people saw no reason not to separate: They had lived for eighteen years under the auspices of the main fishery in Aleksandrovsk and did nothing but toil to relieve Aleksandrovsk of its debts. Now they were doing the same for another kolkhoz in Nekrasovka. The Nekrasovka figures posted in the Rybnoe offices of the kolkhoz appeared to bear this out. In 1989 the 326 kolkhozniks of Red Dawn in Rybnoe and Rybnovsk (10 percent being administrators) produced roughly 6.5 million rubles worth of gross production and cleared 2,170,000 rubles in profits. But this met only 98 percent of the projected total set by Nekrasovka, and workers on the Rybnovsk shore were denied additional bonuses. By contrast, the 270 kolkhozniks in Nekrasovka (79 percent being administrators) logged a 15,000-ruble deficit, but because they met their quotas at 120 percent, they awarded themselves bonuses in the form of cash supplements and consumer goods.

Rybnovsk's decision was made on Monday, and Rybnovsk awaited Rybnoe's decision before going to Iuzhno-Sakhalinsk. On Wednesday morning a motley crew of some sixty-five kolkhozniks gathered in the village House of Culture, in the small auditorium outfitted in red linoleum, stacking chairs, heavily shellacked cedar wainscoting, and a fresh coat of pungently toxic green paint. The House of Culture was a worn gray wooden building that rarely had its doors open and never lost that biting cold drafty feel. The meeting was opened by the slippery Sergei Nikolaevich and taken up by the visiting Russian kolkhoznik, Misha Rezanov from Rybnovsk. Rybnovsk had decided to make its break, he announced, and had plans for a bright future. They will grow potatoes on a collective basis, and they would like very much to develop a system of stocks and bonds. This was quickly interrupted by Misha Kolomyitsev who, only five minutes into the meeting and appearing already like a pressure cooker ready to burst, heartily enjoined everyone (at a very high volume) that Rybnoe could well do the same and more! He did not specify what he meant by "more," or why, if growing potatoes and keeping livestock was so easy and profitable, no one had tried it before. But the mood was such that there would soon be the promise of luxury condominiums if people acted in time. That there was no talk of fish at the given moment seemed to trouble no one.

The revolutionary pace was interrupted by a very drunken fellow who stood up and animatedly snorted his intense feelings on the subject. These were comprehensible to no one, and were followed by a long and unexpected silence. Liuda Kozlova, the Nivkh fish cutter, stood up and wanted to know how they were going to keep themselves busy in the wintertime. Kolomyitsev rose to his feet, insisting, "But we have a program! We'll separate now and then decide on how to keep busy!" This was followed by loud shouting from all corners, including many raucous insults directed at the speakers. The Rybnovsk contingent had noted that Rybnoe was envied for its friendliness, but the uproar already in progress did little to give credence to this compliment.

Another Lidiia Ivanovna, not the postmistress but the Russian head accountant from Red Dawn in Nekrasovka, stood up to defend her much slandered employer. "We never really wanted your fishery anyway. We lived fine before you came along!" This did not seem like much of an argument to keep anyone from separating, and the furor began anew. Two Nivkh women leapt into the fray: Liuda Kozlova shouted that the decision was being made too early, while the normally taciturn Aleksandra Kon, spurred by the maelstrom, enjoined audibly, "We have so many problems, why not separate? Lithuania wants to. Why can't we?" This caused Zhenia of the caviar section to get very red and flustered, and to collapse into a fit of nervous giggling.

Much stir was created by the prospect of voting, and it was at this precise moment, as if by special timing, that the tousled young chairman from Nekrasovka entered in his epaulets and cap. His presence complicated things, for despite his essentially adversarial stance to their designs, no one could deny his good intentions or his personal dismay in watching his new fiefdom crumble. In his disappointment people saw their own hopes of the last thirty years collapse, hopes for a successful collective plan that now had failed.

His arrival put off the question of voting momentarily, and he waited patiently as the leading loose cannon and a heavy-set housewife with badly dyed red hair started a fresh argument, punctuated by her abruptly turning her back to her interlocutor after each volley of invective. Seeing his cue, Dzhunkovskii repeated his avuncular plea to cast emotion from the proceedings. But unable to overcome his own resentment at having been spurned by his underlings, he too repeated the puzzling disclaimer of his Nekrasovka colleague: "No one wanted this marriage anyway. The government arrived like an aging matchmaker, bound us together, and left. We would have gotten on fine without you. If you want to separate, then separate, but it will be you and your families who will suffer!"

This muffled threat appeared to fall on deaf ears. Among the few in the hall who were not already engaged in high-volume debate was one woman in the back who appeared to be sobbing but was actually yawning fiercely. The woman to the left of her, her head wrapped in brightly colored scarves, appeared to be sleeping, and the man on the right, motionlessly gazing ahead, could have been mistaken for his wax mannequin double.

The chairman resumed his carefully prepared declaration that Nekrasovka was being unnecessarily blamed, but this proved to be too much for Kolomyitsev who dismissed his poorly masked politeness and shouted, "We're tired of listening to your stupid presentations! You don't have to be smart to figure out how badly off we are!" With the meeting long into overtime, Dzhunkovskii urged to defer voting, and the small auditorium, still awash in the clucking and banter of unfinished arguments, gradually began to empty. A cold wind whipped up sand around the club as people left to go back to work and drink tea, or go home.

In the days that followed, as the kolkhoz referendum was deferred and then deferred again, a pronounced uneasiness resonated throughout the town. Although throughout Soviet, and some might say, Russian history, there has been a long tradition of criticizing the preceding political generation, this time the vantage point from which to lay blame was unclear. Perestroika had produced a regnant uncertainty, at times hypnotic and, by at least partial definition, destructive. Despite the support of the village soviet chairman, the Russian Boris Ivanovich, who was in favor of kolkhoz independence, there seemed to be little support for the village soviet itself during the kolkhoz meetings, and Rybnoe took to debating the proposal that the village soviet be done away with altogether. Council members snorted in disapproval at the idea: With no village soviet, all administrative functions would have to be performed in Rybnovsk, such as the registration of births, marriages, and deaths; the store, the club, the feldsher, the post office—all were under the dominion of the council. The tension reminded everyone of the long-standing rift between the village council and the kolkhoz over who precisely dominated village affairs. Boris Ivanovich noted disparagingly that when he worked at the kolkhoz, some five years ago, even the workers would badger the supervisors for extra work. There was money to be made and the money was worth something; and the supervisors, he suggested, had their act together. In contrast, workers now sluggishly showed up late to work, often to simply join a card game or wait around in the corridor for assignments. The supervisors shrug their shoulders and explain that there is nothing to do. When work is short, the masters assign it all to themselves; they get the cash, and the rest can take care of themselves.

Throughout early September as most of the meetings were transpiring, a typhoon warning was in effect, leaving the village cold, wet, and overcast, and inclining most people to stay indoors. The rarer members of Rybnoe remained above the fray, such as the postmistress Lidiia Ivanovna. Left by regional shortages without envelopes or stamps, she entrenched herself at her desk behind the omnipresent abacus and the sponge wrapped in panty hose for use as an ink pad, still plotting her victory in the socialist competition.

Television too, for all its expanded capacities to lure viewers, could also be disarming. During the same week in September, in the home of the Nivkh family where I lived during my stay, three of us settled down one morning in front of the television set, myself and two Nivkh women, one of whom worked on the fledgling Nivkh newspaper, *Nivkh Dif*. The feature was a panel discussion on the removal of a statue of Lenin from the main square of the Ukrainian city, Lvov. As hundreds of gathered spectators chanted and jeered, the wrecking ball from a massive crane knocked Lenin in the head. Welders fired at his feet while further blows were made to his shoulders and chest. The crowd applauded wildly. The panel discussants, including the actor turned minister of culture Nikolai Gubenko and three others, winced at the replay of the tape. When the crane lowered a severed Lenin to the ground and lay him horizontally on his back, he was roped about the head for towing as if being blindfolded. When the restrainer fences folded in from the surge of spectators toward the fallen statue, crowds rushed forward to pound their fists against his outsized head.

Normally an editorial household, we watched on in complete silence. Clips of Lenin's funeral from 1924 followed, showing scenes of mourners coming down from the hills through the country snow. "Look at them," one of the Nivkh women said, "For them they had something sacred. Today we've got nothing."

The subject of Lenin came up again when I visited the resident kindergarten cook and bricklayer over lunch, themselves both from Lvov. Over the laundry basin, Nadia said, "I was watching it, and it felt just like it was me they were hitting in the head." Misha, imbibing coffee and vodka in alternating doses, snorted over Ukrainian dissidence and thought that Ukraine should be forcibly separated from the Union before he was made to watch any more nationalist nonsense. Nadia, a bit cooler, went on, "I understand why it was needed, but I almost cried I was so angry." In these last few weeks of my stay in Rybnoe, with a world slowly crumbling around them, everyone in Fishy became a little more disgruntled, a little more confused, a little more angry, and a little more patriotic.

The Centennial Celebration

At the end of September, against this backdrop of the summer fish run having ended, the drive for kolkhoz separation, and the bad weather forcing people back inside, the Rybnoe centennial finally came to pass. Who was organizing it seemed as open to question as everything else. Boris Ivanovich washed his hands of the matter. Olga Afanas'evna, the council secretary from one of the few long-standing Russian families in the village, strangely also said it was the club's work. The club director in turn professed no involvement. Further tension mounted when the Culture Bureau in nearby Okha volunteered its traveling amateur wind orchestra for the occasion. The Culture Bureau had last offered its services on the Day of the Fisherman at the start of July, when forty wheezing musicians arrived by helicopter and deposited themselves in the main square for the purpose of entertaining the proletariat. In a Fellini-esque scene, they played to a scant crowd of three, a glassy-eyed, smiling grandmother and her two pouting teenage wards. Against an almost empty landscape, passersby could be seen intermittently darting behind buildings so as not to be corralled into the audience. Nonetheless the players' concern, then as it appeared again with the centennial, lay not in the size of their audience but with the real purpose of traveling anywhere around the island at the time—strip-mining the general store for available goods and combing the fishery for drunken purveyors of salmon and caviar.

Some hundred people finally gathered in the Rybnoe House of Culture on the last Sunday in September for the official ceremony. It was a rare occasion for so many people from the village to be in one room, let alone for the second time in one season, coming on the heels of the kolkhoz debates. The program opened with a hunched and laconic Boris Ivanovich, who gave a short, prosaic welcome to those gathered, wishing them joy, health, and happiness. "What a fantastic honor," he began flatly, "to actually be the chairman of the village soviet at the very time of the village's centennial!" The mistress of ceremonies, a young Russian woman recently returned to Rybnoe after schooling in the island center, led with nervous speeches of poetry and professed gratitude to the baker ("Bread, O Bread"), veterans, multichildren families, exemplary worker bees, and aging Nivkhi. More than half the prize winners were absent.

The Rybnoe-produced entertainment began in the afternoon, with four Russian women singing short folk songs (*chastushki*). Although not very good, their performance was a stark contrast to the capacities in which most everyone knew them otherwise, dressed in overalls or shouting loudly into telephones to conduct affairs with Okha, and their efforts were loudly rewarded. Alla Viktorovna, on the accordion, and Olga Afanas'evna, on the balalaika, followed with an unlikely duet; this too was well received. Two young Nivkh twins performed an ancient Nivkh dance batting sticks against the ground. This was warmly applauded. Finally came Baba Olia, a Nivkh great-grandmother of some eighty years who crept quietly on stage to perform the dance of the shamaness. Without music or accompaniment, she silently soft-shoed her way about the stage, mimicking the actions of a dancer in the forest, gurgling a tune barely audible to those present. With the rumblings of the audience, it was clear that many thought she was infirm, were it not for the look on her face which suggested that, if no one else could see the forest in her mind, she could. Applause was awkward and less pronounced.

For the Okha portion of the proceedings, we had a choral group of all-Union prize-winning proportions, the well-known group *Song* (five middle-aged Russian women in matching long dresses reminiscent of the Lawrence Welk show). *Song* opened with a rendition of their original composition "Sakhalin," performed in charged soprano overdrive: "Sakhalin, Sakhalin, Russian Island in the Far East! Sakhalin, Sakhalin, Severe Climate, Horrible Weather!" This was followed by a tormented-looking juggler, whose unnatural smile did not hide her apparent terror of her chosen profession; a female contortionist who, despite maneuvering her frame with the required looks of amazement and sexual depravity, was far too young for the comfort of most parents in the room; and, finally, two unfunny clowns. All were taunted by the local drunks to have their photographs taken afterward.

It was only long after I had left Rybnoe that I learned about Grigorii Zotov and the success of Rybnoe's prerevolutionary fisheries; about the early Soviet artels "Pike" and "Jolly" that replaced them; about the former White Guardsmen who took refuge there; about the prize-winning salmon that Rybnoe sent to the World's Fair in Paris in 1937; about the documents relating to Rybnoe and Rybnovsk being destroyed in Okha after the death of Stalin; and about the Sakhalin government declaring Rybnoe to be lacking in prospects. This left me in some respects with the sense that there were two Rybnoes to be considered. There was the Rybnoe filled with people and events that made the upheaval taking place everywhere in the country seem somehow more normal, a place where I lived and worked and used as a base from which to travel to other North Sakhalin towns. The increasingly fine line between the everyday and the absurd that permeated Rybnoe toward the close of perestroika also made the Nivkh narratives of lament easier to put in context. On the heels of this first Rybnoe, however, came a second, one that shared more in common with other rural communities across Russia. With Rybnoe as a locality so capriciously and so regularly redefined by outside forces, there was a sense of the local finally exhausted by the macronarratives of the state. I increasingly felt that one could learn about this second Rybnoe almost anywhere *but* there. In a country so remarkably ruled by the center, where the only radio station available to Rybnoe announced Moscow time, this second rendition of the local was clearly only a smaller part of a larger whole. To know Rybnoe became a process of understanding its precarious place in the Russian and Soviet visions of how life should be in the furthest corners of the empire.

Three

Nivkhi before the Soviets

> Dressed in a black dog fur coat, belted at the
> waist, against which in effective contrast is the soft
> gray skirt made of the skins of young seals, shod in
> boots with narrow tips elegantly tailored in a hat
> of fox paws with earmuffs, and fur gloves that
> cover the sleeve edges, a Gilyak makes a really
> dashing impression.
> (*Lev Shternberg*)[1]

Siberia in Time and Space

During the brief reign of perestroika in the late 1980s and early 1990s the
Soviet general secretary turned president plied audiences with the extensive repertoire of allegiances from the vast state. In Murmansk Gorbachev
proclaimed the Soviet Union's committed membership to the "common
European home." In Vladivostok he declared the USSR "an Asian country." When I lived on Sakhalin in 1990 I often asked Nivkhi I knew
whether they thought of themselves as Asians or Europeans. "Europeans?" came the usual first reply. Europe was London, Europe was Paris,
Europe was maybe Moscow, but Europe did not include Sakhalin Island.
Asia then? This was more difficult. On their enormous coastal island only
fifty kilometers north of Japan, Nivkhi, the Paleoasiatics of scholarly lore
with their ubiquitous bound volumes of Tolstoi, Pushkin, and Dostoevskii, rarely showed much enthusiasm for being known as Asians. Asia
has long represented the dark side of Russia's multiple personalities, and
Nivkhi shared in this unease. To speak of Asians on Sakhalin was also to
invoke the widely held conviction that the Chinese and Japanese who
once held sway over the island did little but pillage the territory of its
resources. "We're Soviets," came the most common reply. And after seventy years of Soviet rule, this answer, to be sure, made sense. Yet for the
current generations, whose parents and grandparents had routinely inter-
married with and spoke the languages of their northeast neighbors, the
new avenues of history perestroika invited made them heirs to a past
many had been determined to forget.

Nivkhi are often referred to as belonging to the "peoples of Siberia," but like all broad labels, this elides much of what sets them apart from the larger grouping. Physically and linguistically, the peoples of Siberia and the Russian Far East are a heterogenous population, with more than 120 languages and dialects tracing from the Turkic, Mongolian, Tungus-Manchu, and Paleoasiatic families, as well as other languages so distinct that they defy broader classification to this day.[2] In the most colloquial way, Siberian peoples fall into two categories based on population. In the first category are the numerically larger peoples such as Buriaty, Yakuty, Altaitsy, Kalmyki, Khakassy, Tuvintsy, and West-Siberian Tatary. The Buriaty, Yakuty, and Tatary dominate this group in population, and their cultures lay to rest the myth that all Siberian peoples were largely illiterate before the Russian Revolution of 1917. The Buriaty have used classic Mongolian script since the thirteenth century, whereas the West-Siberian Tatary have long maintained their ties with the ancient capitals of Central Asia through the use of Koranic Arabic. Although the Yakuty have not had a formal script as long as the others, they are nonetheless renowned for their ancient epic verse known as *olonkho*.[3]

The second category is an assembly of peoples defined by the Soviet government in 1925 for administrative purposes as the "*malye narody Severa*," or the numerically small peoples of the North. This group includes (in descending order by population based on the 1989 census) Nentsy (pop. 34,665), Evenki, Khanty, Eveny, Chukchi, Nanaitsy, Koriaki, Mansi, Dolgany, Nivkhi, Selkupy, Ul'chi, Itel'meny, Udegeitsy, Saami, Eskimosy, Chuvantsy, Nganasany, Iukagiry, Kety, Orochi, Tofalary, Aleuty, Negidal'tsy, Entsy, and Oroki (pop. 190).[4] By demographics and the most immediate effects of colonization, the Nivkh experience is most directly comparable to this second category. What unites all Siberian peoples is a long history of Russian and Soviet state intervention and the changing notions of what Siberia has meant to outsiders.

Cast as a land of snowy expanse, suffering, and oblivion, Siberia suggests emptiness and alterity in a way that few of the other great nether zones of history can. In stretching from the Ural Mountains east to the Pacific, Siberia covers over 8 percent of the world's land mass. Siberia acts as home to more than forty million people and would constitute the largest country in the world, still larger than Canada, were the rest of Russia cleaved from its western flank.[5] When Siberian accounts include mention of the non-Russian peoples living there, their history is traditionally told as a chronicle of physical survival in the face of tough natural odds. Yet their real struggle has not been with the environment, to which their cultures have long been well adapted, but with the changing aspirations of the Russian state under whom they have been ruled for roughly three centuries. At this level their story reflects the turbulent and often brutal history of colonization. But at another level their fate speaks to the alternating visions of Siberia as the land of promise or, as in Dostoevskii's novel, the House of the Dead.[6]

Siberia's reputed promise, now as it has been for centuries, arose through its potential as a resource-based colony of Russia. Some of the earliest Russian records of exploration into the area date back to the eleventh century when explorers from the medieval Russian city of Novgorod first ventured across the Ural Mountains. It was there, "in the midnight lands," that they heard stories of "impure people of Japheth's tribe who ate all sorts of filth . . . and also ate their dead instead of burying them."[7] However, it was not until the broader colonial expansion under way in Europe in the seventeenth century that Moscow began to turn its eye to the east. Hungry for profits from the fur trade, they looked to the *inozemtsy*, or "people from a different land," as a new path to wealth.[8]

By initial accounts the Russian newcomers often impressed their native hosts with unknown foods and wares. In a meeting between Russians and the reindeer-herding Evenki, one Evenk "chewed some bread for a while—and liked it. He said in Evenk: 'Good.' Then he took a cracker, ate it, and said: 'Delicious.' Then he ate some sugar. 'Don't even think about killing those good men,' he said [to the other]. So they threw away their bows and began to eat."[9] The goals of the newcomers were nonetheless economic rather than altruistic. In order to extract a regular supply of pelts from the native "foreigners" who were drawing increasing attention in the Russian court, they instituted a fur tax known as *iasak*.

On paper, it became the obligation of every native male aged fifteen and older to provide a fixed number of sable pelts or the ruble equivalent once a year to the Russian state. In practice, the institution of fur tribute began what was to be almost three hundred years of organized plunder and degradation. Enforced by unlettered provincial tyrants, the Russian policy was frequently to take hostages in order to ensure payment. *Iasak* debts were shared collectively and could be inherited. Hence entire peoples carried the burden of payment in perpetuity under the threat of marauders and the military. Numerous battles attested to native resistance, and in rare cases, groups, such as the Chukchi from far northeastern Siberia, fought off the Russian invaders entirely. For Siberian peoples as a whole the toll was staggering. In the 1640s alone, almost a third of the entire revenue of the Russian state came from the fur trade.

In the eighteenth century the promising image of Siberia gained added weight in the eyes of the Russian colonizers. In the 1730s the Russian geographer and historian Vasilii Tatishchev effectively redrew the border between Europe and Asia by declaring Siberia's eastern boundary along the Ural Mountains, rather than along the Don River as previously held.[10] Tatishchev's revision defined Siberia in a way that had a wide-ranging impact on its peoples: Whereas the Russians represented European culture, Siberian peoples were now Asian savages in need of civilization. Indeed this new civilization was expected to flourish. During the reign of the Russian empress Catherine the Great (1762–96), utopian plans for the colony envisioned the building of "our India, Mexico or Peru."[11] In 1763, in an optimistic gesture, Catherine sent an emissary to Siberia to "punish those responsible for the ruin of the 'timid and helpless *iasak* people,'" but also to find a way to raise the fur revenues still higher.[12]

The new Russian Peru of course never materialized. Because of the frigid climate and expansive distances of these vast new territories, the government persuaded few merchants and settlers to take a chance living there. But the growing official interest in Russia's eastern colony resulted in a number of new measures to bring the natives under state control. Hundreds of Russian Orthodox missionaries spread out to convert the Siberian savages, whose cultures in many cases already leaned toward pronounced Islamic, Tibetan, and shamanic faiths. Despite the absurdity of mass baptisms being conducted in languages unknown to the converted, many natives acceded since conversion signaled the end of their "foreignness" and hence (at least on paper) an end to their *iasak* obligations. In 1720 the Siberian Metropolitan Filofei Leshchinskii was congratulated for having converted more than forty thousand native pagans.[13]

The outlook for improvement in Imperial Russian-Siberian relations showed its greatest promise in 1822 with a series of reforms instituted by the Siberian governor-general, Count Mikhail Speranskii. Speranskii's "Statute of Alien Administration in Siberia" divided Siberian peoples into three categories: settled, nomadic, and wandering. The new law did not absolve the obligation to pay fur tribute but it granted greater native autonomy in land use, governance, and religion. An integral part of the plan was the eventual conversion of the nomadic and wandering peoples to a settled way of life through the introduction of farming and the influence of the growing number of Russian settlers.[14]

Not all newcomers to Siberia went voluntarily, but a number of early-nineteenth-century noblemen and intellectuals in exile there took heart in what they found. The Decembrists, military officers exiled to Siberia after their failed uprising against Tsar Nicholas I in December 1825, were a prominent example. The absence of serfdom and rigid social hierarchies in Siberia made a particular impression on them, making Siberia, in their eyes, more egalitarian and democratic than European Russia. "The Siberians better understood the dignity of man," wrote N. V. Basargin, "and valued their rights more highly."[15] The Russian intellectual Aleksandr Herzen, who followed the Decembrists in Siberian exile in 1835, wrote with equal earnestness:

> What is Siberia?—here is a country that you do not know at all. I breathed in the icy air of the Urals: it was cold *but fresh and healthy.* Do you know that Siberia is an entirely new country, an America *sui generis*, precisely for the reason that it is a land without aristocratic origins, the daughter of the Cossack and brigand, which doesn't remember its forebears, a country in which people are renewed, closing their eyes on their entire past. . . . Here everyone is an exile and everyone is equal. . . . Back there [in European Russia] life is enjoyable and enlightened, but the most important things are freshness and newness.[16]

For Herzen, closing one's eyes on the past paved the way for a new beginning, and the same theme was echoed decades later when one of the best-known Siberian patriots, Nikolai Mikhailovich Iadrintsev, wrote, "The *Siberiak* has forgotten not only the history of the land he has left, but his personal history as well."[17] In the early nineteenth century, geography and the virtues of oblivion conspired to produce what has perhaps been the most enduring image of Siberia—the land of suffering. As the fur trade waned, willed forgetting became Siberia's leading commodity. This was the darker side of Siberia's Janus face.

It was originally the Russian emperor Peter the Great who introduced hard labor as a widespread form of punishment in Russia in the early 1700s; Empress Elizabeth, who reigned from 1741 to 1761, linked hard labor to exile in imperial decrees; and Catherine the Great, reigning from 1762 to 1796 touted her policy of "assisted emigration" to populate the Siberian kingdom with the most available bodies.[18] However, with the failing economic performance of the enormous eastern colony, it was Nicholas I's (1825–55) foreign minister, Count Nesslerode, who formally proposed that Siberia become a dustbin for Russia's sins, a dark colony of convict labor to which criminals and political prisoners alike were banished.[19] Exile became a veritable growth industry for the flagging colony, leading in turn to the entrenchment of Siberia as being the imagined equivalent to horror and oblivion.

From the point of view of Siberian native peoples, the new exile policies added to an already burdensome position. The Speranskii reforms, intended to promote greater native autonomy, added further taxes to already heavy *iasak* obligations. Where exploitation of the native population by imported Russians was already the established custom, the added arrival of the most hardened criminals from European Russia increased the pressure to defend indigenous lands and ways of life. Russian emigration to Siberia reached its peak in the early years of the twentieth century;

in 1908 alone more than 759,000 people crossed over the Urals to "close their eyes on the past."[20] Competition over good land and fishing waters became fierce, and, as a rule, the surest indication of prosperous areas were native villages.

The Island at the End of the World

We have had this island for fifty years, but over
this half-century it has given us nothing but
gloomy stories about the burdens of forced labor
and the horrors of the tyranny that reigns there.
    (A. A. Panov, 1905)[21]

For many of the early years of the Russian colonization of Siberia, Nivkhi fared somewhat more easily than, for example, their counterparts in northwestern Siberia such as the Nentsy or the Khanty, mainly because the Nivkhi were so much less accessible. Where so many visions of Siberia were predicated on distance, Sakhalin entered these ranks as the most distant outpost of them all. At some sixty-five hundred kilometers and eight time zones from the Russian capital, Sakhalin remains farther from Moscow than Newfoundland. Despite its most northerly tip being on the same latitude as Hamburg or Dublin, the island is routinely thought of as being Arctic; despite being only fifty kilometers north of Japan, it is more often thought of not as the Far East but "the Uttermost East," or more commonly "the end of the world."[22]

These literal and metaphoric distances worked against the local island populations in the mid-nineteenth century when the tsarist administration saw in Sakhalin the perfect outpost for its growing exile population. Officials began considering the idea of a penal colony in 1870, and by 1881 the island prison system was established. The tsar accorded Sakhalin its own governor, and from 1884 on, more than a thousand exiles were shipped to Sakhalin each year. "By 1888 Sakhalin had become, in the words of George Kennan, 'The largest and most important penal establishment in Siberia.'"[23] Indeed, although exiles were banished all across Siberia during the tsarist (and Soviet) period(s), often to places much farther than Sakhalin, such as Chukotka or Kamchatka, the island's choppy seas and perceived isolation made it one of the most dreaded exile destinations. Any man with a sentence of more than two years and eight months qualified to be sent to Sakhalin; any woman under the age of forty with a sentence of two years or more could go; and political exiles of any stripe qualified automatically.[24] Aleksandr Ermakov, who was awaiting sentencing in the Russian capital in 1901 for having distributed revolutionary pamphlets, could not at first understand why his fellow St. Petersburg prison inmates were not only refusing their food but generally doing all they could to deteriorate their health. Soon he realized: Only the healthiest men were thought resilient enough for Sakhalin, and inmates were tripping over themselves to be considered too weak to survive there.[25] Solid health and perceived depravity became the main criteria for selecting Sakhalin's assisted emigrants. As one observer noted,

> The island has not a single port worthy of that name, and the two or three anchorages thus used, are so guarded by troops, that ingress and egress, except by exceptional permission, are considered alike impossible. Hence this island has been reserved chiefly as the final destination of the unshot, the unhanged, the convicts and exiles who by frequent escapes or repeated murders have graduated perhaps from other prison stations throughout the vast territory of Russia and Siberia. It will hence be easy to imagine the vague terror which all through Russia, and even in the mines throughout Siberia, is inspired by the appalling and almost prohibited mention of Sakhalin.[26]

James McConkey concurs that by the end of the nineteenth century Sakhalin had become synonymous with hopelessness, bestial callousness, moral depravity, obliteration of the self, despair, and miasma.[27]

Many turn-of-the-century writers chronicled the senselessness and terror of Sakhalin's notorious prison system,[28] but undoubtedly the most prominent was the restless Anton Chekhov, who made the unpredictable journey to Sakhalin at the height of his career in 1890. Chekhov's plans puzzled his friends in Moscow who could not understand why he would want to impose exile upon himself and risk the dangers of the trip. Whether he went out of altruism ("In our time a few things are being done for the sick, but nothing at all for the prisoners"), to enlist public consciousness ("I'm sorry I'm not sentimental or I'd say that we ought to make pilgrimages to places like Sakhalin the way the Turks go to Mecca"), or to supplicate anomie ("Granted, I may get nothing out of it, but there are sure to be two or three days I will remember with rapture and bitterness"),[29] Sakhalin clearly met his requirements of distance and difference. In the words of literary critic Cathy Popkin,

> Chekhov views Sakhalin . . . as "separated from the entire world by 10,000 versts," so remote that it would take "a hundred years to get home again." "This is where Asia ends"; "This is the end of the world"; "you can't go any farther than this" (45). That Sakhalin is "far, far away" (42) to the very edge (41), to elsewhere . . . It is the exotic Orient, where people seem to exchange greetings by waving geese (45), that the climate is "fierce" and the inhabitants are fiercer still (41), that it is "not Russia," "not Russian," "not ours" (42–43), not Europe, not continent and most saliently not known.[30]

Alterity embodied, Sakhalin was, if not a blank slate, an imperfect slate waiting to be righted.

Despite his efforts to have the book be a chronicle of humanity and the victory of the human will, Chekhov's *Sakhalin Island* is more a testimony to the constant struggle between the alternating visions of Siberia as heaven and as hell. Of the arduous sixty-five-hundred-kilometer journey across tundra and through forest, Chekhov wrote to a friend that he saw "prose before Lake Baikal and poetry afterward."[31] But in other accounts he wrote of the fabulous tedium and depressions he endured, passing town after town inhabited by people "who manufactured clouds, boredom, wet fences and garbage."[32] The prospect of describing Sakhalin upon his arrival was less vexing since, in its pre-redeemed state, Chekhov expected the island to be horrible. As his boat neared the Sakhalin shores for the first time,

> I could not see the wharf and buildings through the darkness and the smoke drifting across the sea, and could barely distinguish dim lights at the post, two of which were red. . . . On my left, monstrous fires were burning, above them, the mountains, and beyond the mountains a red glow rose to the sky from remote conflagrations. It seemed that all of Sakhalin was on fire.[33]

Early into the trip the horrors of Sakhalin were not just the vales of suffering, but the trauma of senselessness that pervaded the prison administration.

Absurdities and inversions abounded. Chekhov had wondered what became of exiles after sentencing, but even on Sakhalin this was not clear. There was an almost complete failure to distinguish prisoners; the warden could not be bothered to sort out the sick from the well; the forced labor and the free labor could not be differentiated.[34] Chekhov ignored the northern half of the island, but referred to the center of the island as northern. "By the end, after countless claims that the South is more 'x' than the North, and the North is more 'y' than the South, Chekhov concedes that they are probably just the same. North, which is really center, is the same as South."[35] The strait that insulated Sakhalin and was supposed to render it the impenetrable island of the damned froze over in the winter, thus negating the insularity. In sum, nothing on Sakhalin was quite what it seemed. Sakhalin, Chekhov ruminated, evinced a "vague mood" (*febris sachaliensis*).[36]

Chekhov's odyssey through the island's heavenly and hellish qualities extended to the Giliaks (Nivkhi). The invocation of the native population on Sakhalin was intended by Chekhov to contrast the errors of the man-made environment. Giliaks are "a wonderful and cheerful people . . . always intelligent, gentle, naively attentive"[37] yet they are also dirty, repulsive and prone to lying.[38]

Other, non-Russian gentlemen travelers made their way to Sakhalin around the same time and were less constrained by the noblesse that bound Chekhov. All claimed to be the first of their kind (the first Englishman, the first Frenchman, the first American); all met beautiful young women on the boat going over whose tragic fates had sent them in search of meaning; and all had disparaging things to say about Nivkhi. B. Douglas Howard, an Englishman traveling to Sakhalin just before Chekhov in 1889–90, brought with him trinkets he wagered would be "pleasing to savages anywhere,"[39] but found the (Giliak) food repulsive, the women's hair like horserakes, and the clothing grotesque.[40] The Frenchman Paul Labbé, traveling to Sakhalin ten years later in 1899, might well have concluded that Howard had spoiled things for him: In efforts to enrich his private collection at the Trocadero, Labbé complained that Giliaks charged for being photographed—which he construed as evidence of the corrupting influence of the Russians living around them.[41] Harry de Windt evoked the same theme when he traveled to Sakhalin in 1896. Giliaks, with "their repulsive mask-like faces [which] leered out at us like evil spirits . . . may be summed up in three words: dirt, drink and disease, the two latter having been greatly augmented since their intercourse with Europeans."[42] Only the Englishman Charles Hawes, who traveled to Sakhalin in 1901, ventured a more sympathetic portrait. After visiting Giliaks in the northern interior he wrote at length on problems of Giliak-Russian contact: Native hunting preserves had been overtaken, the best fishing spots had been appropriated, increases in clearings had chased off game, and Giliak dogs could no longer be left to roam and feed themselves since they frequently attacked Russian cows; once tied, they had to be fed, further depleting Giliak fish supplies.[43] Nor had the exile community added any good, for "If a purse is almost indispensable in Regent Street, a revolver is absolutely so on Sakhalin."[44]

Early Accounts of Nivkhi

What all these writers shared were two of the official Russian presumptions about their subject that echo throughout accounts of the period: (1) that the island was wholly Russian; and (2) that the natives existed in a vacuum. Both these visions later took root as commonplaces in the Soviet literature, but neither was very effective in dealing with the complicated history of Sakhalin or Nivkhi.

Sakhalin's Russian pedigree grew in importance after World War II when the Soviets reclaimed the southern half of the island occupied by Japan from 1905, at the close of the Russo-Japanese War, to 1945. Yet the Russians were far from the first nation to either explore, settle, or claim Sakhalin as its own.

Archaeological expeditions undertaken on the island in the 1960s yielded a number of stone industry artifacts from the preceramic period, dating from thirty thousand to seven thousand years ago. More recent investigations into the Neolithic period (5000 B.C.–A.D. 1000) on North Sakhalin have produced a portrait of a material culture greatly resembling that of the Nivkhi in the nineteenth century, but Soviet scholars have hesitated to assert that these were expressly Nivkh productions.[45] The subject of Nivkh ethnogenesis in general has long been a source of debate among Russian and Soviet ethnographers.[46]

Early Chinese sources on Sakhalin have been studied little in the West, as historian John Stephan has pointed out, though the Chinese influence on Sakhalin dates back much further than many realize. Chinese Han period sources (202 B.C.–A.D. 222) refer to native peoples on the extreme northeast of Sakhalin who wore fish skins and covered their hair, possibly denoting either Nivkhi or the more predominantly southern Ainu of Sakhalin. Chinese earrings and beads dating from approximately A.D 600. have been excavated on Sakhalin, suggesting early trade with China. By 1287 the Yan dynasty had erected garrisons on Sakhalin, and some records indicate Giliak-Chinese clashes.[47] The decline of Chinese influence by the seventeenth century on Sakhalin and the Amur region was followed by the rise of Manchu power. In 1644 Giliaks, Tungus, and Ainu established tributary relations with the newly established Ch'ing dynasty, and from approximately 1700 to 1820, Giliaks, Oroks, and Ainu from Sakhalin each sent tribute missions to Manchu posts on the Amur River.[48] However, it is known that Manchu officials made few efforts to actively colonize the indigenous inhabitants of Sakhalin.

The work of the Japanese explorer Mamiya Rinzō (1776–1844) leaves us with one of the most detailed portraits of Nivkh life from the Manchu period. Rinzō had been a minor government official on Hokkaido and was instructed in 1807 to make a study of Karafuto, the Japanese name for Sakhalin. He set off in June 1808 at the age of twenty-six and remained until November 1809. In the interim he spent a good deal of time among Ainu, Orokko (Orok), and Sumerenkuru (Giliak) communities.

Rinzō's remarks about North Sakhalin Nivkh/Sumerenkuru life are remarkable for the level of sophistication they convey, contrasting so starkly with the travelogues of Russian explorers of the same period. Rinzō reported active trade and tribute conducted between Giliaks and the Manchu administration, facilitated not only by dog sledges over the frozen Strait of Tatar in the winter season but via seven ferries that traversed the strait regularly at seven different points between contemporary

Pogibi (*Noteto*, in Japanese) and Moskal'vo (*Tamurao*). On the north-western shore to the north of Pogibi, Rinzō wrote of a Sumerenkuru community more refined than the reindeer-herding Oroks. They wore Manchurian-made cotton clothes, washed their mouths and faces every day "to keep their looks clean and handsome," and were amiable to strangers. Rinzo made particular note of the women's facility for complex embroidery. The Sumerenkuru diet consisted mainly of fish but also included millet, buckwheat flour, wheat flour, and beans imported from the mainland, although these were expensive and not eaten as staples. Japanese lacquerware was present in most homes, as were wine bottles, tin cups, and earthenware brought over from Manchuria. The Sumer-enkuru did their own forging but the dearth of ironwares was a continual problem.[49]

Rinzō's account also notes the limited extent to which the Manchurian administration attempted to inculcate authority within the Nivkh communities: "Among the Sumerenkuru of this island who make the annual trip to the Chinese government post in Manchuria to present tribute of animal skins and to return with gifts, are those called Harata (headmen) and Kashinto (second men). They receive their appointments from the Manchurians."[50] However, Rinzō also contends that with the increasing availability of goods through the Japanese on South Sakhalin, Nivkh-Manchurian relations began to wane: "The islanders formerly crossed over to Manchuria several times a year but, of late, Japanese goods have become so widespread in Hatsushima that they cross over once every two or three years."[51] Instead, both Nivkhi and Oroks would travel south to Shiranushi (approximately modern Nevel'sk) to trade and sometimes work on farms. While the Japanese generally offered hides, liquor, axes, cotton, tobacco, and kettles, the northern peoples could offer brocades, jewels, pipes, sables, and fish.

Rinzō likely erred on the side of courtesy when he described certain aspects of the Nivkh/Sumerenkuru way of life. His illustrations of Sume-renkuru interiors, for example, suggest a far greater degree of good housekeeping than any other prerevolutionary account. It was also salient that he spent time with Nivkhi from central and northwestern Sakhalin, who had a history of much greater contact with their Asian colonizers. Had he fraternized with Nivkhi from the eastern shore, whom Russian administrators would later refer to as Sakhalin's "Dark Giliaks," the portrait might have been different.[52] But his matter-of-fact renderings of Sumerenkuru commerce, industriousness, and affability provide, however briefly, a rare portrait of Sakhalin aboriginals outside conventional na-ture-culture continua. It lays the ground, in turn, for questioning the politics of backwardness and isolation so often ascribed to Sakhalin Nivkh communities upon the arrival of the Soviets.

5. A Nivkh summer village on the Tatar Strait, 1892, as photographed by Lev Shternberg early on in his exile stay.

Still other aspects of Rinzō's account jar the reader even from a modern perspective. To imagine not even one but seven public ferries running between the Amur and the northwestern shore of the closed military zone that Sakhalin went on to become seems impossible by either cold war or post-Soviet standards—the monopoly of state transport and the attendant atmosphere of closure remain too powerful. Japanese lacquerware? Manchurian pottery? This produces nothing but cognitive dissonance in the same land where, for so many decades, contact with foreigners constituted treason. It produces still further cognitive dissonance on an island where even Chinese wares remain absurdly out of reach for consumers left behind amid the ruins of the Soviet state economy. And where were the Russians? Could Rinzō really have been talking about the same island?

Indeed the Russian presence began to increase not long after Rinzō departed. As Manchu sovereignty over the area faded, Sakhalin increasingly became a disputed zone between Russia and Japan. The first documented Japanese landing on Sakhalin had taken place in 1635, though Japanese proximity to the island suggests that they may have been there earlier. The Dutch explorer Maerten Gerritszoon Vries reached Sakhalin's Aniva Bay in 1643. And one year later, in 1644, Vasilii Poiarkov lead the first Russian expedition to the area, although there is no firm documentation that he went to Sakhalin.[53]

By the 1800s both the Russians and the Japanese were maintaining a more substantial presence on the island. Following a long record of clashes, both countries made mutual territorial claims beginning in 1853, to be resolved temporarily by the Treaty of St. Petersburg in 1875, which granted all of Sakhalin to Russia in return for the several most southerly of the Kuril Islands, known to Japanese as *Chishima*. By the late 1880s, when the Russian government began the shipping of political and criminal exiles to the island, Nivkhi entered a new set of relations with the Russian administration. For along with economic and political transformations at the end of the nineteenth century came ethnographers.

Nivkhi in Nineteenth-Century Russian Ethnography

The first and most marked incursion of a Russian investigation into the Nivkh world came in 1859 with the commissioning of the German ethnographer Leopold von Schrenk by the Russian Imperial Academy of Sciences. The assignment was part ethnography and part foreign policy: Schrenk's mandate was to understand the influence of non-Russian interlopers among the local populations of Sakhalin and along the Amur. In what became a weighty three-tome report, Schrenk's research confirmed what imperial officials conscious of their diminutive presence throughout the area likely expected: As of 1860 Schrenk wrote, Amur peoples had far greater ties with Chinese and Japanese traders than with Russians, nor were many Amur peoples, including Giliaks on Sakhalin, apparently well disposed to the Russian administration.[54] In the same spirit the Russian scholar P. Tikhmenev observed in 1863 that, for whatever reasons—Japanese intimidation or distrust of the Russians—Sakhalin Nivkhi preferred to purchase goods at Japanese stores, even when the same products from the Russian-American Company were less expensive.[55] On the other hand, as a tsarist representative traveling with no small contingent, it seems clear that Schrenk met mainly with the Nivkhi already best inserted into the North Asian networks of the day: Though most of his Giliak interlocutors spoke to him in Russian, they addressed him by the Chinese word *dzhangin'*, a vocative term reserved for well-placed bureaucrats; and on the whole, he found Giliaks to be active traders of fish and fur, with a love of wealth and a strong predilection for gambling at cards.[56]

Although Schrenk noted divisions between rich and poor among all Amur peoples, he was struck in particular by evidence of "natural communism" among the Giliaks: The rich, he contended, lent charitably to the poor and there were few disputes over access to fishing and hunting territories.[57] Schrenk's ruminations on this particular aspect of Giliak life set in motion what would become a long debate over the inherent appropriateness of socialist government to primitive communities across Siberia.

Much folklore surrounds the work of Schrenk's ethnographic successor, the idealist revolutionary Lev Shternberg, who was arrested in Odessa in 1886 for his participation in the populist movement, *Narod-*

naia Volia (People's Will). In a proto-Malinowskian turn, Shternberg went on to spend eight years as a political exile on Sakhalin from 1889 to 1897. Through the publication of one of his earliest ethnographic dispatches, Shternberg's description of Giliak kinship rites caught the attention of Frederick Engels, who saw in the Giliak system of levirate—the shared access of wives among designated brothers—proof that group marriage was alive and well in the Siberian hinterlands. Engels's endorsement not only raised Shternberg's stock in socialist circles, it linked both Nivkhi and Shternberg's work, in what went on to become an almost legendary way, to the belief that primitive life revealed communism as man's truest state (see the appendix for a reprint of Shternberg's article and Engels's prefatory remarks).

Having been held in a prison in Odessa for three years following his arrest, Shternberg arrived at the Sakhalin port of Aleksandrovsk in April 1889. His status was that of a political rather than criminal exile, which permitted him to reside in special housing in the small administrative town and perform physical labor during the days. However, by March 1890, penal officials cited Shternberg's harmful ideological influence over other local exiles, and relocated him to the remote community of Viakhta some hundred kilometers north of Aleksandrovsk on the Tatar Strait. That the playwright Anton Chekhov was known to be en route to Sakhalin at that very time, likely making authorities fearful that Shternberg might brief Chekhov on the finer points of the tsarist penal system, was an additional factor often observed in later Soviet writings.[58] Viakhta consisted of five houses for exiles who had finished their prison terms, and was a way station for Giliaks in the surrounding area. "It was here," Shternberg wrote, "that I was ethnographically baptized."[59] In his "Russian Palestine," "A grim land!" where the sea was "eternally stormy," and where the true inhabitants were "bears, powerful winds, punishing hellish blizzards and destructive hurricanes," Shternberg had greater access to investigations of local Giliak life, and by February 1891 he was allowed to undertake what would be the first of dozens of excursions to Nivkh communities across North Sakhalin.[60]

For Nivkhi, Shternberg arrived at a time when outside influences were deeply restructuring their access to fishing and hunting grounds. Nivkhi had long been integrated into trade networks with neighboring indigenous groups and the Amur mainland Manchurians, but they were clearly under new pressure to define their rights to resources when Russian and Japanese fishing fleets began sparring over prime waters. The arrival of industrialists such as the Petersburg fishing magnate Grigorii Zotov introduced the additional lure of paid seasonal labor, by which many Nivkhi took disadvantageous salary advances and fell into considerable indebtedness.[61]

Although by the late nineteenth century some Nivkhi had begun to build Russian-style houses, the majority still lived a seminomadic life between summer and winter homes, in variance with access to seasonal fishing and hunting grounds. The traditional Nivkh summer dwelling was a large one-room wooden cabin perched on posts four to five feet above the ground, whereas winter dwellings were partly underground to ensure warmth. On Sakhalin, both shores of the northern portion of the island as well as the banks of the central Tym' River were lined with Nivkh villages approximately every five kilometers. Anywhere from one or two to ten families constituted a village, with the maximum number of residents usually around fifty. Almost every family kept a team of dogs, for winter transport, and shared narrow wooden boats carved from logs for navigating the famously hazardous coastal waters.

Fishing dominated the Nivkh economy in almost all respects. Summer was the busiest period given the intensity of the fish runs and the volume of *iukola* (dried salmon) to be prepared. Winter, by contrast, was set aside for periodic hunting and, as Shternberg wrote, "*dolce far niente*," sweet doing nothing, and almost constant socializing.[62] The Nivkh diet consisted of fresh or dried salmon, a variety of wild berries prepared plainly or in custards, and a range of products adopted from Japanese and Manchu traders, such as the low-grade brick tea, millet, sugar, alcohols, and tobaccos. Traditional Nivkh clothing, in the form of tunics and pants for men and long tunic-style dresses for women, were made from a variety of textiles, including complexly crafted salmon skin jackets. As with the clothing of other indigenous peoples of the Amur area, Nivkh designs borrowed heavily from local Chinese influences. Few if any Nivkhi were known to be lettered, though many had practical knowledge of Chinese, Japanese, Russian, and other indigenous languages for trading purposes. Though Shternberg expressed surprise at the number of Nivkhi who knew Russian, he worked largely in Nivkh. Noted for its grammatical complexity, including twenty-six ways to count from one to ten based on the spiritual and material qualities of the objects being counted, Nivkh is so unique that it has no known linguistic affiliations with any other language.

Despite the fact that Nivkhi, as both Shternberg and later anthropologists observed, came the closest of any Far Eastern peoples in the nineteenth century to adopting Russian ways, generally little effort was made to convert Nivkhi to the Russian Orthodox faith. Into the early twentieth century, reports suggested a Nivkh worldview that remained deeply animistic, recognizing four spirit masters presiding in turn over the Sky, the Hills, the Water, and Fire. Nivkhi recognized each of these figures through feeding rituals, such as in a ceremonial feeding of the sea with tobacco and *mos'* (a potato and cranberry purée) before commencing a fishing expedition. By the same token, Nivkhi had a complex symbolic relationship with the animal world: Bears in particular were regarded as ritual kin, and would often be kept in pens inside or alongside family homes for several years as visiting guests, culminating in a carnivalesque bear festival that marked the high point of the winter social season. And across the spiritual spectrum, shamanic spirit mediums negotiated healing rituals pertaining to a variety of what were perceived to be spiritually based illnesses.[63]

By virtue of language, clothing, systems of counting, or sheer physical appearance, there was much to set Nivkhi apart from the rapidly growing Russian community around them. Between bear sacrifice, shamanic healing rituals, and Nivkh forest feedings, there was much fodder for the nascent practice of ethnography, which my briefest description only begins to touch upon here, and which has been so excellently treated elsewhere.[64] What is so striking about the corpus of literature on Nivkh life, however, are the shifting tides of what was considered useful or important knowledge from one political era to another. This was perhaps most evident in the Soviet period, when Shternberg's careful work on the clan system, for example, was published posthumously to ensure "the liquidation of patriarchal clan survivals."[65] But with the regnant intellectual trends at the time of Shternberg's field research, it was Nivkh social organization, and its implications for burgeoning socialist theory, that rose to the fore.

By the time Shternberg arrived on Sakhalin in 1889, the American scholar Lewis Henry Morgan had already published his path-breaking book *Ancient Society* (1877), and Frederick Engels had responded to Morgan in the influential *Origin of the Family, Private Property, and the State* (1884). Shternberg had first read Engels while in prison in Odessa, and wrote of relaxing with Engels's book in his tent at nights during his first trip through Nivkh villages in 1891.[66] Thus began a brief intellectual reciprocity between Engels and Shternberg.

Engels's book had been fashioned as a response to Morgan's sweeping comparative investigations of kin terminologies. After meeting with Darwin, Morgan began to think of family structures as evidencing different stages in human social evolution: To the stage of savagery, Morgan located group marriage—the rights of sexual access between all husbands and wives of a designated group; to the more advanced period of barbarism, Morgan traced a loose pairing arrangement between husband and wife; and to the more recent period of civilization, Morgan tied the monogamy we are more familiar with today.

While Morgan concentrated primarily on the first two stages of sav-

6. Portrait of a Nivkh clan, as photographed by Lev Shternberg, outside a semi-underground winter home by the Tatar Strait, 1892.

agery and barbarism, Engels focused more on the civilizing process and how family relations intersected with the rise of private ownership. Whereas in savagery and barbarism, descent was often marked through the female line, Engels argued, civilization saw the rise of male descent rights through monogamy and the perceived facility for identifying a hold over private resources. When descent was traced through the female line, Engels reasoned, paternity, or more specifically precise rules of material inheritance, could not be firmly held. "Once it had passed into the private possession of families and there rapidly begun to augment, this wealth dealt a severe blow to the society founded on pairing marriage and the matriarchal gens," Engels wrote. "Monogamous marriage comes on the scene as the subjugation of the one sex by the other."[67] While modern states presented themselves as products of natural social evolution, "the image and reality of reason," as Hegel set forth, Engels countered that states were products of society that bound up specific interests in the ac-cumulation of private wealth by a few, and families governed under a pa-triarchal system of monogamy structured to serve that end. "Full freedom of marriage," Engels wrote, and by extension human freedom as a whole, "can therefore only be generally established when the abolition of capitalist production and property relations created by it has removed all the accompanying economic considerations which still exert such a powerful influence."[68]

Where did Nivkhi fit into all this? Like many indigenous peoples across Siberia, clan affiliation prescribed a great deal of Nivkh political, economic, social, and religious life. There were roughly a dozen active clans among Sakhalin Nivkhi at the turn of the century. Although only one clan or lineage traditionally prevailed in a given village, mixed settlements had made the system more variegated by the late 1800s. Shternberg's descriptions of the Nivkh kinship system were famously labrynthine: Nivkhi were exogamous, in that they married only outside their lineage in a complex system of reciprocities that bound together, in Nivkh terms, the wife givers and the wife takers.[69] But what made Nivkhi unique, Shternberg claimed, was a triangulated system of marital exchange, based on a tri-clan phratry or alliance group (from the Nivkh, *pandf*) which underwrote a complex web of mutual social and economic obligations. Following Morgan's terminology, Shternberg charted Nivkh kin relations under the heading of "group marriage," since he found the kin system remarkably similar to the Punaluan system in Hawaii which Morgan had documented. According to the classificatory nature of Nivkh kin terminology, any married man or woman had several "husbands" or "wives" from their marrying generation. As a result, "all men of a given lineage had rights of sexual access to women of their own generation in the wife-giving lineage"; by the same token, women had the same access to men of their own generation in the wife-taking lineage.[70] In practice, the system was a loose kind of monogamy: Many Nivkh men and women initiated discreet but permissible affairs, particularly with visiting guests; under more formal circumstances of the levirate, women, if widowed, often married their husband's younger brother. Public displays of affection were uncommon, and most Nivkhi considered it indiscreet to discuss extramarital activities in public.[71] However, what is crucial here is the reference to group marriage, for, according to Morgan's taxonomy, any group still practicing group marriage could only fall under the category of savagery.

When Engels came upon this first article of Shternberg's in the Moscow newspaper *Russkie Vedomosti* in 1892, he seized on the case as an example of group marriage still extant, and within days had it translated into German for reprinting.[72] Shternberg's report was important for Engels not only because it suggested the existence of group marriage in general, but because the perceived backwardness of Nivkh life resonated so well with Marx's and Engels's evolutionary frame. The proven existence of group marriage, which Engels reported had recently been under attack by the "dry-as-dust" jurist J. F. McLennan, validated Morgan's theory of developmental stages.[73] What made the Nivkh case compelling is that "it demonstrates the similarity, even their identity in their main characteristics, of the social institutions of primitive peoples at approximately the same stage of development."[74] What was good for Morgan, by association, was good for the evolutionist theory of class struggle that Marx and Engels were proposing. Engels's pleasure with the discovery overrode some of his more tautological turns: "That the actual exercise of these rights is gradually dying out," Engels wrote, "only proves that this form of marriage is itself destined to die out." Hence, that Nivkhi were proven to be a primitive people with backward customs became, in its own way, a necessary building block in the edifice of Russian socialism.

For Nivkhi the die was cast. Their role as the quintessential savages of Engels's favor made them famous in Russian ethnographic literature. Moreover, although he would contradict himself on this point many times, Shternberg also provided a portrait of a people with "virtually no sense of land ownership" where "communism and individualism coexist without tension."[75]

What was lost in the process is that the article that found its way into *Russkie Vedomosti* was one of Shternberg's first, and one outlining a clan system which Shternberg would later come to recognize as far less fixed than he first perceived it. Looking back he once reflected, "I took them all for pure-blooded aristocrats."[76] Given the swell of non-Nivkhi into the area, increasing dislocations through travel and trade, and the demographic havoc wrought by disease, he realized that much of what he had been presented was an ideal system. The Soviet ethnographer Anna Smoliak also pointed out that intermarriage with Nanai, Evenk, and Manchurian Chinese prefigured the character of many Nivkh settlements in a way that made close adherence to the marriage rules described by Shternberg somewhat difficult; further, Chuner Taksami noted that actual examples of Shternberg's labrynthine systems were few.[77]

That the clan system may not have functioned as methodically as suggested, that group marriage was not as licentious as it sounded, that Shternberg himself was not wholly loyal to the Marxian strain of materialism for which Engels had recruited him (he once called Marxism "a hackneyed reworking of the Hegelian triad"),[78] or that Nivkhi at the turn of the century were far from an isolated tribe waiting to be discovered, were moments soon to be lost in a handful of popular and scholarly accounts. Such lost moments were early but not final examples of the ways in which Nivkh lives would be redetermined over succeeding generations.

Nivkhi on the Newcomers

In 1990 the recollections of Nivkhi I knew who were old enough to look back on the pre-Soviet period spoke to the images of a cosmopolitan island at the crossroads of the mainland and the Pacific Rim. Their accounts stood out sharply from the empty island at the cold edge of the world that I had read so much about. One Nivkh woman in Okha explained to me,

> My father was born in 1892. He used to talk about all the Japanese that used to be on Sakhalin and the Amur. The Japanese used to hire the Nivkhi as workers. There were Chinese too; one of our relatives was married to a Chinese man. She eventually left for China and stayed there. They used to send us letters, but we didn't hear from them after the war [World War II]. As for my grandfather, he was Ainu, he was a very famous hunter. He used to tell us about how they kept horses, and used the horses to go across to Manchuria. Straight from Sakhalin—on boats across the strait and then with the horses into Manchuria. Most of the time they traded furs for Chinese silks and brocades. My father spoke a little Evenk, and a little Chinese. He spoke Japanese best of all, quite well.*

Another retired fisherwoman born in 1929 recounted,

> Sure, my father spoke Japanese. He worked as a brigadier on a Japanese artel. He worked with them before the revolution and then during the war. . . . We used to do a lot of trading. Before we used to live better off, even better than the Russians do now. When I grew up on Baidukov Island [in the northwestern Tatar Strait], we used to have a large wooden house. When we moved to Sakhalin in '35 I had never seen a *zemlianka* [semi-underground Nivkh winter dwelling] before. I couldn't imagine that people lived in it. I thought that it was for keeping dogs. My father took me along once to visit some of our relatives and I wouldn't go in. I wasn't about to walk into a dog house! I thought the dogs would eat me on the spot. On Baidukov we used to have a large house with a verandah. It's still there today. I have some relatives there still. Most of the houses left on Baidukov were built by the Japanese.
>
> Still, it was not like we were cut off from Nivkh life. Every year my father would find a bear den and make off with one of the bear cubs. We would raise it for a year, feed it, and then when it was one year old, we would have a bear

---

* All field quotations are taken from interviews I conducted in the North Sakhalin villages of Nogliki, Chir-Unvd, Okha, Moskal'vo, Nekrasovka, Rybnoe, Rybnovsk, and Romanovka between April and November 1990 and between June and August 1992.

festival. I remember them especially. We had all kinds of Nivkh dishes: *mos'*, *muvi* [blueberry and fish skin custard], *iukola* . . . everything you could want or imagine.

Grigorii Pakskun was only eleven when the Japanese purchased a fishing concession on the northwestern shore in 1922. In the few years after the October Revolution, when the tsarist Whites and the bolshevik Reds were struggling for control of the Far East, Japan assumed control of the entire island from 1920 to 1925.

> I remember the Japanese but they were only in Grigor'evka for three years. They arrived by some agreement in 1922 and left when the Soviets came in 1925. Most of them were fishermen who arrived with their families. They seemed to get along pretty well with everyone. There were a few Russians in our area, like the artel "Pike" in Rybnoe, "Sazan" in Grigor'evka, and "Swan" in Tengi. But mostly there were Chinese merchants, selling dry goods. They had the strangest jewelry and the most beautiful brocades. But by 1925 they were gone too.

Raisa Taigun, born in 1918, was living in the village of Vereshchagino just to the south of Rybnoe when the Japanese worked there.

> Vereshchagino was the prettiest place. Beautiful! In the middle of the village there were trees and flowers—that was when we were still little. There was a Nivkh cemetery. That's where we had the little mortuary houses [*raf*, in Nivkh] where people's ashes and amulets were kept. But eventually people gave that up. The schoolchildren used to play there and take the amulets. Cleaned them out. Today it's all sand. Sand from old houses. Beside the town was the Japanese fishery, from 1915 on. That's gone now too. It had "1915" written right on it . . .
>
> They say that they took all the Chinese and Japanese away in 1925. They recruited them, they said. My mother talked about how my older brother would go up to the Japanese at the Third Fishery and—how do you call those big Japanese dishes?—he would ask them for rice to try. They would always give him some and he would run back home. They gave him sugar too. It was all of half a kilometer from Vereshchagino to the Third. The Chinese, they said, used to marry our Nivkhi, and they lived in Vereshchagino. What good cooks they are, the noodles and broths they would make . . .
>
> Sometimes our parents would go ask us to mail a package at the Japanese station and we would come running back saying, "The Japanese chased us away!" Everyone was afraid of them. They didn't have any women. That's what my mother said. I didn't know any myself. We had a Chinese store too. A little house. A little bigger than this room maybe [3m × 4m]. They had everything! Real honey! What they didn't have! The beads were so beautiful. My mother used to take me there. And little boats. Little sailboats.

There was one woman I met over the course of my stay who was in her nineties, and who could look back on the period from personal experience. Her name was Kalrik and she lived in the predominantly Nivkh village of Chir-Unvd ("New Life," in Nivkh), which was created when the Soviets consolidated four smaller Nivkh villages in the area in the 1920s. She was the only Nivkh I was to meet over my eventual nine months on Sakhalin who did not rely regularly on the Russian language, and I traveled along with Galina Dem'ianovna Lok, a Nivkh ethnographer from nearby Nogliki, in order to meet her.

Visiting Chir-Unvd had held a strange appeal for me since I first began reading about Nivkhi in Moscow. Both Shternberg and his young graduate student Iurii Kreinovich had both worked there, and travelers like Charles Hawes had written in 1901 of the fine French tastes of the adjacent Russian community of Ado-Tymovo. Ado-Tymovo, built on the ashes of a Nivkh village that had been burnt down to make way for Russian settlers, had been a popular way station for people moving across the island from shore to shore. In a stranger twist, it was a matter of some civic pride that the actor Yul Brynner's father had been one of the area's leading merchants, before he fled with his family to China with the advance of the bolsheviks.

But the Ado-Tymovo of the current day was an unexpected shadow of its former self. With the Nogliki-Iuzhno-Sakhalinsk train barely coming to a halt along its edge each morning to exchange a few passengers, the town was a cluster of some twenty abandoned shells of houses overgrown by huge thickets of grass and trees. Some five families still lived there, and in what surely should have been one of the great discoveries of the USSR-in-perestroika, it still housed its own store in an abandoned apartment, with a respectable selection of goods and family-run service. Were it not for the crumbling houses slumped down amid groves of trees, it would be hard to believe that this deteriorating way station had ever been anything but a grassy clearing in the forest.

Chir-Unvd, ten kilometers away by motorcycle, is a small village with a population of approximately 280, of whom 200 are Nivkhi. Settled alongside the Tym' River amid forest and distant hills, it was quite beautiful, with rich soil and verdant pastures. Until the 1960s it had been a prosperous collective farm, but with the drive to reduce the number of villages on Sakhalin under Khrushchev and Brezhnev, the farm was gradually dismantled; the government reassigned the local work force to a cattle-raising operation in a neighboring village ten kilometers away. Since then the government had been paying only sporadic attention; in 1990 half the village was unemployed and most of the villagers lived by raising their own food and fishing out of sight of visiting officials. The true disinterest on the part of the state was evinced, ironically, when regional officials agreed to improve the decrepit housing situation by building twenty-five new homes on the side of the main pasture. In this forested valley where winter temperatures drop to as low as −40 degrees Celsius, government engineers chose an Uzbek enterprise to construct Central Asian-style homes with large windows, thin walls, and light foundations. Contrary to the normal tradition of taking several years to build anything at a snail's pace, these houses were turned out and signed over at lightning speed in the winter some six months before I arrived. Only when spring thaw set in did the new occupants realize that the plaster had never actually dried but had simply frozen. Huge plaster patches inside and out were caving in about them. Radiators, inadequate for the harsh winter, had to be re-piped at the residents' expense, along with replacing the faulty wiring. Rather than dividing Chir-Unvd into "old" and "new" as everyone had expected, the juxtaposition of the old and new produced a strangely organic look, with the older wooden houses in various postures of slump, stoop, and outright abandonment, and the newer, decomposing plaster efforts of the previous year, looking easily twenty years old, fast collapsing on their own.

Kalrik lived with her niece in a two-room cabin near the cemetery. The house was sparsely lined with three beds and two tables, a refrigerator, and a television, but was dominated in all respects by the central Russian wood stove found in most of the village homes. Every wall seemed pitched at a different angle.

> Before the revolution, when the Russians first appeared here, they started immediately to distribute rations . . . rice, sugar, and flour. We had never seen these things before and we were delighted. It had been a hungry year: There had been few fish that season and people were starving. The food meant a lot to us. When my younger sister was born in 1916, my parents called her Paek [ration, in Russian]. That's her Nivkh name!
>
> Still we didn't see the Russians very often. There were four stores in Ado-Tymovo—Japanese, Chinese, Russian, and Korean. Four stores that all served Nivkhi! But I mean, ones that accepted fur instead of money. Most of the time we didn't have money. Our people would come in from hunting, and there would be an exchange. They would give in the fur at the Chinese store, take their groceries, and go home. We bought grain mostly, rice and flour. . . . Everyone liked the Chinese silks most of all. We would make our own clothes from them. But we would shop around. All the stores took Kolchak money. . . .[79]
>
> In Ado-Tymovo the Chinese also had a school, for Chinese children. It was pretty. We didn't see as many Russians then. Most of the Russians we saw were fugitives from the prisons [*varnaki*, in Russian]. We used to call them "bolsheviks." They were frightening because they were so desperate. They

would steal from villages to keep themselves going. Sometimes they were nicer, and would stay longer and hide. They sometimes asked us to make shoes for them. I had a Russian friend in Ado-Tymovo though, Mitia Torlov. He used to have a gramophone. We would go over to his house and dance to jazz records. That was just before it all changed.

The Russian Administration

What, then, was the extent of the Russian colonial administration of Nivkhi on Sakhalin at the turn of the last century? Russian archival documents provide an inherently partial account (here Japanese and Chinese accounts would make a larger contribution), but this sense of incompleteness may stem from an administration that was itself inherently partial.

Despite sporadic state policy shifts regarding the administration of Siberian indigenous peoples, the tsarist government at the turn of the century had no overarching plan for native development.

> Thus, even at the time when the indigenous peoples of Siberia were better known than ever before, they hardly mattered as part of the empire and were totally irrelevant in terms of the "accursed questions" that the politicians and the intellectuals grappled with. They were not even history: as far as most people (and history narratives) were concerned, the conquest of Siberia ended with "Ermak's rout of Kuchum."[80]

The most frequent observation found in Russian state reports of the late 1800s and early 1900s was that, since the northern half of the island had no administration to speak of, no one except exile ethnographers like Shternberg and Pil'sudskii knew much of anything about the native inhabitants. In 1911 the Sakhalin government wrote to the maritime governor-general in Khabarovsk that Giliaks had been miscategorized as nomadic when they were in fact sedentary. "Despite their number and the fact that they occupy the enormous northern portion of the island rich in fish and animals," he wrote, "the island administration has paid little attention to them."[81] Other officials noted that Nivkhi were "completely outside administrative control."[82] As of 1909 only 194 Russians were residing on North Sakhalin, spread out in the communities of Rybnoe, Astrakhanovka, Nevel'skoe, Uspenskoe, Valuevo, and Liangery. They were attended to sporadically by government *strazhniki*, or rural police constables.

Occasionally the government's attention turned to the use of Nivkh artworks as ornaments for the empire, and the attention could be elaborate, as was the case with the Amur Nivkh Pozvein in 1862. Pozvein had worked as a guide for Nevel'skoi (and later Tikhmenev). In recognition of the furs, birch baskets, and fish nets made from nettles that Nevel'skoi took back with him to St. Petersburg, the Imperial Economic Society of St. Petersburg initiated eighteen months of correspondence between three governors-general, an admiral, and a prince to ensure that Pozvein was rewarded for his contributions with a gold medal on the proper imperial ribbon.[83]

On Sakhalin, as one official noted in 1883, Russians generally did as they liked, and Giliaks followed suit.[84] In practice, this meant that the Russians forcibly appropriated native fishing sites, leaving Giliaks with little recourse.[85] The role of convict settlers on Nivkh communities should also not be underestimated. By 1893 more than thirteen thousand convicts, former convicts, and exile settlers were living on the island.[86] Forsyth has noted that the Nivkh population dropped dramatically during the early years of the Sakhalin prison administration—by some estimates, up to a third of Nivkhi died from associated diseases or by foul play.[87] It was former convicts who originally razed a Nivkh village to make way for Ado-Tymovo, later murdering entire Nivkh families who persisted in staying on.[88] There are no records of Giliak insurrections, though that too may only remind us of still further partiality.

Politically, efforts were begun in the 1880s to create a network of native officials, or *starosti*, who would act in the service of the colony. Although Shternberg would later write of the futility of the *starosta* system, his original agreement with prison officials, who permitted him to travel to Giliak areas, enabled Shternberg to appoint the native overseers himself.[89] Rinzō indicates that the Manchus had attempted to institute a similar system approximately a hundred years earlier, but as Shternberg noted from his own experience, the few willing *starosti* tended to be among the most obsequious and least influential in the Nivkh communities.[90] In 1911 Gondatti, the regional governor-general, discouraged a campaign to make Sakhalin Nivkhi eligible for military service; the idea had been that military service would aid in their gradual Russification while their numbers would add to the strength of the forces. "Natives knew the backward regions," Gondatti conceded, but that "to expect that the *inorodtsy* [people of a different birth] will be promising and loyal soldiers is difficult to assess, since many of them spend more time with the Chinese than they do with they Russians."[91]

Economically, the picture is equally disparate. Some Nivkhi found wage employment on a Russian artel, such as that of Grigorii Zotov in Rybnoe where more than five hundred Nivkhi worked in high season. But what they were paid and how they were employed is unclear. More notoriously, others worked as bounty hunters in the service of the prison administration, hunting down fugitive prisoners and returning them to the authorities. Felling a "white sable" brought Nivkhi not only financial remuneration but the morbid respect of the administration. Prison officials, such as the officer who penned the following 1887 letter, were effusive in their praise for Nivkh efficiency in this regard.

> The Giliak Vas'ka has long distinguished himself by his energetic participation in the search for fugitive exiles. Only recently he personally returned six men. . . . Further, the antagonism expressed by exiles toward him is a clear sign of his diligent efforts. In light of the above, I have the honor of awarding the Giliak Vas'ka a special monetary award in the sum of three rubles for each prisoner caught, in recognition of his exemplary service.[92]

When Nivkhi went wanting in times of famine, as was the case when storms and low tides curbed the salmon runs, the government made a number of efforts to organize food relief to native communities. This was often a complex operation, however, since, as the island's military governor observed in 1909, there was not a single government official on the northern half of the island.[93] At one point in 1908 foodstuffs such as rice from Saigon, flour, and sugar were shipped through private merchants on the northwestern shore, leading to a myriad of investigations when the supplies immediately disappeared.[94] Particularly bad years were 1908, 1914, and 1917.

To understand the famines affecting Nivkhi during these years, particularly in contrast to the bucolic picture offered by Rinzō of the same area only a hundred years earlier, one has to consider the impact of the intense and repeated Russian encroachments upon all the most prominent fishing and hunting sites. Colonial officials routinely remarked on Giliak laziness as the root of the problem, but the Polish émigré ethnographer Bronislaw Pil'sudskii countered with a spirited defense:

> To attest to Giliak laziness is to never have seen them at work, for example, during the fishing season when, to not even speak of the men, women work from morning to night with such energy that their hands start to swell. . . . Laziness cannot possibly be the leading marker of a people that look upon it as a vice. In the winter . . . they are also obliged to work. They hunt deer, bears in their dens, and the sable with traps. They gather wood, repair tents, work on skis, the sled, dishes, and so on; finally, they must travel to distant locations . . . to exchange nettles and nets for seal oil, seal skins, and other things they don't have in the Tymovsk Valley. As for women, there is nothing to say—they are eternally at work.[95]

Pil'sudskii pointed out that Nivkhi normally lived in their own houses for their entire lives, but that by 1900 many had been forced to move three or four times because of Russian encroachment, creating a drain on their resources. "After all this, could anyone be surprised that Tymovsk Giliaks live in such ramshackle lean-to's . . . They hardly know whether next year they will be obliged to move and start all over again."[96]

No particular efforts at Russification were made in the cultural sphere since, as we saw above in the military recruitment example, the perceived questions of loyalty and cultural difference seemed too great. In contrast to the Japanese, who had set up twelve schools on South Sakhalin for Ainu children by 1917,[97] no schools were established for Giliaks.[98] Only one Nivkh was known to have been formally educated by the turn of the century, Imdin, who had been sent by Pil'sudskii to study in Vladivostok. It was Imdin who reported to Charles Hawes the legend of a group of brothers who traveled with their writings long ago during a storm. With the storm at its peak, the wind carried away the papers of two of the brothers, the Giliak and the Tungus, and the art of writing was forgotten to them soon after. The other brothers, whose descendants went on to become the Chinese and the Japanese, saved their writings and traveled on to a new country.[99] In early Soviet accounts, it became popular to cite the example of the tsarist Sakhalin administrator in 1913 who expressed interest in education for Giliak children, were it not for the "certain odor" that precluded their being exposed to Russian children. As one early Soviet reformer put it, "Such was the dilemma: either shed the 'certain odor' or remain in darkness. The latter alternative wins by default, since the Giliak native—politically and morally forgotten—has had no chance to attempt the former."[100] Other prerevolutionary officials were more solicitous. In 1911 the Sakhalin governor wrote the governor-general of the Amur region requesting that the Sakhalin aborigines be upgraded from the status of "wandering" to the status of "semi-sedentary," a legal change that would have afforded them greater social services. "[Giliaks and Oroks]," he wrote, "are hardly inclined to run from culture," but his arguments appeared to have little sway.[101]

Efforts to convert Nivkhi to the Russian Orthodox faith appear to have been equally minimal. As early as 1887 the prison administration in Dué sent missionaries to North Sakhalin, but without clear results.[102] By 1901 the Sakhalin military governor cited only two Nivkh men and two Nivkh boys who had been converted.[103]

While local administrators debated the implications of nomadic and sedentary statuses for Nivkhi, the one real legacy of the legal debates remained the symbolic change brought about by the 1822 Speranskii reforms. By the early nineteenth century the aboriginal Siberian *inozemets* (man of a different land) graduated to *inorodets* (man of a different birth), as the historian Yuri Slezkine has shown.[104] Politically, the term *inorodets* was applied to anyone not speaking the Russian language, such that even Ukrainians were sometimes included in this category; but legally the list was considerably shorter, ranging from Siberian natives to hill tribes of the Caucasus to the Kirghiz. In a 1910 article Shternberg argued that neither the political nor the legal uses of the term was appropriate, since the reliance on language "characterizes neither the level of culture, nor the degree of national (*natsional'nogo*) self-awareness of a given individual." When neither race nor religion managed to satisfy Shternberg's criteria, he arrived at the one determinant that seemed to link all *inorodtsy* together—alienation from European culture.[105] In the years leading up to the October Revolution, Nivkhi were defined as non-Europeans; they were also about to become much less Asian.

Four

1920s and the New Order

> Vulgar philistines say that socialism is a structure
> of total stagnation. Rubbish, the crassest rubbish!
> Only with socialism does real progress begin. Man
> will look for the first time at himself as if at raw
> material, or at best, as at a half-finished product,
> and say: "I've finally got to you my dear *homo sa-*
> *piens*, now I can get to work on you, friend!"
> *(Lev Trotsky, "A Few Words on How to Raise a*
> *Human Being")*[1]

> One thing Vas'ka knew for certain: Soviet power,
> like the sea, washes over all shores. And didn't he
> like the sea?
> *(from Ruvin Fraerman, "Vas'ka Giliak")*[2]

The Building of Soviet Power in the Far East

While the October Revolution echoed around the globe in November
1917, the news took some time to reach Siberia's northern natives. It was
a full eight years before the Soviets were able to establish a unified government straight across to the Pacific, and still a few years more before
they fully made themselves known in the remotest corners of the former
empire. For most native northerners the overall breakdown of the established order was enough to signal that change was at hand. Others came
into direct contact with prolonged fighting, since Siberia was one of the
last holdouts of the imperial forces. In the Far East, fighting went on
directly in Evenk, Nivkh, Nanai, Ulchi, and Udegei territories. "One can
say with certainty," the Russian scholar G. Lebedev wrote in 1920, "that
the Russian Revolution has saved [the northern peoples] from their
'friends' forever, from theft and deception, but on the other hand, the
Civil War has affected them in the most harmful way. Before these small
nationalities were shamelessly and inhumanely taken advantage of by our
[Russian] 'Kulturtrager' [culture-bearers]. . . . Today . . . trade has
ceased, there is no bread . . . no salt, no needles, no thread. . . . The situation is completely tragic."[3] However, it was not only their perceived

helplessness but their backwardness that made these peoples unique. It was a backwardness at once borne from their perceived primitiveness, and one that left them, in Engels's mind, closer to a communist life-style than were many of their new modern compatriots. It was this kind of backwardness that made the progress of Nivkhi so emblematic of what the Soviet state had to offer. The aboriginal peoples, Lebedev suggested, "for whom modern life is a bona fide fairy tale on the scale of *A Thousand and One Nights*," were by consequence "the truest proletarians," and they deserved state assistance.

In the Russian Far East, the Civil War continued through the early 1920s. A pro-bolshevik Far Eastern Republic was established in 1920, tenuously declaring administration over the Transbaikal, Amur, Primor'e, and Kamchatka regions, as well as northern Sakhalin. It eventually merged with the RSFSR in 1922, but not until after several fundamental decrees had been made, decrees that would later be instrumental in the charter of the Moscow-based Committee of the North. The Far Eastern Republic's minister of nationality affairs was Karl Ianovich Luks.[4] One of Luks's first and most important acts was the decree, "To all Peoples of Non-Russian Nationality of the Far Eastern Republic," issued in 1921:

> The constituent assembly of the Russian Far East ensures the right of all nationalities of the Far Eastern Republic to an independent cultural life. Every nationality or tribe has the right to independently determine all aspects of their national life free of pressure on the part of the state. The Russian working masses, having taken power into their own hands, have triumphantly turned away from the policy of pressuring and badgering smaller nationalities, as practiced from the time of the tsars. . . . Henceforth the state aspires only to the general governing and control over the overall way of life of each nationality, without which the existence of a united, powerful state would be inconceivable.[5]

Nonetheless a responsibility accompanied the new directives: "Each individual citizen of each nationality must carefully remember that these rights have been apportioned by the working masses, and their significance will be manifested only through the maintenance and strengthening of the workers' state."[6] Luks was fast to map out a vision of aboriginal government within the new Soviet system. Native autonomy would be based on a three-tiered system of administration, beginning at the bottom with clan councils, mediated by native coordinators, and convened regularly at Clan Council Congresses. Native courts were slated to have the main voice in resolving local disputes. The ministry barred traders from native areas, pledged to establish trading points to ensure access to essential goods, and also set aside funds for native education.[7]

The problem Luks had in implementing these reforms grew not only from the exigencies of the ongoing civil war but from the very nature of the autonomy being drawn up. The bolshevik agenda for cultural development called for all the nationalities of the new Union to draw together, while others, such as the Russian ethnographer Vladimir Bogoraz, saw virtues in having the northern peoples live apart. Bogoraz was an influential player in the early development of aboriginal policy in Soviet Siberia and the Far East. Having been exiled to Kolyma in 1890, he had impeccable political credentials. His monumental study, *The Chukchee*, which resulted from his internment, made him one of the foremost ethnographers (along with Lev Shternberg) to lead the new field of Soviet ethnography. But while the closing line to Bogoraz's 1908 monograph on the Chukchi made his sentiments about Russian-native contacts clear, "In modern times, the same as two centuries ago, Russianization for this nomadic and primitive people would bring destruction and death,"[8] he went out on a limb still further with a 1922 article pressing for native reservations before a largely unreceptive readership.

> Currently the state approaches the natives with the same line as before: "Hand it over." They take their fish and nets, they kill reindeer for the meat, never at the proper time and always in excess, with no idea of the environmental or economic circumstances. For the sake of competition, they propose to compare the natives with the local Russians, to merge them together, even where it concerns the division of reindeer, to count the natives as the same as everyone else and limiting them to monthly rations. This kind of merger is a virtual end to the natives—they are crushed into smithereens like an earthenware pot tossed in with iron kettles.[9]

Here and in another 1923 article Bogoraz argued in favor of the North American and Scandinavian experiences of creating territorial reservations.[10] The idea was stopped short by the *Narkomnats*, the People's Commissariat on Nationalities in Moscow, which directed native affairs in Siberia until 1924. The reaction of later historians, such as Mikhail Sergeev, writing in 1955, sums up the problem Bogoraz faced:

> [The reservations proposal] found itself in scandalous contradiction with Marxist-Leninist teaching on the noncapitalist development of backward peoples and their passage to socialism through the active assistance of the victorious proletariat. It ran counter to the objectives of national construction and the socialist development of the North, and testified to the profound lack of understanding of the very nature of the Soviet nationalities policy. Its author was not aspiring to give backward tribes a new culture, but to leave them in isolation, to artificially preserve an exotic "museum culture." Such a "conservation" of backward "races" through their isolation in special "human reser-

vations" advocated the theory and practice of modern reactionary Anglo-American science, dedicated to the service of imperialism. . . . It goes without saying that such a vain and politically harmful concoction did not even merit discussion among Soviet authorities.[11]

It was clear early on that Siberian peoples were to play an integral part in the new society.

As the Civil War dragged on in the Far East, Sakhalin's fate hung in the balance more than people realized. As the bolshevik-led Far Eastern Republic tried to gain an administrative foothold in the region, a 1923 meeting of the party politburo in the Kremlin, attended by Stalin, Trotsky, Zinoviev, and others, resolved to sell off Sakhalin altogether to the Japanese for one billion yen. Under the 1905 agreement following Russia's defeat in the Russo-Japanese War, Japan already owned the lower half of the island, known as Karafuto. Japan later took control of the entire island in 1920 and had begun to develop the northern oil and coal deposits in earnest.[12] In June 1924 the politburo again discussed how long it would take to evict the island's residents were the island to be sold.[13] However, by 1925 the Red Army gained control of Russia's northern half of Sakhalin and began to call on all Whites to hand themselves in.[14]

Since much of the Sakhalin population had landed there as punishment by the tsarist government in the first place, many were content to see the White administration fall; still others were eager to see the departure of the Japanese, whose appropriation of North Sakhalin in 1920 was protested by the Americans, as well as Sakhalin residents, who were witness to the uncommonly zealous development of the island's natural resources.[15] The problem, however, also lay in convincing the dwindled Russian population to return to work—some Soviet officials claimed that the Japanese had paid North Sakhalin residents so extravagantly that "young women were walking about in silks, thinking this to be normal, not even realizing their humiliation."[16]

By 1925 approximately 2,000 people remained in the Rybnovsk district: 1,017 Russians, 620 Nivkhi, 273 Koreans, and 53 Chinese.[17] Armed with newspapers and Stalin's brochure on the results of the Fourteenth Party Conference, Communist Party coordinators set out through the district to cultivate membership. In one of their earliest memos they urged representatives to focus on youth, work up to antireligious themes gradually, and not to alienate women by leaping pell-mell into discussions of sexual diseases. However, they also advised, "Don't even think about working among the Giliaks."[18] This task would be left to specialists.

The Work of the Committee
of the North

In 1922 the Soviet government entrusted the welfare of the Siberian indigenous population to the ethnographic bureau of the *Poliarnyi Pod-
otdel*, the polar political division of the People's Commissariat on Nationalities (*Narkomnats*). With the dissolution of the *Narkomnats* in
1923 a more broadly based planning body was proposed, and in 1924
this came in the form of the Committee for the Assistance to Peoples of
the Northern Borderlands, or the Committee of the North.

With the founding of the Committee in June 1924 the Moscow-based
working group set out three main priorities for northern native development: native self-government, economic reorganization, and social enlightenment. Immediately proposals were made for creating a network of
northern correspondents, for starting a special fund for northern problems, for releasing native peoples from payment of direct taxes, and for
recruiting students to work in the North. Given their ambitious program,
what is striking about the Committee's early work was the shared high
regard for existing native channels as an avenue for reform.[19]

One of the central means for achieving this compromise between the
"traditional" and the "modern" became the establishment of *kul'tbazy* or
"culture bases," all-purpose social service centers that would serve as the
main avenue for information collection and program implementation.
During the ten years of the Committee's existence, eighteen such bases
were established. The idea was that they would serve nationalities rather
than regions, and would look to the "furthest, darkest, least accessible,
and least studied" groups as their constituents.[20] In 1929 the third of
such bases was established in the town of Nogliki, on Sakhalin's north-
eastern shore. Within a few years the Culture Base comprised a hospital,
a two-storied boarding school (*internat*), a reading room (*izba-chi-
tal'nia*), three houses for the staff, a storage wing, an ice house, a dog
stable, trade workshops, and administrative offices for the district clan
council, the Communist Party, the Youth League, and the local newspaper, *Bolshevik Fish Run*. Still more buildings, such as a veterinary unit,
were planned.[21]

By locating the Culture Base at Nogliki the Committee of the North
was following its pledge to serve the farthest and the darkest of native
communities. Sakhalin officials rarely if ever visited Sakhalin's eastern
shore since they took up active administration of the island in the late
1800s. Nogliki's location at the intersection of the only three roads in the
area also made it ideal for the work of the *Dom Tuzemtsa*, or House of

the Native, which formed an integral part of the Culture Base's work. In prefatory remarks in a 1931 *Bolshevik Fish Run* piece about the House, correspondent Nikolai Rutkevich saw public relations in overnight accommodation.

> Natives pass through Nogliki for many reasons . . . to the hospital, school, and cooperative . . . or simply to look at the big village. In the House of the Native they will be able to warm up, have something to eat, and stay overnight. . . . Representatives of the district council will tell the natives in their own language about Soviet cultural construction, about how Soviet power is improving the lives of the natives through the Culture Base. . . . Doctors will read lessons about the human body, about epidemic diseases . . . Teachers will organize discussion groups with the magical flashlight about cultural construction . . . The Technical Director of the Culture Base will tell them how to best build their house, dog houses, and *iukola* racks . . . The veterinarian will tell them how to help their dogs and reindeer.[22]

While there was much emphasis on political and cultural enlightenment, rapid modernization with a sensitivity to local circumstances was the express objective: "Class work should not occupy too much time—not only because of an overload of unfamiliar, intellectual activity which may be discouraging to the natives, but because bookish questions are less of what they need. . . . The goal is to give practical knowledge and to apply modern culture and technology to local culture."[23] Correspondingly, the formation of hunting and fishing artels, small collective enterprises of up to twenty members, were formed among the Nivkhi through the *kul'tbazy*. Sakhalin's *Okhottovarishchestvo*, a hunting union, was founded in 1925. Intended to eliminate exploitation in the fur trade, the union started with fourteen "hunting cells" bringing together 206 native members.[24] Like many early collective unions it was a share-holding operation, originally under the organization of the Sakhalin Joint-Stock Company (*Aktsionernoe Sakhalinskoe Obshchestvo*). Fishing artels were easier to establish, partly because many already existed before the revolution, and partly because Nivkh fishermen frequently worked in groups. *Sovetskii Rybak* (Soviet Fisherman) was established in 1927 to lend credit to local fishing entrepreneurs.[25]

Images of the "magical flashlight" predominate in the literature of the early years of Sovietization among Sakhalin Nivkhi. Culture volunteers known as "Red Delegates" taught Nivkhi to make bread, "and soon Nivkh women were comparing bread and competing." Nivkhi were taught to plant potatoes, "and soon they were harvesting bushels."[26] In 1926 one Russian reformer wrote of the first instance when he screened motion pictures to a Nivkh audience:

[They] had virtually no idea precisely what a movie was, or how it was that living people, horses, moving cars, ships, and crowded battles could take shape on the screen. Some ran away in fear that there really were armed crowds, that it was not simply a picture, but something sent by an invisible power. However, little by little they began to request certain films such as *Death Bay*, *Battleship Potemkin*, and other revolutionary works.[27]

What such accounts took for granted was the childlike fear of and fascination with the Russian prestations of modernity. But they also overlooked many of the difficulties in implementing the Soviet agenda.

While artels were established relatively quickly, for example, the question of native self-government came about more awkwardly. The main difficulty was in defining the Nivkh community as a political unit: the carefully triangulated Nivkh clan structure had largely atrophied toward the end of the 1800s, and there were few parts of the island where Nivkhi lived apart from the Russian community.[28] Documents outlining the formation of "clan councils" were interpreted to local officials as simply meaning "Nivkh."

The structure of native self-government was highly organized, at least on paper. Karl Luks played a hand in the design of four tiers of governing in his 1926 "Temporary Administrative Position of the Native Tribes of the Far Eastern Province."[29] The lowest level was the "General Clan Meeting" open to all members of a given clan (*rod*) over the age of eighteen. It was to meet once a year; voting was to be open and decided by a simple majority. The second level was the "Clan Executive Committee" (*Rodovoi ispolnitel'nyi komitet*), or RIK. Having an RIK required at least fifteen clan families. The RIK elected a chairman and two officers, one of whom would serve as deputy chair. The third level was the "District Clan Executive Committee." This committee united the various clan committees in a given district or *raion* under the guidance of a district chair, elected for a one-year term. It was at this tier that natives had the power to resolve local conflicts, except those involving political crimes, murder, robbery, violence, forgery, and speculation. Finally, at the highest level, all voting natives would attend the "District Clan Congress" held at least once a year. The Congress was the highest organ of Soviet power in the native community; it required at least four hundred members and had its own deputies—one deputy for every twenty-five people but no more than twenty-five deputies. This same structure was reaffirmed in a 1936 directive, although the names of committees were altered slightly.[30]

By 1928 a network of fourteen Nivkh village councils (*tuzsovety*) were developed in tandem with two Nivkh district councils (*tuzriki*)—one in Nogliki, on the eastern shore; the other in Viskovo, on the western shore. However, the Sakhalin Nivkh councils were run more as information posts than administrative organs. Not a single chairman of all the councils was literate, and, as one Sakhalin official reported, none of the councils functioned much at all.[31] But despite the disjuncture between theory and practice, a performative gesture was achieved in spurring Nivkhi to realize their potential roles in the new system. As the Russian ethnographer Erukhim (Iurii) Kreinovich, one of the Nivkhi's first political organizers, observed,

> To speak of a high quality of work of the native councils in their first year of existence, given an almost complete absence of literacy, is not called for. But nevertheless in the protocols of the meetings, one can see that the majority of questions are directed at the cultural-economic organization of native lives . . . the development of private plots, the organization of fishing artels, schools and literacy units, as well as Houses of the Native, as has already been implemented in Chaivo.[32]

What the Viskovo council did organize, however, was one of the first Nivkh schools. In 1927 the school year opened with a play featuring scenes of Giliak life and a speech about Soviet government. Over the course of that year twenty-four Nivkh students learned to read and write, evidently a testimony to the virtues of a good instructor, since other reports routinely indicated the reluctance of Nivkh parents to release their children into the hands of Russian educators. When Russian Petr Tuganov served as the teacher (*shkol'nyi rabotnik*, or *shkrab*) in 1927, parents eagerly sent their children to him. When he left because of the conditions—classes were held at the home of a Chinese resident where five regular guests smoked and drank in the same room as the students— interest dropped off. Tuganov was succeeded by Kotovshchikov, a Russian instructor who drank along with the adult guests, who was then replaced by a Korean instructor by the last name of Kim, who traded in furs, and so on.[33] Circumstances were similar in the central Sakhalin Nivkh town of Chirevo (near Ado-Tymovo), where the first school was held in a bathhouse.[34]

With time it became clear that certain aspects of the agenda of the Committee of the North were not just difficult to implement, but fundamentally at odds with the exigencies of regional development charging alongside. One stream of the Committee's work was to empower Nivkhi to assert political and economic control over their territory. Yet on Sakhalin, this goal was becoming increasingly quixotic. Newcomers from European Russia were settling in large numbers as a move to stabilize the northern Soviet half of the island. When the new arrivals predicted the imminent extinction of local Nivkhi, one local official noted, it was increasingly difficult to tell whether this was a regret or a request. He observed, "While it's clear that the Nivkhi aren't going anywhere, it is also clear that the problems of the Nivkhi are not going to stop either mining or agricultural colonization."[35]

However, what the Committee may have lacked in political or economic clout, they made up for in energy and innovation, with early reformers such as Shternberg's protégé Kreinovich, now enshrouded by Nivkhi in an almost legendary status. Bogoraz, who through the ethnography department of the Institute of Geography from 1922 on helped to train many of the young officials who were to go eastward, looked upon his early work with a messianic vision.

> We must send to the North not scholars but missionaries, missionaries of the new culture and the new Soviet statehood. Not the old ones but the young ones, not the experienced professors but the recent graduates, brought up in the new Soviet environment and ready to take to the North the burning fire of their enthusiasm born of the Revolution, as well as the practical skills perfected by revolutionary work. Before they begin their work, these young agents of the Committee of the North must receive complete and thorough academic instruction—primarily in ethnography—but in the North their main work will be practical, not academic, in nature.[36]

In contrast to the historically uneasy relationship between ethnography and the state in Western scholarship, the mission of Soviet ethnography in the service of the federal administration had always been a clear one: Over the course of ethnographic research, the new missionaries of socialism were to collect information with a view to facilitating Soviet government in the most expedient way possible.[37] In the early years under Bogoraz, Shternberg, and Smidovich, ethnographic research built an almost Jesuitic tradition of syncretic approaches to new Soviet principles and native categories of administration.

Kreinovich, like Shternberg a generation before him, also became interested in ethnography after reading Engels's *The Origin of the Family, Private Property, and the State.* After his studies in a provincial gymnasium, he went to Leningrad where Bogoraz advised him to study Nivkhi since Shternberg could help him with the language. Against the wishes of his family who protested on the grounds of his health (he had tuberculosis) and his sanity, Kreinovich asked to be posted to Sakhalin in 1926 at the age of twenty, in order to be part of a "bright epoch."[38] Whereas Shternberg had gone to Sakhalin under a repressive order, Kreinovich followed as part of a new vision. Unsure of what to do with the young recruit when he arrived on "the island of my dreams," the Sakhalin Revolutionary Committee in Aleksandrovsk placed him in a native school in Khanduza. However, there Kreinovich quickly succumbed to the epidemics of measles and smallpox that were claiming the lives of Nivkhi around him. He relocated to the central Tym' River valley, where Chir-

Unvd would soon be founded, in order to establish the first *likbez*, or center for the liquidation of illiteracy. From 1926 to 1928 Kreinovich was formally affiliated with the Sakhalin Revolutionary Committee in Aleksandrovsk, first as an assistant to the Commissioner for Native Affairs (*Upoltuz*) and later as the Commissioner himself.

Yet, for an idealist looking to bring light to a dark outpost, Kreinovich found his efforts frequently diminished both by the fledgling infrastructure behind him, which was rarely able to deliver the financial credits he pledged to new Nivkh cooperatives, and by the initial indifference of many Nivkhi themselves. After a year of disappointments Kreinovich wanted to leave, and he wrote to Karl Luks, his supervisor in Khabarovsk who then ran the activities of the Committee of the North in the Far East. Luks's response in June 1928 eventually plied Kreinovich back to work.

> I especially want to get you away from the point you made about ethnography only being of use to [the Nivkhi's] great-grandchildren. We are not doing ethnography in the old sense of the word. All words that end in "—logy" or "—graphy" are bound up in that process or activity, call it what you like, that divides subject from object, "us" (the scholar or researcher) from "them" (the studied, our wards), who in the best instance we "feel for." We want to *erase* this line between subject and object, between us and them. The process of serious Soviet native work is really the nativization [*otuzemlivaniia*] of you and me, in keeping with the ideas of the party. And gradually, from the first few natives who come over to the Soviet way of life, there will be dozens, then hundreds, and then thousands. The objects of study must become subjects![39]

Luks's response was in step with the zeal of the day and persuaded Kreinovich to stay on. Ironically, however, at the close of this new call to arms, Luks advised Kreinovich to give up political work for a time and work on a Nivkh dictionary, so as to renew his energies.[40]

Kreinovich traveled widely during his tenure on the Sakhalin Revolutionary Committee, and he described his overall assignment in 1926 as being six fold: (1) to look for survivals of organized debt servitude; (2) to send evidence of the above to the courts; (3) to organize financial credit to the natives; (4) to train native village chairmen; (5) to help develop hunting and fishing cooperatives; and (6) to compose a native dictionary.[41] But it is not surprising that Kreinovich made more enemies than friends when he began to travel across the island frontier which, by definition, was home mainly to convicted criminals or newcomers looking to make fast money off the fish and fur supplies.

Transforming Nivkhi into masters of their own fate—indeed into the subjects of Luks's manifesto—proved difficult when so many Nivkhi were

7. On the eve of Kreinovich's departure for Sakhalin in 1926, his mentors and colleagues in Leningrad gathered to see him off. (*Top row from left to right*: I. A. Dyshchenko, Saul M. Abramzon, Zakharii E. Cherniakov, Stepan A. Makar'ev; *Middle row*: Ian P. Koshkin, Vladimir G. Bogoraz, Erukhim A. Kreinovich. Lev Ia. Shternberg, Pavel Iu. Moll; *Bottom row*: Sergei N. Stebnitskii, N. G. Shprintsin, Elena V. Talonova.)

in considerable debt to others. One of Kreinovich's reports from 1927 charts a long litany of Russian and Chinese exploiters who had outlasted the transition to the infant Soviet system on Sakhalin. On the eastern shore, Vinokurov, the director of the state *faktoriia*, or trading station, was working for the Japanese, Kreinovich reported, and should be exiled from the island.[42] In Nyivo, to the north of Nogliki, where ten Chinese traders lived, the head trader Yun-Dziun-Fu claimed to be poor, but all the Nivkhi were in debt to him.

> A Giliak will go to visit Yun-Dziun-Fu. Yun-Dziun-Fu's wife is a Giliak. She serves the visitor tea and the Giliak will start to ask Yun-Dziun-Fu to sell him flour and Manchurian tobacco. But the Chinese man always answers the same: If I give you the little I have, the price will be high. And so the Giliak pays, as they all do . . . three to four times the price.[43]

Kreinovich's early documents, now in the archives of the Russian Far East, are covered frequently with sections blackened from censorship, either self-imposed or external. The documents testify not only to the personal antagonism he encountered from most Russian locals, but his own frustration with the contradictions of the new state. Many Sakhalin

8. Photographed here, by Kreinovich, are Churka (*left*) and his son Zagan (Aleksei Churka) (*right*), a Nivkh student, before Zagan's departure in 1926 to a boarding school at the Institute of Northern Peoples in Leningrad. Selecting Nivkh students for the boarding school was one of Kreinovich's first objectives on Sakhalin. Churka agreed to send his son out of professed loyalty to Shternberg, whom he had known forty years earlier during Shternberg's exile in the 1880s.

Russians evidently looked upon Kreinovich as a hangover from an era better forgotten. One Russian asked him, "What's an old bourgeois like you supposed to do to help us? Couldn't they find someone better?"[44] On the same trip, Kreinovich wrote,

> It's time to pay for old sins, and they are indeed many. How does a group of Russians, let alone former criminals condemned to hard labor, get by when they neither sow nor reap their own bread? How did they support themselves before? To me there is no more striking evidence than the look of fear the natives have when they are around them. Can the Revolutionary Committee really think that the presence of people like Kalevskii, Krotov, Boiko, Chervinskii, Meriniuk, Zelinskii, and the Chinese act favorably upon the natives of the eastern shore? I know it not to be the case. Their continued presence on the island can only be seen as silent forgiveness for their actions.[45]

Kreinovich's supervisor Aleksandr Il'in made his own expedition to the Rybnovsk district on the northwestern shore in 1925 and expressed many of the same frustrations:

In the villages of Rybnovsk district, located alongside Russian settlements, Giliaks live somewhat more cleanly. Here, along with the art of card playing, drinking, and cursing, the Giliaks have absorbed a number of aspects of Russian life. Many Giliak yurtas [tents] are fashioned after Russian houses. In many, soap can be found. However, the presence of dirt in Giliak yurtas should in no way be looked upon as a consequence of their cultural heritage. It is the direct consequence of the continual economic oppression of the native and absolute absence of political rights. From the arrival of the Russians, the natives have been hounded from the favorable fishing grounds where they have lived for centuries. From the de facto master of the land, he has quickly been transformed into the object of shameless exploitation. With the loss of the fishing grounds, the haul has diminished but the demand has remained the same. . . . Hungry years have become more frequent and the native has been confronted with the pressing dilemma: What to buy now? Buy a net and forget about a hunting rifle? Or buy a rifle and forget about a net? And how do you get the fish in order to trade for one or the other? Do you feed less fish to your family and dogs in order to sell more? What then do you eat?

Under such economic conditions it is no surprise that Giliaks have been reduced to the dirt and sloth of which it has become so popular to speak, dirt and sloth which indicate the absence of any purpose in life excepting the pursuit of a full stomach and the most immediate of needs. "Soon our Giliak will die out altogether"—is how the surrounding population looks to the future. At the start this might have been posed as a question. However, after years of oppression, darkness, illness, and work of cabals, it is looked upon as fact with the greatest of certainty.

The Sakhalin climate and the surrounding environment do not especially incline one to either laziness or the contemplative mood. On the contrary, they incline one to energy and the urge to struggle. To suggest that dirt and laziness are characteristic of the Giliak people is nonsense. The Sakhalin Giliaks long ago began to make strides to improve their living conditions and continue to do so today. They began to build "Russian-style houses" already thirty-five years ago, and if you visit the village of Viskovo, you will see that they wash their floors too.[46]

From Local Autonomy to Soviet Cultural Construction

Looking back on the early reforms of the Soviet period, the ethnographer Il'ia Gurvich suggested that the process of Sovietization among Siberian indigenous peoples could be divided into several phases:

1917–24: Release from the past
1924–29: Early Sovietization
1929–34: Early collectivization

1934–41: Completion of transition to socialism
1941–45: War years
1945–56: Accelerated industrialization and cultural advancement[47]

The difference on North Sakhalin was that, given that region's late incorporation into the Soviet Union in 1925, there was little distinction between the release from the past and the headlong charge into the Soviet vision of the future. People like Kreinovich, Il'in, and other reformers were recruited and banished from the island long before most Nivkhi became literate. In contrast to the sympathetic accounts of the earliest reformers, Sakhalin news articles of the late 1920s, which appear to have been much closer to popular sentiment than the reports of native affairs officials, focused almost entirely on dirt and the prospects for redemption: "Once, going into a gloomy cabin, I was surprised: Amid the disgusting grime, the smell, and the smoke was a white brochure on the wall with the slogan, 'Lenin said: The Giliak Will Be Clean! Cut Long Hair!' . . . A Giliak boy had brought it home from school."[48]

By the start of the 1930s the mandate of the Committee of the North narrowed, largely owing to the advance of other ministries eastward to assume responsibility for the economic and political reforms. This was also in step with changes taking place at the Institute for Northern Peoples in Leningrad, which had evolved into the main training ground for new native cadres. Under the new directorship of Ian Petrovich Koshkin, a research division for Soviet Cultural Construction was established, which placed new emphasis on the political significance of students not only receiving an education but becoming active facilitators of Soviet policy.[49]

In the field a new rigor was expected from researchers. Many, like Kreinovich, found new ways to meet the political requirements. When he returned to the Far East in 1931 to organize meetings among mainland Nivkhi living along the Amur, his notes were the usual scribbles on current issues—a visiting doctor or disputes over kolkhoz administration. But for the first time since he began field studies in 1926, he added the rubber-stamped tracts of officialese that would be the mainstay of official documents through to the 1980s. On 31 January 1931, in the village of Kol', he recorded in an immaculate longhand,

> *Heard*: Lenin and the national question. What kind of person was Lenin? What role did he play in the formation of the Soviet state? Lenin as leader of the proletariat. What Lenin said about national identity.
>
> *Decreed*: Lenin's enormous role in the liberation of workers, peasants, and peoples was noted. Only thanks to Lenin, smaller nationalities have the right to citizenship, the opportunity to take part in the building of our country, and to be free. It was thanks to someone like Lenin, leader of all leaders.[50]

Scribbles followed thereafter.

With the new banner of "cultural construction," the important difference for reformers such as Kreinovich was that the culture at the forefront was expressly now Soviet, rather than those of the indigenous Siberians. For Nivkhi it inaugurated what would become a dizzying turn in state policy. Whereas Russian Orthodox missionaries on prerevolutionary Sakhalin had hounded them for their pagan ways, Lenin praised them. Yet by 1930, only five years into membership in the Soviet system, icons of native life were again subject to Russian censure.

This narrowing of the Committee's mandate, and the partial conflation of cultures local and Soviet that it detailed, represented the start of a new balancing act that went on to define Stalin's nationality policy; in that policy the languages and cultures of individual nationalities were promoted so long as they contributed to the flourishing of a pan-Soviet community. In the native context the formula mapped neatly onto the professed dialectic between modernity and tradition. Embracing a Comtean brand of evolutionism, the state supported indigenous traditions early on in order that native peoples themselves would recognize the errors of their ways. It was clearly not a new policy for Soviet theorists but one that was gaining greater currency. As the nationalities ideologist S. I. Dimanshtein argued in one of his early 1919 articles, "Soviet Power and the Small Nationalities," the overt distinctiveness of peoples like the Nivkhi would gradually diminish but, like salt, would lend flavor to the Soviet character.

> We as Communists should not make it our business to cultivate nationalism among the smaller nationalities, to become its ideologues or advocates . . . but on the other hand we should avoid the fate of Aesop's donkey,[51] who found himself between two virtually identical haystacks and could not decide which one to start with since there was no reason to prefer one over the other; the donkey died from hunger because of its indecision . . .
>
> We are making it clear to all small peoples on the road to development: we will help you develop your Buriat or Votskii language and culture and so on, since that way you will become more familiar with culture known to all mankind, with revolution, and with communism. Through this development process, you yourselves will be convinced, by your own experience, of the extent to which your nationalism, your national language, confines you. . . . The qualities that distinguish various nationalities [*narodnosti*] will not disappear without a trace but will be, let us say, like salt or sugar sprinkled on food—though they may not be visible, they lend a recognizable flavor.[52]

The shift to Soviet cultural construction of the early 1930s did not reduce Nivkhi to ornamentation or flavoring, but it began a process whereby the state appropriated control over the definition of what "Nivkh" meant. As of 10 February 1930, when Sakhalin Nivkhi, Oroki, and Evenki held their first District Clan Congress in Nogliki, Nivkhi were humble, forward looking people who thought little of their past and their former land-lords. The Nivkh Pimka presented this testimony:

> We—we are a dark and uneducated people. Before Soviet power, people thought of the natives as there to be trod upon [*podmetka*] and said, why not let them die off? The Japanese gave us vodka and little else. Under the Japanese, everyone died off because the Japanese didn't pay us. The Soviet authorities prohibited the sale of vodka and paid us wages. We are grateful. . . . We have become farmers.[53]

This approving nod to Soviet rule was characteristic of the increasingly effusive public discourse of the day, but it was not characteristic of its author, Pimka, who was described during a 1928 expedition to Chir-Unvd as uncooperative and recalcitrant.[54] Rehabilitated for political advantage to the state during the Nogliki native congress of 1930, Pimka was downgraded by 1931 to "that *polukulachnik*," an exploiter of others, according to *Bolshevik Fish Run*.

> At the time of the elections Pimka aspired to the downfall of the kolkhoz, spreading the rumor that those who enter the kolkhoz will be sent to prison; he tried to prevent people from sending their children to school. . . . These facts speak for themselves. The moment has come for the entire native population to lead a decisive battle against class enemies, to strengthen the party, the Communist Youth League, and the kolkhoz. The moment is approaching when, through total collectivization, worker natives will destroy the kulak as a class.[55]

The erratic rise and fall of someone like Pimka was characteristic of the political turbulence of the decade; however, already by the close of the 1920s, official appropriations of native life had begun to present a far more edited version of events.

The state may have tightened its control over the presentation of native identity, but the new rigor did not represent any shortage of idealism. As the years advanced, the process of cultural construction became more standardized, assuming in some instances an almost paramilitary quality. Typical of the new mass emphasis on cultural revolution throughout the Soviet Union was a 1931 *kul'testafeta*, or "culture relay race," organized jointly by students of the Khabarovsk Polytechnical Institute for Peoples of the North and the Communist Youth League. Using the language of an actual race with a start and a finish, the idea was to relay or "bring culture to the taiga and tundra" across six Far Eastern districts which included the town of Viskovo on northwestern Sakhalin.[56] The goal was to liquidate illiteracy among native adults and to produce *kul'tarmeetsy*, or

"Soldiers of Culture," as the graduates of the literacy courses were called, who would in turn pass the baton of culture on to their compatriots.[57]

Spirits were high among the twenty student participants when they presented their manifesto for the race.

> We, participants of the culture relay race, students of the Khabarovsk Polytech-nical Institute for Peoples of the North, welcome the plans of the Central Of-fice of Culture Excursions and the Committee of the North for the cultural storming of the taiga and tundra. We look upon our participation in this great political event with joy. Our firsthand experience in this culture relay race through the districts of the small peoples of the North is a test of our readiness in the battle to reconstruct the semiprimitive North along a new socialist line. We assure the party and all workers that we will bring to bear all our energy and all our years of training to meet this task with honor, in the spirit of the Com-munist Youth League and the bolshevik way. All twenty of us pledge to meet this task as shock-workers [*udarniki*],[58] and to persevere through to the final training of the [new] Soldiers of Culture. . . . We will fight hard for culture, for a new way of life, for the collectivization of the native economy, for the liqui-dation of exploitation [*kulachestvo*], for the correct implementation of the Leninist nationality policy, and for the general line of the party.[59]

"The illiterate man stands outside politics," Lenin wrote, "so first one must teach him to read."[60] This was the mobilizing credo for the students when they arrived in the Viskovo district in July 1931. Eighty-six percent of the local Nivkh population were estimated to be illiterate, but the ex-isting infrastructure of native affairs programs enabled the students to move quickly. Viskovo itself already had a district native bureau (*rai-kul'tshtab*), and three villages—Viskvi, Iuk, and Vas'kvo—had corre-sponding village units (*sel'tuzshtaby*), permitting Soldier of Culture courses to be established in all four places. Twenty-four Nivkhi enrolled in the course in Viskvi, for example, where classes were held in the fishery. Shamans reputedly attempted to disrupt the courses, spreading rumors that participants would be charged for the literacy lessons. A number of women were reluctant at first to participate, until two Nivkh mothers completed the first course and began to enjoy the respect of others.[61]

The Khabarovsk students wrote with particular pride of the forty-nine-year-old Nivkh chairman of the Viskovo district committee, Mikhail Pe-trovich Kul'pin. Although almost completely illiterate at the start of the *kul'testafeta*, Kul'pin had already done much to distinguish himself as a leader among Nivkhi in the new order. As chairman of the Viskovo *tuz-raikom* (native district council) since the start of 1931, he was com-mended in a number of Sakhalin newspapers and state documents for having initiated special sanitation measures among Nivkhi—the digging of garbage ditches outside homes, the daily cleaning of benches and floors, and the construction of a bathhouse and special fish-drying areas. Kul'pin's commitment to social hygiene extended with equal diligence to errant kolkhozniks, many of whom he purged from the fishery. Since Kul'pin himself could not write, V. Kim, the Korean secretary of the native council, prepared a number of dismissal notices for kolkhozniks such as the Russian Plamskovskii who propagated antinative sentiment and "messed up the artel finances like a Black Hundreds element."[62]

Despite his educational handicaps, Kul'pin pledged to become a literacy shock-worker himself, entering into competition with Ugnun, the Nivkh chairman of the village kolkhoz, and spending all his free time with a pen and paper. "To help the collectives produce qualified cadres," the Khabarovsk coordinator wrote, "This is the task before us. . . . The Ivans, the Kul'pins, and the Ugnuns represent the start of this work."[63] Returning to Khabarovsk in October, the six student brigades who had fanned out to native communities across the Far East celebrated the fruits of their efforts. They had planned to train 60 native Soldiers of Culture, but had managed to train as many as 227. Of these, 39 were women, 204 were kolkhozniks, and 38 were members of native councils.[64] "Taking into account our experience, we will arrive at the next finish with even greater results, particularly when in this very year northern peoples are receiving new textbooks, and lessons will be conducted in their native languages. . . . Illiteracy will be liquidated in even the remotest corners of our Union."[65]

Language and the Politics of Knowledge

Accordingly, one of the most important reforms of the 1930s was the creation of a written language for Nivkhi under the aegis of the Committee of the New Alphabet, formed in 1932 to work in tandem with the Down with Illiteracy Society. The most radical aspect of the new literacy campaign was the choice of the Latin alphabet rather than the Cyrillic for the new scripts. The Latin alphabet was not only thought to be more internationalist, it departed in a bold way from the Russificatory overtones of the recent prerevolutionary past, thereby attempting to sidestep both local nationalism and Russian chauvinism. But the new alphabet was not just for unlettered Siberians: "Only on the basis of the new latinized alphabet, easily accessible to the proletariat and the poorest peasantry, can the cultural revolution of the peoples of the Soviet East be fulfilled for those who previously employed Arabic or other complex writing systems which were inaccessible to the broad working masses."[66] The Committee intended its new alphabet for use among a broad range of non-Russian nationalities in a strategy that would not only represent a break from the past but would give far greater control over what broad working masses would be reading. A campaign was launched to drape the new alphabet in the cloth of reform by referring to it as "the new alphabet, born of the October Revolution" and "the Octobrist alphabet of the peoples of the USSR."[67]

The Far Eastern wing of the Committee of the New Alphabet focused on three groups: Chinese (of whom there were still ninety-two thousand in the USSR in 1926),[68] Koreans, and the northern natives. As in the manifesto of the unionwide Committee, a direct link was made between language and politics.

> For the working masses of the peoples of the Soviet Far East who were previously schooled in hieroglyphic or other difficult scripts, or who were with-out writing systems altogether, the path to socialist culture hinges on the crea-tion and cultivation of a new latinized alphabet as a powerful tool of cultural revolution.[69]

The task before them clearly was an enormous one. In their 1932 plan they set up traveling expeditions to study various dialects, orthographies, grammars, and the viability of publishing facilities. As soon as possible, they were to produce primers and readers for eleven nationalities, gram-mars for eight nationalities, special typewriters for ten nationalities, and special support staffs among all fourteen of the nationalities under their jurisdiction.[70]

One reason for the success of the Committee's ambitious plans was that they had the support of existing infrastructures already in place. Party members, local RIKs, ethnographers, Culture Base workers, Red Dele-gates, Soldiers of Culture, and the *rabsel'kory*, a network of proletarian news correspondents (these categories not being mutually exclusive), all joined in the work of the local literacy cells consisting of three to fifteen members. The Sakhalin Committee worked only on the Chinese and Nivkh languages. Kreinovich developed a written script for Nivkh based on one of the language's three dialects,[71] extra teachers were hired in the villages of Nogliki, Viskovo, and Viakhta, and Soldiers of Culture traveled to present the lecture, "Toward a New Alphabet."[72]

Here Kreinovich's mastery of the complex Nivkh language was put to full use. Kreinovich authored the first Nivkh primer *Cuz Dif* (New Word, in Nivkh), which appeared in 1932, and translated a second-grade reader, which appeared in 1933. The texts were intended for use by children in schools, as well as adult workers, through a system of *likbezy* (illiteracy liquidation units). Though both efforts were considered equally impor-tant, it was noted on Sakhalin, as elsewhere, that "social reconstruction of the native economy can be accomplished only with the patience of the younger generation, and not of the older ones still living in an outmoded century, whom it is difficult to reeducate, who have years of outdated customs and old views that they bring to bear on their new life."[73] Kreinovich emphasized that the material was politically oriented against Nivkh exploiters, kulaks, and shamans who resisted the implementation of Soviet institutions. To overcome resistance hidden and overt, he urged local teachers to concentrate their efforts on the poorer echelons of Nivkh society (*batratsko-bedniatskie sloi*) and to set examples from among local Nivkh Communist Youth league members. Particular emphasis was placed on the conversion of women to the Soviet worldview.

> The working Nivkh women represent the most forgotten, exploited part of Nivkh society. Nivkh domestic law, to a large extent created by Nivkh elders, shamans, and kulaks, denies women the same rights assigned to the male producer. The woman is given the worst spot in the house to sleep, on the edge of the bench by the door; in the home of a Giliak with two wives the second wife lives in poverty; the woman is defenseless from the moment of her birth— she is an object to be bought and sold; she is not permitted to take an active part in clan ceremonies. As a result we have almost a complete absence of women in meetings, in the councils, and in the kolkhozes.[74]

Indeed native women across Siberia came to play an increasingly important role in the 1930s as potential builders of culture, not only because of their manifest influence on children but because of the paltry successes of early reforms on older native males.[75]

The new Nivkh textbooks introduced local vocabulary and the stuff of children's readers everywhere: "Boat. Horse. Fish. . . . The little boy goes to school. The little girl goes to school. The children go to school!" But learning to read went hand in hand with learning about the nature of new social institutions. Throughout *Cuz Dif* and the companion reader, Nivkh children were versed in a panoply of social and political topics, including past exploitation of Nivkh fishermen by capitalists, the virtues of daily hygiene, the importance of agriculture over fishing and foraging, the idea of voting and socialist competitions, and the lingering threat posed by shamans.

> In our village we have a reading hut. Every evening men and women visit the reading hut. They read books. They listen to the radio. We children also go to the reading hut to listen to the radio. Radio. Does your village have a reading hut?

> Today in our village we had a meeting. Men and women gathered and said, "We don't want to catch fish the old way. It's hard to catch fish when you have a small net and you are on your own. Let's form a kolkhoz and catch fish with a big net and a pier." Everyone agreed. We workers didn't admit shamans and kulaks into our kolkhoz.

What is a kulak? . . . A kulak is someone who lives off someone else's labor. We have a kulak in our village. His name is Koinyt. Koinyt has a long net and lots of equipment. Koinyt lies to the poor and the hired hands [*batraki*]. When fish come, he gathers the poor workers and gives them his net to catch fish. When they are done, he takes fish for himself, his wife, and his little children, but he doesn't give enough to the workers to feed their wives and children. Having enslaved and deceived the poor year after year, he has become rich. A kulak gets rich by taking orphans, enslaving them, and selling the orphan girls. Do you have a kulak in your village?[76]

The life of Nivkh women is hard. As soon as we are born, they sell us. . . . We aren't masters of our own lives. . . . Comrade women, what do you think, are we not people? Can we not live by our own minds? Are we to live by the minds of shamans, the rich, and kulaks? Women, let's cast off the old laws, let's live in the Soviet way.[77]

By training native cadres, the Committee sought to create a "native high culture,"[78] but most Nivkh parents were reluctant to release their children to unfamiliar schools where tuberculosis, among other diseases, was rampant. However, the minimal progress that was made permitted a small number of students to be sent to the Institute of Northern Peoples in Leningrad, including four sent in 1932 who were drawn into service to the new order by the last pages of *Cuz Dif.*

Voksin, Nengun, Pen'guk, Sarat: As Nivkh students in Leningrad we speak to working Nivkhi on the Amur and Sakhalin:
Working Nivkhi, cast off shamanic law, live only by Soviet law.
Don't elect kulaks or shamans to your soviet.
Strengthen your soviets and your kolkhozes.
Boys and girls, join the Pioneers and the Communist Youth League.
Read this Nivkh book well.[79]

In the first years after North Sakhalin's incorporation into the USSR in 1925, Nivkh life began a process of rapid change that set the pace for the remarkable decades to follow. Between the sharp drop in the Japanese presence, the gradual withdrawal of the Chinese, the nationalizing of operations such as Zotov's in Rybnoe, and the fanning out of Russian officials to even the remotest areas after generations of only the most nominal state interest, the Soviet intervention in Nivkh lives marked an uncertain contract that dramatically transformed the trade and social networks they had known with Asian neighbors.

It was clearly an era of excitement, with a new sense of what it meant to be modern guiding the Soviet cultural project. While Moscow experimented with conductorless orchestras, and the Commissar of Public Enlightenment, Anatolii Lunacharskii, set as his goal the virtual reorganization of human consciousness, nationality policy saw its own early turns. Having previously been shut out of village sites and access to fishing grounds, most Nivkhi looked favorably on the new steps in native autonomy, medical care, and literacy programs. Whereas tsarist officials did little but occasionally hound Nivkhi for their pagan ways, the new government was eager to distinguish itself as a liberating force. Reluctant to recognize a history of Asian influence in the Nivkh sphere, the Soviets officially looked upon Nivkh ties with the Chinese and Japanese as early capitalist errors, from which a new life, too, brought emancipation. The more cultureless the Nivkhi could be portrayed before Soviet administration, the better an indicator they would be of the changes afoot. The very earliest days of Soviet intervention in Nivkh life bespoke an ambiguity that created a balancing act over the entire Soviet period. Releasing Nivkhi from the bonds of tsarist rule, the government encouraged Nivkhi to express their cultural uniqueness, and the 1920s was a high period for all icons of Nivkh life—native dress, native language, and trained native cadres. However, as the poster children for primitives seeking civilization, Nivkhi were also a tableau by which the success of the new Soviet cultural project, an internationalizing project, would be measured. With the social and political flux of the 1920s, Nivkhi filled a handful of often contradictory roles set for them by the state. However, their malleability also left them open to the sudden policy shifts that marked the succeeding decades.

Five

The Stalinist Period

Overcoming the past is a prerequisite for full
membership in the family of peoples of the USSR.
(from the masthead of the Sakhalin newspaper,
Bolshevik Fish Run, *1930s)*

Structural Changes

The new social forms and new tools of cultural transmission reflected the
dramatic social changes rapidly transforming North Sakhalin. In less
than ten years most Nivkhi had made the shift from a family economy to
artels, and from artels to kolkhozes. By the spring fish run of 1930 *Sovry-
bak* had become *Rybakkolkhozsoiuz*, which set about creating thirteen
kolkhozes from the forty-seven fishing artels that operated on the Soviet
part of the island.[1] In the East Sakhalin district where Nivkhi had the least
contact with Russian settlers, the state reported that adult literacy had
risen to 28 percent.[2] By 1933, 223 Nivkh, Evenk, and Orok elementary
students, making up 76 percent of the entire student-age population,
were enrolled in government schools.[3] In the more active trading area of
Ado-Tymovo on central Sakhalin, as mentioned in chapter 3, four Nivkh
fishing villages were incorporated into the agricultural collective Chir-
Unvd, or New Life, an operation that developed quickly and thrived.
Most Nivkhi by this time were living in Russian-style homes; Nivkh dress
and the braids once worn by men were increasingly abandoned; and the
ranks of Nivkhi enrolled in schools, visiting hospitals, and joining the
Komsomol [Communist Youth League] were swelling. By 1934 well
over half the Nivkhi in the area of the Nogliki Culture Base were listed as
Russian-speaking.[4]

By most accounts the substantial process of collectivization went relatively smoothly, partly because of the attendant distractions of modernization. As one Nivkh fisherman from West Sakhalin recalled in 1990,

Representatives came from Nikolaevsk-on-the-Amur to organize meetings.
They said, "We're going to gather it all up. You'll work as you did before.

You'll fish as you did before." But everyone had to give his things in. Someone had a net, another a boat. We voted in a chairman of the village soviet,
who was a little more literate than the rest of us. That's how it went and went
and went.

   We didn't catch any fewer fish than before. . . . We fished and gave it in to
the kolkhoz. Generally people were happy. The main thing is that before we
didn't have a store. They built a store, a club . . . they began to bring in films.
The shamans, though, they would run away as soon as the Russians came. If
the shaman were in a trance during a performance and someone shouted,
"There's a Russian!" he would stop and go away.

   After that it was all kolkhoz, kolkhoz, kolkhoz. It was all about potatoes and
kolkhozes. About how to give your things in. People gave their horses, their
ploughs. We began to plant potatoes. We learned everything: how to give in
the horses, how much to plant and how much to give to the kolkhoz, how
much to fish and how much to give to the kolkhoz. We processed the fish
ourselves and then handed them over in barrels to the state.

Since many Nivkhi had already been participating in a market economy,
the transition for them to a more routinized system of production was
potentially less disruptive, for example, than for Siberian hunting and
herding peoples. Among the nomadic Evenki of central Siberia, publicly
planning ahead was considered bad luck and therefore taboo. Then, how
were they to take part in a five-year plan?[5] Among herders on Chukotka
and Kamchatka, ancient beliefs maintained that a spiritual bond existed
between a reindeer and its owner. Even when reindeer were held by families, each deer was tied to a specific individual. To collectivize them was
a clear transgression of local codes. Across the entire North, herders
began to slaughter their reindeer rather than collectivize them, resulting
in a drop of as much as a third of the entire Siberian herd in only three
years.[6] In the mid-1930s Anatolii Skachko, the acting head of the Committee of the North, assessed the debacle by noting, "We have paid for
the transferal of [only] 20 percent of the herd into the socialist sector by
destroying 35 percent of the reindeer."[7] Iurii Kreinovich had the same to
report from a northwestern Siberian Nenets kolkhoz that dispersed more
than half its herd in protest of the new rules.[8]

   At the same time, however, the entire process of collectivization on
North Sakhalin, and perforce the expansion of the fishing industry there,
was predicated on the appropriation and restructuring of Nivkh villages.
Where prerevolutionary Russian settlers may have hounded Nivkhi from
many of their ancestral homes, Soviet planners kept their eyes on the
shores to which Nivkhi had relocated. Collectivization by definition
meant that the entire populace would have to be concentrated into

fewer settlements in order to streamline production. Hence, in 1930, when *Rybakkolkhozsoiuz* transformed forty-seven artels into thirteen kolkhozes, the government reduced the twenty-five villages in the Rybnovsk district to six.[9] But the interesting aspect to these first series of village closings on Sakhalin is that native villages were the ones kept open; that is, they were the ones to be redeveloped into larger fishing centers dominated by Russians. A report of the same year explained the situation matter of factly:

> In order to develop the fishing sector, economic planners should focus on the sites where natives live. As the Giliaks have located their villages in the most convenient locations, and occupy the very best bodies of water, this is where large-scale development should begin. By building up native areas, natives will be crowded and eventually excluded from the best fishing grounds. The natives will be unhappy, since this not only goes against their interests but transgresses the decrees of other directive agencies. But given their diffuse dispersion, there can be no other alternative. Some natives are taking this into account, and now realize that living in such small villages is no longer possible.[10]

Such radical acts of displacement did indeed fly in the face of the efforts of the Committee of the North, who argued that it would be harmful to so extensively overhaul the native communities. But the rapidly changing political climate had been working against the Committee of the North since Stalin's entrenchment of power in 1929. Of their three central goals—native self-government, economic reorganization, and cultural enlightenment—only cultural enlightenment remained under the Committee's aegis by the early 1930s.

The new order represented a break from the past that many Nivkhi embraced. But the official intent was more specific: What began as a series of profound changes became an express "war against the past," and as the 1930s advanced it became more difficult to determine which changes were voluntary and which were coerced. As resistance to collectivization mounted, the government struck back everywhere by singling out the wealthiest capital holders as *kulaks*, from the Russian word for "fist." The term *kulak* quickly became a catchword for anyone in opposition to state policy. Among Siberian peoples this meant particular trouble for shamans, the spirit mediums and healers who acted as religious figures across the continent.[11] For northern social planners, a war against the past called not only for the eradication of shamans, kulaks, and class enemies, but the aggressive jettisoning of all forms of traditional life in favor of a new Siberia in step with history. It marked a decisive turning point for Siberian peoples' great leap forward.

Reforming the Reformers

Although the Communist Party had advised its faithful to leave Nivkhi to themselves when they set up government on North Sakhalin in 1925, nine Nivkhi were candidates for party membership by 1930.[12] One of the key roles the candidates were assigned to was vigilance in matters of political and economic sabotage. Though Stalin's war on the past is most often associated with the *Ezhovshchina* of 1936–38[13]—the period when Nikolai Ivanovich Ezhov, the new head of the state security forces or NKVD, presided over the arrest and killing of hundreds of thousands of Soviet citizens—on Sakhalin, as elsewhere in the country, organized campaigns of terror clearly began to take root much earlier. A 1931 Communist Party circular from the Rybnovsk district noted that the exposing of kulaks was being stepped up in earnest with the announcement of total collectivization in the area. Of twenty-seven households under investigation, twenty were slated to be "dekulaked" (*podlezhat raskulachivaniiu*), causing district party officials to be castigated for having failed to expose these class enemies earlier. Still worse for the local officials, a significant number of persons under investigation had already had their voting rights revoked for their roles in religious organizations or the tsarist state apparatus, and should therefore have been more readily identifiable to government agents as bad elements. In response, the party office in Rybnovsk urged all its members to dekulak the area down to the last offender, particularly in Nivkh settlements where work of this nature had been undertaken only haphazardly. Outlined in the box on the following pages are the procedures established in 1931 for arresting kulak families and delivering them to Rybnovsk NKVD officials, though it is unlikely that the process ever went as smoothly or as systematically as described.

Whereas any citizen with a dubious past was at risk, so too was anyone perceived to have prospered financially under the new Soviet system and who, in all likelihood, would be trying to unload their movable goods in an attempt to ward off the inevitable. "Bearing in mind that with the announcement of total collectivization in the district, kulaks will undoubtedly attempt to liquidate their assets by selling them off, destroying them, or spreading them among friends and relatives—party cells, Young Communists, the working poor, and all Soviet organizations must be on full alert."[14]

The elderly fisherman Koinyt was one of the first Nivkhi whom officials offered up for sacrifice, singling him out in the pages of the children's reader *Cuz Dif*. Both the ethnographers Bronisław Pil'sudskii and Lev Shternberg had forty years earlier heralded the young orphan Koinyt as a

Technical Instructions

[Rybnovsk, 1931]

1. All kulak families should be retrieved and delivered to the commissioner of the OGPU (*Oblastnoe Glavnoe Politicheskoe Upravlenie*), or Main Regional Political Directorate, in the village of Vereshchagino.

2. The delivery time in Vereshchagino should be agreed on with the OGPU with sufficient accuracy so that kulaks do not have to wait for the steamship in Vereshchagino for more than one to two days.

3. Once the delivery time has been agreed on definitively, the district council (*raiispolkom*) should appoint particularly firm and self-restrained representatives, at least one for each village from which kulaks will be removed.

4. The council representatives, on arriving in the appointed village, will gather the village's most active members of the worker-peasant ranks and prepare a presentation on the liquidation of kulaks as a class as a result of the total collectivization of the district. A decree will be prepared regarding the eviction of kulaks indicated on the list. (The time of eviction is not discussed at the meeting but is delimited by the general phrase, "the fastest removal from our village.")

5. On the same day a general meeting of the kolkhozniks and the worker-peasants will assemble to hear the presentation and endorse the decree of the village poor (once again without indicating the exact time of removal).

6. At the conclusion of the general meeting and the endorsement of the decree on the removal of kulaks, the council representatives will summon that same evening the most active kolkhozniks and activists from among the members of the village soviet—strong, staunch, and restrained comrades—among whom the task of undertaking the immediate removals will be assigned.

7. Immediately thereafter the comrades head to the kulaks' houses, where the eldest among them will proclaim the will of the village poor and kolkhozniks: that the kulaks are to be evicted immediately and are expected to be completely ready to leave by morning.

8. From this moment no one will be allowed in or out of the kulak's house until the moment the kulak departs from the village.

9. In the kulak's presence one must first remove any firearms, money, or valuables (except personal crosses) and conduct the most thorough search possible, beginning with the kulak and then searching family members. According to instructions, the kulak will have the right to take along items of utmost necessity, but by no means valuable, and foodstuffs—up to a total weight of 30 puds [1,080 pounds].

10. During the confiscation of property, comrades must demonstrate the utmost restraint and steadfastness, by no means harping on trifles or permitting excesses.

11. All items the kulak selects for transport should be carefully packed in strong sacks together with necessary instruments such as axes, saws and so on. Food items are to be packed in separate sacks.

12. A list is then drawn up in the presence of the kulak or an adult family member indicating the nature and value of all remaining belongings to be given over to the village soviet according to instructions.

13. Two trustworthy comrades are to be posted at the kulak's house until morning.

14. Early in the morning appointed comrades will bring around carts for the transport of women, children, and the kulak's belongings.

15. The carts, accompanied by the village poor, are delivered to the commissioner of the OGPU in Vereshchagino and are surrendered as kulak families along with the listed belongings.

16. The district council at the kulak receiving post in Vereshchagino should oversee the provision of lodging, food (if the kulak supplies are insufficient) and, in the same manner, if necessary, medical care for the kulak families for a period of one to three days.

17. During this entire operation it is essential to remain restrained and steadfast, under no circumstances deigning to crude remarks or excesses. One must strictly remember that kulaks are not merely under arrest or persons being removed by administrative means, but strangers, hounded from their surroundings by the poor laboring and kolkhoz peasantry.

[*5 copies only*]

NTs./IL

27.V.1931.

[Source: *TsGADV*, f. R-4549, o. 2. d. 16 (1931), ll. 226–227.]

great poet and a celebrated shaman, but Koinyt's shamanic talents served him poorly in the new atheist state.[15] A Nivkh youth group in Viskovo followed suit in 1931 by voting to disenfranchise the shaman Upan in upcoming elections, suggesting a pattern whereby Nivkhi who had most distinguished themselves in opposition to state policies over the previous decade—elders and shamans—were the first to be harassed.[16] In Rybnoe, party secretary Ivannikov and his coworker Krylov were arrested for drunken behavior, for keeping religious icons in their homes, and for recruiting tsarist bandits into the Rybnoe kolkhoz "Bolshevik" and the neighboring Liugi kolkhoz "Stalin."[17] Similar campaigns were going on in Lupolovo, Nai-Nai, and other regions with large Nivkh communities.[18] In a largely clandestine 1934 campaign known as "The Islanders Affair," V. M. Drekov, the head of Sakhalin's Border Patrol and the island NKVD, culminated three years of investigation into undercover Japanese espionage movements with a sweep through twenty-two North Sakhalin settlements; 115 people were arrested and killed, 40 of whom were Nivkhi and Oroki.[19]

Kreinovich, returning to Leningrad in 1929 to teach at the Northern Division of the Institute of Eastern Languages (renamed, in 1930, the Institute of Northern Peoples), found an environment much changed. Around the time of Shternberg's death in 1927, class-based quotas had become the main criteria for selecting students, and the curriculum had become increasingly politicized.[20] Across Siberia the pressure to identify class enemies in what had effectively been stateless, classless societies required ethnographers to extensively revise the role of indigenous social organization.[21] At departmental meetings Kreinovich resisted claims that Nivkh social organization had been by nature exploitative, and was censured for his views. Kreinovich's colleague Koshkin, working with Shternberg's widow, put out a posthumous 1933 collection of Shternberg's essays, *Giliaki, Gol'dy, Orochi*, most of them written in the twilight of the tsarist period, with the professed hope of providing information for antireligious causes.

Patriotism was not so much the issue here. Looking back, many friends of Kreinovich expressed surprise that he remained committed to the Soviet system through thick and thin. For someone who was always one step behind most political changes, he steadily maintained that the Soviets had given him an education and a career he felt would have been unattainable in the tsarist world. By the same token, the same Shternberg who once called Marxism a "hackneyed reworking of Hegel" appeared to be firmly committed to a role for politicized ethnography in the new socialist state.[22] What was at stake, however, were new codes of propriety that were changing faster than even those who set them could adapt to.

In the offices of the Committee of the North in Moscow, the ideological upheavals were equally turbulent. Having resisted central government efforts to forcibly render the northern indigenous communities sedentary for several years, the Committee had lost much of the minor sway it once held. In 1935 Stalin sent a letter to members of the Committee congratulating them for a job well done, and then formally dissolved the Committee. The Committee's work was transferred to the Main Administration of the Northern Sea Route (*Glavsevmorput'*), an organization eminently wealthier and notably less interested in native affairs. The role of Glavsevmorput' was to oversee the rapid industrialization of the North; its reputation as "the absolute ruler of all of northern Asia above the 62nd parallel" was challenged only by the industrial giant *Dal'stroi* in the Far East. "Thus," as Yuri Slezkine observed, "most native northerners became part of two quasi-independent fiefdoms bent on industrial development."[23]

By 1936 the Committee of the New Alphabet found its new Latin alphabet declared to be old, and plans were under way to rewrite the new Siberian scripts on the basis of Cyrillic orthography. In a July meeting of the committee's Far Eastern division, members gathered to lambaste the errors of latinization. Years earlier, when Kreinovich had introduced a written script for Nivkhi, the Far Eastern committee praised the virtues of the Latin alphabet for best responding to Nivkh phonetics.[24] Koshkin in turn, in 1932, further advocated the latinized *Edinyi Severnyi Alfavit* (*ESA*), or "single northern alphabet," as internationalist and less Russificatory. But four years later committee members took issue with the slander this implied for Russians: "Do the authors [of the *ESA*] truly equate the prerevolutionary missionaries with their vodka and their Bibles alongside the hospitals, schools, kolkhozes, and councils that the Russian bolsheviks brought to the North?"[25] Another delegate ruminated, "I don't understand why someone who is for the Yakut language, which already exists in the Russian alphabet, is a nationalist and a chauvinist, while someone who is for the alphabet of the French and the Italians [of the 1930s] is an internationalist."[26] The Committee of the New Alphabet, fittingly named, introduced its second new alphabet in five years. The revisions were in keeping with the reinstating of the Russian people under Stalin as the leading members of the new fraternal Soviet Union; they clearly spelled trouble, however, for the northern reformers who had been advocating native autonomy in the interests of limiting exploitation of the northerners by Russian newcomers. It was a marked downturn for Nivkh fortunes, and an ironic twist for people who had entered into the Soviet state on the promise of new cultural freedoms.

Comrade Razumov from Leningrad complained that the very work of the Institute of Northern Peoples, responsible for the teaching of native languages among other things, was harmful. "Peoples of the North," he argued, "are hungry for the Russian language, for the party literature in Russian, for the central newspapers."[27] Regardless of whether Siberian peoples hungered for the Russian language, it is evident that the linguistic isolation brought on by being in the latinized minority had little place in the increasingly centralized state. On Sakhalin cursory efforts were made in August 1936 to distribute flyers with texts in both scripts so as to let Nivkhi themselves decide which was easier to read;[28] but by December the Presidium of the Council of Nationalities of the USSR reversed the latinization policy. In the Far East the alphabets of the Nivkh, Nanai,

Stalin

Kommunist parţija nuḫinivx Stalin.

Stalin Leṇin nəḍ jukrgur nəḍra.

9. Kreinovich's 1932 primer *Cuz Dif*, or "New Word," was in circulation for only four years before the government declared the latinized Nivkh script, shown here, to be a bourgeois alphabet. The text reads: "Stalin is the leader of the Communist Party. Stalin carries on the work of Lenin."

Even, Evenk, Chukchi, Koriak, and Eskimo languages were Russianized, while the written languages for the Udegeitsy and Itel'meny were abandoned altogether because of the small size of their populations.[29]

The form of native languages may have been settled by the 1936 decision, but the question of the content of the children's readers and adult primers for Siberian peoples came under increasing fire, illustrating the ideological tightrope that fewer and fewer authors were deft enough to negotiate. In Konstantin D. Egorov's 1938 review of children's readers in northern schools during the 1930s, case after case is lambasted. Some errors were minor: I. Ia. Chernetseva's book for the Mansi overlooked the role of the working class before 1917; O. P. Sunik's book for the Nanaitsy failed to mention the role of the peasantry in the October Revolution; Sunik "speaks about soviets, schools, and Red Yarangas,[30] but not one word about kolkhozes"; and Prokof'ev's book for the Nentsy mentioned Lenin's name only once in eighty-eight pages.[31] Other errors were considered more fundamental, such as distorted ideas about proper discipline in the work place.

> Stebnitskii included the following conversation between "eager workers" in his primer:
>   —What are you doing?
>   —Nothing.
>   —And what is your comrade doing?
>   —Helping me.[32]

Egorov explained that Stebnitskii's problem was, in part, that he "gives no examples of the lives of heroes, Stakhanovites,[33] Shock Workers, or the warriors of socialist labor discipline." But Stebnitskii's real problem may have been that he wrote a children's primer with children in mind. Egorov complained that Stebnitskii's primer for the Koriaks was "filled with almost nothing but fairy tales. . . . Fox stories predominate, including 'The Fox' (p. 52), 'Fox' (p. 55), then in succession 'The Sly Fox,' 'The Fox and the Wolf,' 'Foxes,' 'The Little Foxes,' and 'The Story of Kovak' (again about a fox)."[34]

> All these distortions are the result of sabotage by bourgeois nationalists, the absence of efforts to combat the consequences of such sabotage, and the extremely weak supervision over the publication of these textbooks on the part of *Narkompros* [People's Committee on Enlightenment]. . . . Only through the battle for party-mindedness in scholarship, and by preventing the oversimplification of pedagogic ideals in the northern schools, will we be able to root out the Trotskyite-Bukharinist gangs, the bourgeois nationalists and saboteurs on the ideological front.[35]

Mistranslations in the Nivkh textbooks also spelled trouble for Kreinovich and the other scholars who worked on the negotiation of the three Nivkh dialects for publication. The Nivkh word *kolanivkh* was intended to signify *kulak*, but came out contextually as "the leader, the distributor of wealth, the rich man who helps others." The Nivkh word *krygris* was intended to signify the Russian *batrak*, a term for "hired hand" which was ennobled by the Soviets; instead it came out as "slave." The use of the Nivkh *khutikhumnivukh* was intended to mean *sredniak*, or middle peasant; however, its use in context suggested only "the one living in the middle of the village" or "a man of average height." Equal suspicion was cast on the expression used for "joining the kolkhoz," which was the same expression in Nivkh for getting caught in something, such as a net.[36]

The War against the Past

By the mid-1930s, when the mass purges started in earnest, Nivkhi were especially at risk. Given the rampant xenophobia that dominated the country during Stalin's reign, the Nivkhi's prerevolutionary history of co-operation and trade with Japanese, Chinese, and Korean merchants made them particularly vulnerable. It is difficult, of course, to comprehend an era of such stunning excesses, to reason through a time when few reasons were given for mass disappearances. Forty percent of the entire Kazakh population died between 1931 and 1933, and between four and five million Ukrainian peasants died in 1933 alone.[37] Yet we can lose sight of the workings of terror if we accept the traditional interpretations of the purges long regnant in Western scholarship—that they were carefully engineered by Stalin as part of a methodical scheme to establish dictatorship. As the historian Robert Weinberg has pointed out, local party officials and bureaucrats, eager to demonstrate their vigilance, quickly took up where the central directives left off.[38] With local Sakhalin officials under duress to produce enemies of the people in increasingly greater numbers, it is not surprising they turned to Nivkhi who, as a group, were far from full members of society in the first place.

What was striking about the purges among Nivkhi was the speed of the turnaround. Native leaders who had been celebrated as model Soviets one year became enemies of the people the next. Manifestations of a traditional way of life, which were praised and encouraged as signs of new political freedom in the 1920s, were now grounds for arrest and disappearance.

Aleksei Churka had been one of Kreinovich's first Nivkh guides on Sakhalin. He was the first Nivkh under the Soviets to receive a higher education at the Institute of Northern Peoples in Leningrad. He had been a party member since 1934, and became chairman of the East Sakhalin RIK that same year. On 12 October 1936 he was fired on the grounds of an undisclosed state crime. His wife recalled in 1990,

The first chairman had already disappeared and the second had been fired without reason, so we had an idea that Churka would be taken away too. One day we had gone for a long walk and then to the bathhouse. When we got back, the house had been searched and the militia were there. He just went and that was that.[39]

Following his arrest, the East Sakhalin District Party Committee excluded Churka from the party on the grounds of "Japanophilism and local nationalism." On 20 September 1937 the NKVD sentenced Churka to five years of hard labor "for inciting nationalist antagonism between Russians and Nivkhi for speaking out against government plans, for giving away state seal resources, for opposing the merger of two state kolkhozes, and for praising Japanese culture."[40]

When I inquired about the Stalinist period on Sakhalin's northwestern shore, it was exceptional to find someone who did not have relatives who disappeared in the 1930s. Six older Nivkhi made the following comments:

All the good people, all of them, all of them, through to Rybnovsk. They put them in prison. All the brigadiers, all the people who would speak at the meetings, those were the kind of people they put away.

In 1937 they took a lot of good people. Men, women, and sometimes even children. The Tungusy [Evenki] especially. A lot of people were taken away. As if they were kulaks. Who was a kulak? Some people had more than others but there weren't any kulaks. There were families with seven or eight children and they took the fathers away. In one village not far from ours they took almost all the men away.

No one knows why they took my father away. We never saw him again. Sometimes it was enough that one wore Japanese glasses. This meant you were a collaborator. Or that you found a candy wrapper, with Japanese writing on it, that had been floating down the river. People would ask, "Where did you get that from?" Or they wouldn't ask at all, and the police would come all the same.

I was young, but I already understood. When the police would go around the yards, the NKVD, you knew what they were doing. They would look for that material—the shiny silk, it was Japanese or Chinese. They don't make it here anymore. A few people had the material in their homes, and as soon as the police found out about it they would immediately take them away. I remember once how my father got angry at his mother. She had some silk and wanted to bury it, but he wanted to burn it.

Whole villages! All the elders. All the supervisors. They came, they took people away, and that was it. My grandfather they took. And my brother, and my uncle. A lot of them were sent to work on that tunnel they tried to make

across the Tatar Strait. That's where a lot of them died, during construction. . . . There were no good reasons. What reason could there be? The old
men, they worked on the kolkhozes, they fished and they hunted. None at
all. . . . They would simply come in one of those big trucks, a five-ton truck,
the kind they used on the kolkhoz for transporting the fishing nets. They
would go up to a door and say, "Let's go. Get ready." They'd put you in the
truck. Where to, they didn't ask.

The police never told us why. When they came to the door, they referred to
our order to leave as a *putevka*, a tourist pass. But we were hardly tourists. We
spent four years moving from town to town on the mainland looking for work.
It was the dead of winter the night we left and the baby was only seven months
old. He fell ill on the trip and died. "An enemy of the people." What kind of
enemy was I?

The sum result was a stunning level of repressive terror. A 1948 Ministry
of the Interior document concerning anti-Soviet activities in the
Rybnovsk district asserts that from 1917 on, and particularly during the
Japanese occupation of North Sakhalin from 1920 to 1925, Japanese intelligence cultivated a network of counterrevolutionary agents among
Nivkhi and Evenki living in the district. In the village of Viskovo, the site
of the native executive council founded in 1926, the ministry credited
Japanese intelligence with the formation of an anti-Soviet Nivkh group
known as "the Viskovo counterrevolutionary organization" headed by
the former Nivkh council chairman, Mikhail Petrovich Kul'pin. Kul'pin
was the same man so praised in 1931 by the visiting Culture Army from
Khabarovsk for his assiduous efforts to combat illiteracy and prerevolutionary traditions.[41] He was working as one of the directing brigadiers at
the "Red Baikal" fishing kolkhoz in Viskovo at the time of his arrest in
November 1937. He was convicted in March 1938 on grounds of espionage and was shot in nearby Okha later that month. Kul'pin's main transgression, his granddaughter later recalled, was that he had a Japanese
watch. But his mistake may also have been speaking out against the work
of the party at a district meeting in April 1937.

Self-criticism is the guiding principle in our work. Nivkhi have much to be
thankful for: before 1926 we lived in twenty-seven lousy villages around the
district, and now we are grouped into seven kolkhozes. This is a real achievement. . . . But we won't stand on our laurels. We receive little assistance
from district organizations. Mass cultural work is no longer conducted in
Viskovo, despite Central Committee directives requiring this. It would be better if these directives were observed. We have had Soviet government in our
district since 1926, but I rarely see [any government officials]. You could
organize party meetings in our village but you don't. In 1930 we had ten

Nivkhi who were nominated to the party. Now there are only three and they have nothing to do, so they are dropping out. No one organizes discussions about the constitution. Nivkhi don't know about their own achievements under socialism, and yet they are interested.[42]

In turn, Kul'pin's son and a Red Baikal coworker were arrested on the grounds of harboring an enemy of the people and remaining silent about espionage activities they were presumed to know about.[43] Ironically, following the recommendations of the Soldiers of Culture who so admired Kul'pin when they encountered him on their campaign in 1931, other writers continued to celebrate him as a model native long after he had been liquidated by the state.[44]

Through NKVD operations, "the Viskovo counterrevolutionary organization, consisting of eleven members, most of them from the Nivkh population, was summarily [*operativno*] liquidated."[45] Likewise, an unspecified number of Nivkhi from the nearby village of Grigor'evka were arrested for anti-Soviet activity and collaboration with the Japanese in the same year. On the whole:

> As a result of repressive measures undertaken against counterrevolutionary and rebel elements among peoples of the North in 1937–38, approximately 36 percent of the adult population was removed [*iz"iat*], composed mainly of Nivkhi and Evenki from forty to sixty years of age, while the remaining 64 percent expressed their understanding and support for the measures undertaken by the Soviet government. A persistent but insignificant anti-Soviet element continued their activity; although most came to support the Soviet government over the years, those remaining were arrested as necessary.[46]

The NKVD report also asserts that Nivkhi were active supporters of the All-Union Council of Evangelical Christians (*VSEKh*), a "counterrevolutionary umbrella group" based in Leningrad with ninety-one registered members throughout the Rybnovsk area. A number of *VSEKh* members, who evidently had influence over the native population through public chapels in the Rybnovsk region, were also liquidated during 1937–38.

The few remaining foreigners on the island became fewer still. A number of Japanese oil interests and traders remained on North Sakhalin through the late 1930s following an agreement concluded when Japan ceded North Sakhalin to the USSR in 1925.[47] However, the hundreds of North Sakhalin Koreans who had been recruited by the Japanese as immigrant labor in the North found themselves in increasingly tenuous positions.[48] The 1936–37 ledgers written from the Korean settlement of Kefi, three kilometers north of Rybnoe, were like those of any other village council, recounting the dividends of the year and making plans for propagating the new Stalin constitution in 1938. The notes end abruptly one day in 1937, when trucks arrived to close the village and relocate the Koreans off the island, most to Kazakhstan and destinations in Central Asia.[49] One woman recalled in 1990,

> In 1937 a boat arrived. I was already twelve. And they took away everyone from Kefi and Naumovka, two Korean villages. They came to Vereshchagino too and took all the Koreans away. An old man escorted them to the shore and sat there for hours after they left. He was probably crying. They gathered them together, got them on the boat, and went away. My mother was against it. They had to break up families, leave wives and children behind. We got one letter from a man in Tashkent, he wrote from Tashkent. At least someone else wrote for him—he was illiterate.

Back in Leningrad, Kreinovich, guilty by association, was arrested in 1937 on grounds of conspiring with "a Trotsky-Zinovievite terrorist spy organization in league with the Japanese."[50] He later recounted being beaten and held without sleep for five days, and then being required to sign documents attesting to his participation in antistate bombings.[51] He served his ten-year sentence in exile in a Magadan camp in far north-eastern Siberia, only to be sentenced again, for the same crime, to another ten years upon his release. When he attempted suicide at the outset of his second term, he was allowed to work as a medical assistant for prisoners in a village outside Leningrad until 1955. At the close of his eighteen-year odyssey, the state rehabilitated him for lack of evidence. His life was a stark reminder of how much had changed (and how much had remained the same) since his mentor Lev Shternberg had himself been exiled to Siberia and had gone on to lead ethnography in the brave new world.

Throughout all this, the Culture Base in Nogliki managed to remain open but not without trials of its own. In 1934 the *Bolshevik Fish Run* pronounced the Nogliki base to be "a dead institution" and "a refuge for vagrants."[52] The staff commanded little respect in the community, anti-religious work was reported to be weak, mass cultural work was not being conducted, the school and hospital were not heated in the wintertime, and Nivkhi traveling through the town were no longer offered a warm place to stay since the House of the Native had been given over to Russians. Perhaps most problematic given the Culture Base's original charter, only four of the forty-four students enrolled in the elementary school were actually native (Nivkh, Evenk, or Orok). Moreover, five adult students had returned from their training in Leningrad (Utkin, Lanzhero, Mariia Kofkan, Semroiden Chikht, and Churka), but the Culture Base had refused to hire them and they were left to fend for themselves. The Culture Base's director, Comrade Krames, in a separate report, offered a simple defense: As he himself was the target of accusations and threats, local organizations had ceased to cooperate with him, and allotted funds from Moscow had not been forthcoming.[53] Krames, in turn, was replaced by Kniazev in 1936, who was in turn dismissed for taking the name of the proletarian writer Maksim Gorkii in vain, and for excusing himself over extended periods on the pretext of illness.[54] Kniazev disappeared in 1937 to be replaced by Golovin, who, in one of the first documents indicating his stewardship, was accused of being an enemy of the people. He was replaced the same year by Vasil'ev. On it went.[55]

Throughout the 1930s and 1940s the Culture Base accounting ledgers and director's files present a stark series of dismissals, discharges, firings, removals, and early retirements. The Base's operation was not a small one: In 1934 there were forty employees in addition to occasional hired hands.[56] Yet in 1936 the Base's director fired twenty-six employees for transgressions, accepted eight resignations, and issued warnings to several others. Tramenko, the first teacher to be fired, was dismissed for failing to provide proper socialist education to children, for spreading rumors, and for sabotaging the Stakhanovite movement. The second teacher was fired for improperly harboring Communist Youth League documents.[57] On it went.

It was an era of total politicization of almost all spheres of life. In 1938 the town of Nogliki voted to change its street names from the original Nivkh and Russian ones to more patriotic incarnations already ubiquitous around the country such as Soviet Street, Communist Youth League Street, Pioneer Street, Freedom Lane, First of May Street, Partisan Street, Physical Culture Street, and Red Army Street.[58] On the kolkhozes, accountants listed fishing boats by names such as Construction Worker, Shock Worker, Freedom, October, Activist, Stakhanovite, Bolshevik, Commune, Decembrist, Avant Garde, and Spy. On the Freedom kolkhoz in Vereshchagino, names for horses such as Five-Year Plan, Courageous, and First of May were common, while cows, perhaps the only collectivized commodity with a pulse to escape the patriotic gambit, were nonetheless filed under vaguely menacing names such as Falcon and Eagle.[59]

Much of the zeal demonstrated on North Sakhalin kolkhozes at the time attested to real patriotism and the spirit of building a new society of which many if not most saw themselves a part. But the quest to maintain appearances became equally crucial on kolkhozes where simply not working hard was sufficient grounds for being labeled an enemy of the people.[60] Between 1938 and 1940 the Freedom kolkhoz, with 120 members, let 44 members go and hired 72 new ones. In the same period Red October, with 160 members, let 60 members go and hired 89 new ones.[61] Bearing in mind that these communities were quite small, each dominated by one kolkhoz, these were enormous turnovers.

The extent of the purges was consistent with the systematic terror engineered throughout the rest of the country, but as the historian John Stephan has pointed out, the Soviet Far East appeared to have suffered disproportionately.

> On the basis of a recent estimate that 30,000 people were shot in Far Eastern prisons "in the time of Stalin" (i.e. 1929–1953), one can hypothesize that about 15,000 of these perished during 1937–1938. . . . Assuming that about 200,000 were repressed in the Far East during 1937–1938, that would constitute 8% of *Dal'krai*'s population (2,338,095 in 1938), a significantly higher percentage than for the USSR as a whole.
>
> The disproportionately high mortality of Far Easterners is suggested by party statistics. Of 1,956 voting delegates to the Seventeenth Party Congress in 1934 from all parts of the USSR, 1,108 were arrested. Of thirty-two Far Eastern delegates to the Seventeenth Party Congress, *none* appeared at the 18th Party Congress in 1939. Of 139 candidate and full members of the Central Committee in 1934, ninety-eight were shot. *All* Far Eastern members and candidate members of the Central Committee in 1934 were shot or committed suicide. Far Eastern party membership, 44,909 on 1 January 1933, fell to 27,730 by 1 January 1937 and to 24,885 in 1938.[62]

Stephan notes that the Far East was distinguished by durable party elites whom Stalin may have sought to disrupt, but the proximity to Japan appeared to be the critical downfall for Nivkhi who were themselves still different in a society bent on normative homogeneity.

After such wholesale purgings, who was left to run Sakhalin? Kolkhozes managed to make up for their losses by recruiting extra labor often in the same way they did after the October Revolution, by hiring newcomers trying to elude their pasts elsewhere.[63] But finding competent individuals in the government and the party was more difficult since, by definition, almost anyone in a position of responsibility had been at the greatest risk during the purges. Of the six new political enlightenment specialists hired at the Nogliki Culture Base in 1939 to organize reading huts in the district, the youngest was fifteen and the oldest was twenty-two. No one had more than a seventh-grade education.[64] The purges undoubtedly had supporters among educated elites, but in reading through the Culture Base ledgers, as the invective against enemies of the people went up, the erudition of the directors clearly went down. From the 1941 ledger, a four-sentence accusation by the director against one of his political enlightenment specialists contained forty-five errors in spelling and grammar.[65] Rarely was someone returned after having been taken away, and in such a case often the individual was met by neighbors with the same acquiescence as when he or she was taken away. One Nivkh woman in Moskal'vo recounted,

My stepfather was taken away but he managed to escape in Aleksandrovsk and then made his way back up the coast, stopping and hiding himself in villages along the way. He hid himself briefly when he got back to Moskal'vo, but no one objected. After a while he even got his old job back. People didn't talk about it because they knew that most of the people who were taken away hadn't done anything.

Her Russian neighbor added,

What were you supposed to say? At that time it was impossible to talk about those things. You didn't even want to talk about them with your family. People talked in whispers. You would hear that someone was an enemy of the people and you would just stop talking about them. I remember how I was in school in the 1930s and they began to replace some of the photographs in the corridors. Plekhanov had become an enemy of the people, then Bliucher, then Postyshev, Iagodov . . . there were quite a few. Someone obviously objected to them—Beria or Stalin. And yet, it's hard to describe, no one really associated these things with Stalin.

Throughout the Stalinist juggernaut, there were no famous acts of resistance since canonized among Nivkhi, such as the earlier mass slaughter of reindeer to protest collectivization or the rebellion by northwestern Siberian Khanty in the 1930s.[66] But amid the usual rubber-stamped accounts of kulaks and saboteurs that pervade the archival documents of the era are the rarer pedestrian accounts of insolence from the 1930s that stand out for their sheer anomaly: Aleksei Churka being reprimanded by the party in Nogliki for having publicly insulted a local Russian doctor;[67] Andrei Khevtun in Rybnoe refusing to go to work and declaring that he had entered the party by mistake;[68] or Nivkhi on the Five-Year Plan kolkhoz in Tengi vowing to leave the collective if the Russians stayed on.[69] If there were express elements of resistance by Nivkhi, as occurred randomly among other Siberian peoples, one can expect that these were quickly suppressed as the state systematically began to extract "the people who spoke up at meetings," and eventually even those who did not.

Ironically, in its zeal to bring all of society under its control, the state co-opted resistance as well. By regularly arresting ordinary citizens without pretext, and by wildly exaggerating accounts of saboteurs posing as honest citizens, the Sakhalin administration had most Nivkhi pressing to bury their pasts, both metaphorically and literally. After lunch one rainy afternoon in Moskal'vo in 1990, a Nivkh hostess brought out for my inspection a Manchurian dress her mother once owned. It was a floor-length gown in a blinding silk brocade the likes of which I had never seen in any museum. "It's in pretty good condition," she said, fingering stray threads holding prerevolutionary Chinese coins around the hem, "considering how long it was buried in the ground." Her mother had buried the dress, along with other outward trappings of premodern Nivkh life, in a box in the sand in 1937, unearthing it only in the years of Khrushchev's political reprieves, some twenty years later.

World War II and the Integration of Women

World War II proved to be a turning point for Siberian native peoples in the Soviet world.[70] For all the citizens of North Sakhalin, it was a chance to focus on a collective cause rather than the losses of the purges. For Nivkhi, it marked the threshold of their independent entrance into Soviet society. For the men, it was a chance to define their citizenry by taking part in Soviet missions. And with the men off at war, it was a chance for the government to finally coax women into the work force. In manifesto after manifesto, Nivkh kolkhozes on North Sakhalin pledged to give freely of their time to overfulfill their quotas in order to aid the front. On 25 April 1941 the women of "Freedom" challenged the women of "Hammer" in an open competition, with the Freedom women, Nivkhi and Russians alike, pledging to be responsible for 20 percent of the total kolkhoz quota, to complete a new net within a month, to plant four hectares of vegetables, to build a new children's playground, to improve cleanliness among Nivkh families, and to demonstrate the fullest participation in the decisions of the Seventeenth Party Congress. The sixty-two women of Hammer responded by forming a special all-women's brigade called "Seventeenth Party Congress," and by pledging in turn to take on 25 percent of the fishing quota, to submit only fish of the highest quality, and to build a cafeteria by mid-May.[71] Nivkh women on the kolkhoz "New Way of Life" were reported to have regularly overfulfilled their plan by 500 percent.[72]

> "*Vymyt tor, urla tor*"—"Soviet government is good government," the Nivkhi say. "Soviet government has made a good life for us," said Nivkh Comrade Ryskun, a skipper on the "Trapper" kolkhoz and a representative on the Aleksandrovsk City Council. "The bloody fascists," he said, "want to enslave our people, just when, thanks to Soviet government, we have only begun to live. The fascists will never succeed. In fulfilling the orders from the front, our kolkhoz met its ice fishing quotas before all the other kolkhozes in the Aleksandrovsk district and provided the country with hundreds of additional tsentners[73] of navaga. For this the crews worked fourteen-hour days, seven days a week. Each month every kolkhoznik contributes two days' pay to the defense fund, and many more have donated a further one thousand or fifteen hundred rubles to the cause.[74]

The role of women in World War II is particularly important since Nivkh women had long been among the most reluctant of Sakhalin citizens to participate in the new rituals of Soviet life. Before the war, efforts to recruit women into politics and kolkhoz work had been fledgling. Soldiers of Culture organized the first Nivkh women's meeting in the Ado-Tymovo area village of Chirevo in 1928, and held six additional meetings over the course of that year. Three women were elected to a Nivkh women's council, sewing courses were organized in both Chirevo and Viskovo to encourage women to pool their talents in clothing workshops, and the Committee of the North distributed questionnaires to district offices to assist them in measuring the participation of native women in kolkhozes and village council meetings, and to assess the level of women's literacy.[75]

The minutes from a 1933 Vereshchagino meeting, held in the yurta of a Nivkh woman, Paiguk, show that twelve native women attended to hear a visiting Russian doctor lecture on "Native Life Then and Now," and to learn how to encourage other women to use the bathhouse and not to smoke around their children. If nothing else, the Committee of the North was by this time better organized, with lengthier instructions on enlightenment measures among women. In a series of proposed monthly gatherings, instructors would lead with a prescribed topic of discussion, beginning with "Native Life Then and Now," and then moving on to the class struggle, the dictatorship of the proletariat, how to help the party to help the poor, how to create a cultured village, the Pioneer and Komsomol movements in the village, and so on.[76]

It was the absence of men, however, that marshaled the majority of Nivkh women into the work force through all-female fishing brigades. In the excerpts below, three older Nivkh women reflected on the war as a formative time:

Hard work? You can't imagine! All the men were gone during the war. So we had to do all the jobs. We collected wood for ourselves and for the kolkhoz— that meant sawing down trees in the taiga and hauling them away by dog sled. Sometimes we had the horses. One year I delivered the mail between Langery and Tengi on reindeer sled. There were two sleds and about seven or eight deer. The deer are a little faster than the dogs. We didn't have any days off either. That was hard. We normally worked from about eight in the morning to six at night, but when the fish were running, that was another matter.

I was ten when the war started. I had only been in school a year but our mother had no money, so I started working on the kolkhoz. There were other young girls, thirteen, fifteen, but I was eleven—I was the youngest. It didn't seem so strange at the time. My mother had already been working on the kolkhoz Five-Year Plan hauling fish, so I worked with her. Now it's all mechanized, but back then it was hellish work. We had to pull in the fish nets by hand. Most of the time we didn't have gloves, out on the ice, pulling in nets that had been underwater. It really hurt, but if you let go you only had to pull them in again. We cried, we ran around . . . anything to keep warm. But we were pretty good.

There were only fifteen of us in our brigade, but we worked hard. There was another brigade of men, sailors, who sometimes tried to help, but they had a terrible time! They couldn't work as well as us. When the war ended I was only nineteen. That's when I became a Stakhanovite. They gave us the award on August 31, on the beach. Vorobev came from the *raiispolkom* [district executive council]. There were three of us from the women's brigade, and some men too. I still have the Stalin pin they gave me. I wear it on holidays.

The widespread integration of Nivkh women into the work force was an important step for Soviet planners concerned with broader native development. By 1942 Sakhalin voters elected the first Nivkh woman to a local council seat, Tamara Urziuk from the New Life kolkhoz in Chir-Unvd, and her life story became emblematic of women's new role in Soviet society. She represented her people on the native council, won prizes for her potato planting accomplishments, became a Stakhanovite, and was the subject of countless newspaper interviews and articles.[77]

But amid these generic prize-winning homages to Soviet success, handfuls of other, less celebrated stories attest to how much had changed over only two decades of Soviet administration. Zoia Ivanovna Agniun, born in 1918 in the Nivkh village of Ungri along the Amur, recounted her tumultuous childhood.

I lived with my parents in a small house in Ungri. The benches inside all around were clean and white. My parents always kept everything very clean. In the autumn some time, I think I was five, or at least they told me later that I had been five, I went with my parents to pick berries. That's when Eltun, he's the one who stole me, that's when he found me and took me away.

My uncle told me later that I had first been taken to Nikolaevsk, and two months later he and my father followed me there to get me back, but Eltun heard they were coming and escaped with me to Baidukov [Island]. There was a lot of ice and the route was long so they wrapped me up in a bundle, like *pel'meni* [Siberian meat dumplings], to carry me there. That I remember. Then I stayed until I was twelve or thirteen. My parents had died in the meantime.

The living conditions there were terrible. Eltun had enough money, and there was always enough food, but there was a lot of work. The well we had to haul water from was all the way over in the next village, and we had to collect wood every day by the seashore. There was an old woman there,

10. World War II was a dramatic leap for Soviet cultural activists who had been trying to integrate Nivkh women into vital positions within Soviet society. A Nivkh woman and her Russian colleague posed for this wartime portrait in 1943.

Numtuk, she and I chopped wood. We hauled fish with nets and then carried it in on sticks. We spent most of the day hauling water and wood and fish back and forth. When the wind was quiet we would go out on the lake to fish. That's how we spent our time—working. Our clothes, too, they were never washed. Everyone was always scratching. It was really dirty. Finally, in 1932, through the police, my uncle found me and took me away.

I asked why Eltun had kidnapped her in the first place. And she continued:

Eltun was a kulak! He had a son and wanted us to marry. The boy, Ook, they said, was my husband. But even when they came to take me back, I was thirteen or something, I still didn't know what that meant. And we left it at that. That's the way it was.

That summer I began work in the day care center back where my uncle lived, in Vereshchagino. I started going to the bathhouse. They bought me everything, a dress. I had my own clothes. I started washing again and I had a job. Eltun used to come by almost every month that first year to try and take me back, but I heard eventually that he died. Ook finally got married. After work at the day care center, I worked for a while on the collective farm [artel]. We cut down trees in the taiga. The older women and children, we had our own fishing nets.

In 1936, at the age of eighteen, Zoia Ivanovna married her first husband, Ianlan, who was one of the first Nivkh members of the Komsomol on the Rybnovsk shore and a Shock Worker in the Stakhanovite movement. In 1938 they were awarded a one-month pass to a resort south of Moscow for their achievements in the fishing brigades. The trip became symbolic of her passage into a new life, and it was the story she dwelled on most often whenever we talked about the past.

> We left in September 1938 across the strait on a boat to Nikolaevsk, and then we went by train to Khabarovsk to buy the tickets to Moscow. We had to wait for weeks, but when they found out Ianlan was a Shock Worker they gave us special seats on the mail train. Once we got to Moscow, *Rybakkolkhozsoiuz* didn't know how to get us to Piatigorsk so they put us up in a hotel for two weeks. I was nineteen then and I only spoke Nivkh, I didn't know any Russian, but you can imagine what it was like to see Moscow. We went around to look at all the buildings and we went to a restaurant where some Italians were singing the *Internationale*. That's when I really felt myself to be a Soviet. Then we met more people at the sanitarium. On the way back, we had to spend the winter working in a factory in Vladivostok to earn money for the rest of the route home. There weren't any passenger planes then. By the first of May we got to Nikolaevsk, but then the weather was so stormy we had to wait two full months before we could take a boat to Pogibi. Our one-month trip took us ten months!

The Postwar Period

With the defeat of Japan in 1945, Allied forces agreed to return South Sakhalin to Russian hands, ending forty years of Japanese rule on Karafuto, as the island was known to Japanese. The land transfer was a huge boon for the Soviets. While North Sakhalin's population reached only 106,000 in 1941, the Japanese had transformed Karafuto into a wealthy fishing and agricultural colony, with a population of 447,976 by 1944.[78] It also signaled a tidal shift in Soviet human resources from the North to the South. The Sakhalin capital moved from Aleksandrovsk to Iuzhno-Sakhalinsk (formerly Toyohara) and hundreds of Soviet functionaries set about erasing traces of the Japanese occupation. The state relocated dozens of North Sakhalin kolkhozes to the South, necessitating yet another series of village closings and reshufflings. "Stalin may have hurt people," a retired Russian schoolteacher in Moskal'vo once told me. "But it was Khrushchev who did the subtler damage on North Sakhalin by denying us our industry. After the war, everything went to the South." Vereshchagino was closed after moving Freedom and its mainly Nivkh work force twenty kilometers to Romanovka. Tengi was closed when Five-Year Plan went south, and its Nivkh kolkhozniks joined the Vereshchagino emigrants on Freedom.

Such postwar moves were in keeping with an enormous state apparatus already in place for encouraging hundreds of thousands of Soviet citizens to relocate to the Far East. In his history of the Far East, John Stephan cites the case of Valentina Khetagurova, who moved from Leningrad to the Far East at the age of eighteen. When Khetagurova authored a 1937 article, "Girls, Come to the Far East!" in the central newspaper *Komsomol'skaia Pravda*, more than seventy thousand women responded. They would soon be known as *Khetagurovki*.[79] Throughout 1937 in particular, the pages of *Sovetskii Sakhalin* were filled with testimonials of satisfied arrivals who intended to stay on permanently. The oil worker P. M. Kalinin moved from Groznyi to the North Sakhalin town of Okha in 1931. "The people wanting to move to Sakhalin were so many that only the lucky ones were able. . . . Sakhalin has taught me to love the heroic spirit of our working life, Sakhalin has tamed my wandering spirit."[80] Likewise, the Stakhanovite border guard P. A. Burov, in his article, "I'm Staying to Work on Sakhalin," called on all demobilizing soldiers to remain on the island where they were needed.[81] Starting in 1941 cinema houses in Moscow and Leningrad began showing the short film "Around Sakhalin" as a trailer before feature presentations in order to recruit further settlers. A virtuoso tribute to island cornucopia, the film offered rivers swelled with fish, verdant trees straining under the weight of their fruit, smiling kolkhozniks bearing flowers, brimming oil wells, a homage to Stalin ("The Best Friend of Physical Culture"), and Nivkhi, decorated in military honors.[82]

For Nivkhi, the postwar Stalinist period marked a watershed of changes. It was a slightly delayed version of what historian Yuri Slezkine recently described for Siberia as a whole earlier on.

By the mid-1930s the revolution was over. Some reformers had run out of steam, some had to be restrained and silenced by the commander-in-chief, and others achieved their aims through social mobility. Agriculture had been forcibly collectivized, and industry had been greatly expanded. Millions of class enemies had been fired, arrested, or exiled; millions of peasants (including class enemies) had moved into towns, and thousands of workers had become managers. There was no more opposition, and all political, scholarly, and artistic discourse had become official. Ethnography had been declared a bourgeois pseudoscience; the Committee of the North had ceased to exist; and the small peoples of the North had lost their special status as well as most of their reindeer.[83]

Stalin had handed the administration of Siberia's small peoples to Glavsevmorput' in 1935, but this Sea Route Administration declined this responsibility three years later, so that from 1938 to 1957 no administrative body was dealing expressly with indigenous peoples.

Cultural work among Sakhalin Nivkhi continued during this interlude, and it reflected the more streamlined professionalism that resonated throughout the Soviet administration after what was in some places more than thirty years of governance. Over the course of the war the character of cultural work among the native populations changed: In place of Red Tents and Red Boats came *agitkul'tbrigady* (Culture Agitation Brigades) versed in native languages, armed with films, books, and a catalogue of lectures to choose from.[84] Agitation, in the Leninist sense, was any work undertaken on behalf of the party that sought to spread general ideas through slogans, brochures, and posters. *Propagandisty*—propaganda specialists—in turn would tour native communities explaining the finer points of party and government policies to smaller audiences. Cultural construction went corporate.

In 1942 the Rybnovsk district could boast eighteen agitation collectives uniting 298 agitators, the majority of whom belonged either to the party or the Komsomol. In keeping with the required excesses of the day, the Rybnovsk *agitkollektiv* reported logging a fantastic 7,730 conversations throughout the district [1937 pop. 6,602][85] in that year alone. Conversations, or *besedy*, could mean anything from formal lectures to individual exchanges, often on war-related topics such as Stalin's speech on the occasion of the Twenty-fifth Anniversary of the Revolution and events unfolding in North Africa.[86] In 1943 the 196 agitators of the East Sakhalin district [1937 pop. 4,498][87] logged an equally remarkable 100 lectures in a 140-day period with a cumulative attendance of 6,000. On average, this was the equivalent of formal presentations being held 21 days out of each month, with approximately 60 people at each lecture.[88] The East Sakhalin information cadres included 19 Nivkh and Orok agitators such as comrades Sira from the kolkhoz New Life, Voksin from New Way of Life, and Antik from East, who were all commended for their creative use of party brochures and posters.[89]

In 1990 the agitators and propagandists stood out little in the minds of most older Nivkhi, not because of their unimportance but because their near constant presence had made them a natural part of the landscape.

> Agitators, propagandists, disseminators [*rasprostraniteli*]—it all depends who you were talking about. Sure, they used to come around, encourage us to study, to join the kolkhoz, to tell us how Soviet power related to us. But most of all it was to study. To go to school. To go to the literacy classes. In the

11. Six Nivkh students photographed here in the 1960s, with their Russian instructor (*standing, center*) at the Herzen Institute in Leningrad (formerly the Institute of Northern Peoples), were among the generations of native students from Siberia and the Far East trained for teaching and leadership roles in their communities.

> 1940s and 1950s they read mostly political lectures. Lots of people used to show up for the stories about Stalin and Churchill and the meeting at Yalta. Vasilii Kuzenko was the one I remember most. I can't remember what happened to him.

By all accounts large numbers of people, including Nivkhi, did attend the patriotic lectures. The lectures are a testimony not only to how the highly streamlined state wanted to present itself, but to the growing success of winning over the populace to a collective mission. One rainy night in June 1990 I sat with two women who had grown up in a two-family Nivkh village that had since gone on to become a bustling port. The setting itself was a reminder of times gone by, since one of the women now lived in a tumble-down house that was once the main office of the local prison. It was a nostalgic evening as they recalled the different kinds of plants and berries that grew in the area before it was settled, the friends and relatives lost during the purges, and the ways people's lives had changed. It was only late into the conversation, long after I had retired my notebook and desisted from putting forth questions, that the woman whose father had been taken away under Stalin broached the same topic that was to be repeated in brief renditions over and over again during my stays on Sakhalin: "Stalin has a bad reputation now, but he was handsome, don't you think?" "There were a lot of good things that Stalin did too. . . . People blame Stalin for everything now, but an entire system was at work, not just one man. I liked Stalin. I supported him then and I support him now."

The heady years after the war were marked by proclamations of economic triumph. At Freedom's new location in Romanovka the net intake per fisherman was reported to have almost doubled in the three-year period between 1954 and 1957; in 1957 the kolkhoz overfulfilled its plan by 235 percent.[90] Projections through to the early 1960s on all North Sakhalin fishing kolkhozes were comparably ambitious, and plans were approved to diversify into fish processing. Whether these striking figures had any basis in fact is questionable, but their importance here is in the contribution they made to perceptions of social development. By the time the Nivkh ethnographer Chuner Taksami hailed the "renaissance of the Nivkh people," his work reflected the official position that the great stride into history had been made. Nivkh living standards had been increased by such an extent since the 1930s, he contended, that "they differed little from those of the Russians."[91] Moreover, the new way of life had brought about fundamental changes in Nivkh consciousness: "New psychological characteristics developed that were typical of socialist societies—political awareness, a socialist attitude to labor, Soviet patriotism, trust and respect for other peoples, and the feeling of civil obligation toward the socialist homeland."[92] The spirit of change was the order of the day, but sufficient ambiguity remained in the implementation of the Soviet nationality policy for the Nivkhi to maintain some fundamental aspects of an otherwise familiar life-style: extensive fishing rights, a seasonal work cycle, and perhaps most important, residence in favorable territories.

Throughout the Stalinist period the darker sides to Sakhalin's past had by no means disappeared. Secret prisons and labor camps still lined the central artery of the island from Pobedino on Aniva Bay to Pogibi on the northwest shore from at least 1947 on, and possibly earlier.[93] By the start of the 1950s seven corrective labor colonies housed roughly 5,000 prisoners, 70 percent of whom had been arrested under Article 58 of the RSFSR Criminal Code as "enemies of the people." By 1953, 12,500 prisoners were working on two of the most notorious work projects on Sakhalin in the Soviet period—a railway leading from Pobedino to Pogibi and an underground rail tunnel running the seven kilometers under the Tatar Strait from Pogibi to Lazarev on the mainland.[94] When Stalin died in March 1953 and a political amnesty was declared the following month, the number of prisoners working on the project dropped to 3,500. Former subway construction workers were recruited from Moscow to continue working on the tunnel, despite the warnings of engineers that the force of the current at that point in the strait was too strong to permit underground passages. Workers on both the Amur and Sakhalin sides managed to dig underground for three kilometers on each side, leaving only one kilometer between them. In Pogibi, residents speak of the apocalyptic end to the project on a day in the 1950s when workers struck an underground lake, and hundreds were drowned.

"Stalin waves his right hand—a city grows up in a swamp, he waves his left—factories and plants spring up, he waves his left—swift rivers start to flow," went the homage to the Soviet leader in a verse from the folklorist Kovalev.[95] But in an eerie rejoinder to Stalin's resolve was the Nivkh admonition recorded by Kreinovich in the 1920s, "When winter comes, lightning sinks to the bottom of the Tatar Strait, just to the north of Cape Pogibi. This place is called *nyun'u*. There the water freezes first. Lightning lives there like a blind man, not seeing anything."[96]

Despite efforts after the amnesty to rehabilitate those who disappeared during the purges, such as Aleksei Churka, the late 1950s was a time to look forward rather than back.

In 1959 a publishing house was established in Iuzhno-Sakhalinsk that has since issued popular local histories for national consumption. Epithets such as "treasure island," "gem," "Soviet forepost on the Pacific," "order-bearing island," and "beloved island," have been promoted in the hope of ridding Sakhalin of its unfavorable connotations.[97]

Where early activists in the 1920s and early 1930s were prone to look syncretically at Nivkh and Soviet ways of life, a wartime report on North Sakhalin Nivkhi summed up the shift in perspective by noting, "There is no need to write about the position of the peoples of the North before the establishment of Soviet power on Sakhalin. With the arrival of Soviet power, the resurrection of these peoples, in the fullest sense of the word, got under way."[98]

"Overcoming the past is a prerequisite for full membership in the family of peoples of the USSR," read the masthead of *Bolshevik Fish Run* in the early 1930s. But how many pasts were ultimately involved? An Asian cosmopolitan past, in which Russians figured so little that the period could only be traced to an aberrant flirtation with capitalism? The revisionist primitivism of the Soviet imaginary? Or a more recent past, of city-trained native officials, native councils, Latin alphabets, and other persons and objects of reform erased so quickly after their promotion? By the postwar period, the only past that held much currency was one where the state played the redemptive role. The regnant notion of traditional Nivkh life as "cultureless" became a staple in ethnographic and popular writing.

It was a notion by which young Nivkhi were schooled and that many adopted. Having been dismissed by the Russian Orthodox Church, praised by Lenin, and then routed by Stalinist purges, Nivkhi came to find a more generalized, less distinctive place in the new Soviet system after World War II. By the time the Stalinist period had drawn to a close, their stride across a thousand years was considered to have been formally achieved.

"Slogans for the 1935 May Day Celebrations, Rybnovsk"

1. Long live the May Day military review of the revolutionary might of the international proletariat!

2. Class brothers, victims of the fascist terror, prisoners of capitalism: in honor of May Day, our proletarian greetings!

3. Proletarians of the world! Strengthen proletarian internationalism! Stand under the banner of the Communist International!

4. Onward to new battles and victories! Long live the world socialist revolution!

5. Our brotherly greetings to the revolutionary proletariats of Germany! Long live the heroic Communist Party of Germany! Freedom to prisoners of fascism!

6. "We seek not one inch of the land of others. But we will cede not a speck of our own land, not to anyone."—Stalin.

7. "We stand for peace and will defend the cause of peace. But we are not afraid of threats and are ready to respond to warmongers blow for blow."—Stalin.

8. Long live our own invincible Red Army—mighty bulwark of the peaceful labor of the peoples of the USSR, true defender of the achievements of the October Socialist Revolution!

9. Workers and kolkhozniks! We will meet the five-year plan in its entirety! We will achieve the technical reconstruction of all sectors of the economy! Let material and cultural levels rise still further! Let us build a classless socialist society! Onward to new victories!

10. To the army of millions of Shock Workers and distinguished people of our country, to the heroes of socialist construction, our ardent bolshevik greetings!

11. Workers, engineers, and technicians! Master the full strength of our socialist industry! To the mastery of new technology! To the fullest use of the shortest working day in the world!

---

12. Kolkhozniks! Let us strengthen the kolkhoz system day by day! Assist lagging kolkhozes to rise to the level of the best! Let us make all kolhozes bolshevik and all kolkhozniks prosperous! Let us nominate honorable private workers for entrance into kolkhozes. Long live the friendship between workers and peasants triumphantly building socialism!

13. "To join the personal interests of the kolkhozniks with the social interests of the kolkhozes—there lies the key to strengthening kolhozes."—Stalin.

14. Kolkhozniks! To work in the kolkhoz honorably and to maintain the goodwill of the collective—this is the path to a prosperous life!

[Source: *STsDNI*, f. 13, o. 1, d. 24 (1935), l. 213.]

Six

1960s Resettlements and the Time of Stagnation

Ask any Nivkh. We are all from somewhere else.
(Nivkh schoolteacher, 1990)

The Towns Left Behind

In the autumn of 1990, after a long fish run, smoke from the stormy meetings over the future of the kolkhoz began to clear, and as the routine of Rybnoe's villagers began to slow down, I resolved to extricate myself in favor of a trip to the nearly empty town of Pogibi down the western coast. Pogibi had loomed large in my mind throughout the summer of interviews: From the tsarist period through to the end of Stalin's rule, it had been the focal point of the island's notorious prisons and military camps. In the 1930s Vasia Pogiun had driven enemies of the people there on his dog sled from Rybnovsk; those who were not interned there, initially in a prison or later on in the 1940s to work on the notorious underwater tunnel project, were shipped along the next leg down to Aleksandrovsk. For the current day, however, it was also sufficiently peripheral to my research to afford something of a retreat.

Then, as a hundred years earlier, reaching Pogibi was slowed by North Sakhalin's almost complete absence of roadways. As in much of rural Russia at the end of the Soviet period, the local infrastructure was deceptive; for despite roughly 100,000 people living on North Sakhalin in 1990, and the remarkably flat landscape, only the few largest towns could be reached by road. Instead a heavily subsidized fleet of small planes and helicopters criss-crossed the island from town to village like city buses. Though Pogibi is only eighty kilometers down the coast from Rybnoe, it was only after seven hours in a kolkhoz truck headed in the opposite direction, for Okha, followed by two more hours in a cargo bush plane headed there by chance, that I managed to reach my destination. My high spirits from getting away diminished only with the descent of the plane. As it touched down I realized I had propelled myself on the spur of the moment to a town where I knew no one, where, as a foreigner at a time when foreigners were not about, I was arriving unannounced, where I had heard something about there maybe being a place to stay, and where, if no one in particular minded, I wanted to photograph crumbling Stalinist labor camps.

I expressed this realization to one of my two fellow passengers, a health official in a bright pink pants suit, who resolved to take matters into her own hands. Handing me two large bags of unspecified frozen foodstuffs, she commissioned me to pass them on to her medical counterpart on site. We parted with the plane's motors still roaring on the forest airstrip—she, pleased that she could fly on across the strait to other business, and I, satisfied with my flimsy pretext for knocking on strangers' doors. As the plane pulled away, I chose the footpath on the forest's edge that looked the most traveled, and set toward it.

On the other side of the grove stood some twenty tar paper trailers which housed construction teams working on the pipeline that goes across the strait. I wandered from one portable cabin to another asking where I could find the town nurse, and finally planted myself on her stoop with the now dripping bags of melting comestibles. Beside me in the sweltering heat, one of two sleeping miniature dogs rose on its legs to observe my arrival. Its stomach convulsed slightly, and it neatly coughed up an entire fish head, or parts thereof, looked balefully in my direction, and laid down again to rest. We were swimming in the heat and waiting for someone I did not know. Several hours later the Pogibi nurse did show up, received her thawed parcels with grace, and displayed little distress at the thought of a stranger arriving to photograph the lesser sides of Soviet history.

Pogibi is at the narrowest point between Sakhalin and the mainland, where across the Tatar Strait to the town of Lazarev lie only seven kilometers. From Lazarev, Sakhalin's flat stretches of sand and dwarf pine make Pogibi look unreachable, but from Pogibi, the tall hills of the Amur basin rise up sharply against the horizon, making it impossible to believe that the other side is more than a few minutes away. "The hills of Cape Lazarev stand out seductively even during gloomy weather," the Russian exile Ivan Miroliubov wrote in 1901, "and tease the fugitive with their proximity. The novice, perhaps, will set across to try his fortune, but most know otherwise, that Pogibi is a place of death."[1] When the Nivkhi, the Japanese, and the Manchus traveled the area at the start of the nineteenth century, the spot was known as Noteto.[2] Nivkhi had called the spot Pogg'obi, from the West Sakhalin dialect meaning "worm," because of the way the Tatar Strait narrowly snakes its way between the rocky shores. But when Russians established prisons there in the 1880s Pogg'obi became Pogibi, for the way it evoked the Russian *pogibel'*—ruin or death. In later times, by 1970, it had grown into a town of some two thousand people involved in forestry, oil, and border patrols. However, by 1990, save for the few dozen itinerant construction workers refitting oil pipes by the airstrip, only twenty people had stayed among the remainders of camps and schools and stores left behind.

Despite there being no more than a few dozen people in the area at any given time, Pogibi is nonetheless divided into new and old: new Pogibi houses the tar cabins and barracks for the passing oil and construction crews, and old Pogibi, where the nurse and I headed after her return, consists of dozens of empty houses, with doors flapping, set against open pastures and a fallen line of fences. It is in old Pogibi that one of its last older residents, who along with her three daughters, their three husbands, and their children (otherwise at state boarding schools) form the remaining family who maintains the weather station and their own small farms. It was a startling but vaguely romantic kind of isolation (to an interloper), with sporadic electricity from their own generators, water from wells, and mail service only once a month in the remains of a verdant village where it appeared that several hundred neighbors had closed up their homes for short absences and just never returned.

I spent all of three days in Pogibi, having waited a suitable amount of time for the currents in the Tatar Strait to calm sufficiently to allow for travel by motorboat to visit the camps. In this respect I found what I had come for. Along with two men from the meteorological post, I visited two sites at the very narrowest point between the island and the mainland, where the remaining fifty meters of wooden pilings from Stalin's ill-fated bridge jutted out into the water. The first camp was from the Stalinist era, had been closed down in the late 1950s, and had been used on and off until 1985 for military purposes. It was now a popular stopping ground for hunters, and it was evident that someone had been there in the last few days. There were some ten buildings left spread out over an acre, some storehouses and barracks positioned around a stone monument to Soviet power, and an eternal flame, since extinguished, set into the ground by a steel red star. The taiga had grown up around the camp since it had last been used. There was a watch tower, now barely visible through the brush. The floors of the barracks had rotted and fallen through, though the inspirational slogans of "border guard-dom"— "The borders of the Motherland are sacred and impenetrable!" and "We will defend the Pacific!"—were still legible over entranceways. The sense of isolation was formidable.

The second camp, the meteorologists said, was dated from before the 1917 October Revolution. It was all but impossible to find after a few kilometers of wandering through the brush. Said still to be standing ten years ago, with the names of inmates from the turn of the century scrawled on the crossbeams, the structures had evidently succumbed to their own weight, and the remains of five or six very large buildings could be identified through the thickets only by the rooftops and attics that rested on the ground. Each of the buildings had plunged so evenly into the soil around it that to crawl into the vaulted roof chambers was to find an almost perfectly dry, perfectly preserved attic space looking almost to have been built only a few years earlier were it not that the entire first story was now interred in soil.

Both these camps lost their reasons for existence over three different political generations when first the St. Petersburg and then the Moscow central governments called an end to the keeping of prisoners on the island. But to focus on these more obvious remains would be to overlook the more compelling ruins left behind in Pogibi itself. To walk from the construction worker barracks to old Pogibi, as I did each morning, was to pass the concrete hull of the former two-story cinema house, the gaping shell of a now rusting water tower, and some dozen two-room wooden homes from the 1930s now used as hunting sheds. Around the weather station, with its absurdist yard of brightly colored weather vanes, precipitation trays, and mechanical wind gauges, the small wooden buildings left behind had slumped into the pastures on the edge of the strait. My first tour from the oldest daughter and her husband was an act of the imagination. "There's my old school," she said, as we looked at the boarded up remains of a one-room cabin and flag post, "It used to go up to the eighth grade." We crawled our way into the old store, which still had its shelves and display cases. In turn we paid respects to the former post office, and to the homes of several neighbors, now serving as chicken coops.

At the end of the first day, when the sea had been stormy and gray and generally opposed to small motorboats, the health official from the plane trip returned, and we dined with the family at the station in the old part of town. The houses and pastures were plunged in darkness, in stark contrast to the glittering lights that rose on the horizon from the homes in Lazarev across the water. At a table in the yard of the main house, set amid the weather vanes and with a view to the sea, we lingered over a dimly lit dinner of salmon pies, followed by much homemade wine and conversations about UFOs. "But what about those five people from outer space that landed in Canada? There was a ship and they all got out. . . . No, that was Brazil!" Late into the evening when it seemed already too dark to find our way back to the housing trailers by the construction site, it was voted that we adjourn to the club. I had little idea of what a club might amount to under such circumstances, and as we entered a long, dark, windowless shed on the water's edge, I was prepared for grotesque, clandestine rituals. I was expecting something on the order of a damp, decaying barn as we stood with the matriarch, her three daughters, and two of the husbands, waiting in the dark for the remaining son-in-law to fiddle with the generator.

Instead, with the lights activated, it seemed clear that the clubhouse was the one piece of town life that had not been allowed to court oblivion. We found ourselves in an auditorium with rows of wrought iron cinema seats with worn red velvet upholstery, red flocked wallpaper, art deco-style glass light fixtures on the walls, and windows painted over black from World War II. There was an oil barrel wood stove in the rear, and alongside the stove, more than thirty reels of film sent six months earlier by the weather administration. In brighter days Lenin's famous aphorism had called Pogibi to culture: A long, red velvet banner over the stage read, "Art belongs to the People!"

Since it was readily clear that all present had seen each of these films at least once, the evening's film selection fell to me, and we whiled away the evening before a Soviet murder mystery featuring French capitalist spies and a decadent chateau. The chateau paled in comparison with what seemed the more extraordinary splendor of an evening spent in one Soviet cinema that had not lost its appeal for the masses. Over the course of that first summer I had been to many abandoned towns along the Sakhalin coastline. Some were so empty as to have been created by Hollywood rather than Brezhnev; others, like Romanovka and Liugi, had, respectively, either a handful of Nivkhi in their sixties and seventies who would not leave or a few couples who had informally taken refuge from kolkhoz life. But in Pogibi the atmosphere was neither of recalcitrance nor retreat, and the residents were neither of an alternative social vision nor outcasts. In this small, strange remainder of the Soviet past, extant but for another stroke of an administrative pen, it was clear that at least in the minds of the people who lived there, far more of Pogibi remained.

Resettlements and the Politics of the Modern

Hegel once wrote that there is no history without struggle, and to a Soviet population so accustomed to tumult and duress from the first days of the USSR's existence, the 1960s and 1970s could have only seemed a lull by comparison. In the aftermath of Stalin's rule and Khrushchev's relatively quick passage through the Kremlin, many considered the rule of Leonid Brezhnev to be so uneventful, by comparison, that Brezhnev's name gradually became synonymous with the *vremia zastoia*, or time of stagnation. Yet the moniker of *zastoi* can mislead us, for throughout the Brezhnev era truly trenchant changes did of course take place. In Siberia and the Far East the government undertook a dramatic plan to restructure the economy through forced relocations that virtually turned people's lives upside down, and a gauntlet of new policy directives were adopted to upgrade social services across the vast eastern territories. In this sense the idea of stagnation occludes the very sea changes afoot. On the other hand, in the entire Soviet history of northern native development, perhaps never was there a time when more money was spent and less accomplished.

The entire stagnation period demonstrated the inherent contradictions in the two dominant streams of Soviet nationality policy—the streamlining of a pan-Soviet identity versus the freedom of diversity—at their point of greatest tension. It is a time that Sakhalin Russians and Nivkhi alike popularly point to as the source of the USSR's modern ills, yet it is also the time for which both groups hold perhaps the greatest nostalgia. Understanding the nature of the resettlements themselves is key to examining this kind of paradox.

In 1957 the Central Committee of the Communist Party and the Soviet Council of Ministers adopted Decree No. 300, "On Measures for the Further Economic and Cultural Development of Peoples of the North."[3] The federal initiative was spurred in part by the ethnographer Anna Smoliak's indictment of social services for Nivkhi on North Sakhalin, and looked to redress what had been twenty years of a policy vacuum since the Northern Sea Route administration had abdicated its involvement in Siberia and the Far East as a whole.[4] But in practice the decree was overshadowed by a seemingly unrelated resolution introduced by Khrushchev on the strengthening of collective and state farms. The idea was that fewer settlements would mean fewer problems of coordination and distribution.

These were not the first resettlements on North Sakhalin, nor for Nivkhi in particular. Since their concerted colonization of the island from the mid-1800s, the Russians' propensity for perestroikas had been obliging Nivkhi to relocate on an almost regular basis. Before and immediately after the revolution, Russian and Japanese settlers expressly overtook Nivkh communities on the presumption that they were the most auspiciously located. The Vereshchagino native council in 1929 set about reducing twenty-five Nivkh settlements on northwestern Sakhalin to four for the collective benefits that concentrated resources would bring.[5] Collectivization itself was about "concentration" and "strengthening" of the work force, and the impetus from this process meant that across the native North from the 1940s on, as the Evenk writer Vasilii N. Uvachan wrote, small kolkhozes were gradually merged with others.[6] Uvachan reasoned that the first waves of collectivization in the North in the 1930s had brought about an artificially enforced specialization of labor, and therefore kolkhozes needed to merge in order to regain a diversified occupational base. Originally most communities mixed herding, fishing, and hunting until these first kolkhozes dictated a focus on one activity. Hence, as kolkhozes unified in the years following, their numbers dropped. In the Chukotka and Evenk regions, for example, the number of kolkhozes dropped 30–40 percent between the 1940s and 1950s.[7] On North Sakhalin the process of kolkhoz relocations was further accelerated by the total shift in resources from the North to the South after Japan relinquished Karafuto at the close of World War II.

The scourge of the resettlements on Sakhalin in the 1960s, however, was that, in almost every case, when one kolkhoz had to be selected from among many for expansion, the least profitable enterprises on the least profitable sites were chosen. Indeed the only criteria for selecting which communities to expand and which to close appear to have been proximity to existing regional centers and the consequent ease of administration.

For Nivkhi, these latest moves and village closings were the most visible and sobering indication of how much and how quickly their lives had changed. On Sakhalin's northwest and northeast coasts, the number of villages lining the shore between 1905 and 1975 dropped by more than 75 percent. Between 1962 and 1986 alone, the number of settlements on Sakhalin as a whole dropped from approximately 1,000 to 329.[8] These were dramatic changes that signaled profound restructuring for the public and private lives of Sakhalin Nivkhi and Russians alike.

The burden on local government was to legitimize the resettlements in a manner consistent with the policy prescribed by Moscow. The rationales they invoked ranged from balancing the budget to bettering communism. In 1963, on Sakhalin's eastern shore, the collectives "Red Sakhalin" in Pil'tun and "East" in Chaivo were shut down and transferred to the regional center of Nogliki. The Nogliki party committee reasoned that the economic and cultural standards of the towns had become untenable: Salaries at the two kolkhozes had fallen to 920 and 600 rubles a month, respectively, work loads had been decreasing, and the towns' locations—75 and 150 kilometers from Nogliki—made it increasingly difficult for the state to provide proper food supplies, communications, and educational and medical services. They pointed out that sending children to the boarding school in Nogliki imposed financial obligations on parents, and that, "after lengthy absences from their parents to attend school, children want to return to their villages for the summer, avoiding pioneer camp, and thereby weakening the process of collective upbringing."[9]

Yet in contrast to the 1963 explanation, which listed the average salaries of kolkhozniks in Red Sakhalin and East as a disparaging 920 and 600 rubles a month, a 1962 kolkhoz report lists much higher figures of 1,567 and 1,033 rubles a month, which were in fact a marked increase of 9 percent from five years earlier. Moreover, Chaivo's East had been the only regional kolkhoz to meet its yearly plan successfully in 1962, and the

Nivkh brigadiers of both Red Sakhalin and East were favorably singled out for their production.[10] In 1990 one of the same brigadiers described the meeting where the village closure was announced,

> None of us could believe the news when we first heard it. The town had grown to about seven hundred people, about three hundred of us, Nivkhi. The government had spent so many years building us up! There was a school, a laboratory, two clubs, a kolkhoz. . . . They had only just finished a whole new set of houses and a two-storied hospital on the edge of the village. A new rail line too. I had been a party organizer [*partorg*] there before and I didn't know a thing. They called a meeting of the whole village. The *raiispolkom* explained that small settlements were no longer profitable for the country, that they were too broadly spread out and maybe even dangerous. Then they tried to tell us that the town was badly situated, that there was a danger of flooding. There's never been a flood there ever!

The experiences were similar on the northwest coast, where the fishing kolkhozes Freedom, in Romanovka, and Twenty-first Party Congress (formerly "Stalin"),[11] in Liugi, were closed down and amalgamated with Nekrasovka's failing Red Dawn.

The brigadier Vasilii Mikhailovich assured me: "Suddenly they moved us all here. People were frightened into leaving. Sometimes the militia would have to come in trucks and even move people out by force." But across Sakhalin the stories told by both Nivkhi and Russians about the resettlement operations suggested more incremental withdrawal. The younger generations were usually the first to accede to the offers of better housing elsewhere, whereas among the older generations and the hesitant, party members were the first to be told to go. The school would be moved, forcing parents with children to follow. From the stories and archival accounts, one can almost chart a hierarchy of organized oblivion, with the hospital next to go, then the village council, then the post office, then the store, and then the electricity.

> Of course, people didn't want to leave. Here there isn't the same kind of fish. There you'll find everything. Those that didn't want to go stayed behind. But how can you stay behind if there is no kolkhoz any longer? No school? No store? So you move.

Similar stories were repeated again and again.

> The 1960s were a turning point for us, when they began the closings. They closed the Shirokopadskii plant. There were five villages in that area and all five were closed. That's five villages that automatically lost their reason for existence. The Khoenskii kombinat [enterprise] was closed, that was another

six villages. Here in the Northwest we had the villages of Tuzrik, Viski, Astra-khanovka, Nevel'skaia, Uspenovka, Liugi, Kefi, Naumovka, Grigor'evka, Kali-novka, Valuska, Third Station, Fourth Station, Romanovka, Lupolovo, Ten'gi, Pogibi . . . and all the rest around there . . . all gone!

Yet to cast the moves in a roundly negative light would not be accurate. For most of those involved, only in retrospect has the resettlement program come to be so rued. At the time the plan met with few incidents of overt resistance. Most people interpreted the decision as official policy and assumed it would be for the best. As one Nogliki resident re-marked in 1990, "The tragedy is that nothing happened. The empty houses in Nogliki were all ready. The kolkhoz had already been built. Most people just got up and moved. That's the tragedy—that there was no tragedy."

Indeed what sets the resettlements of the 1960s apart from those that immediately followed World War II was the absence of any real economic virtue. By 1968 Nogliki's reconstituted East was palpably failing: Debt was increasing, fishermen could not fulfill the planned quotas, and the kolkhoz recommended more expeditions farther afield, namely back to the abandoned Pil'tun and Chaivo.[12] At both East and Red Dawn the average fish catches were four times lower than the average for the region, and the average kolkhoz salaries were two and a half times lower.[13] In 1969, when the few who did formally object, residents of the defunct town of Venskoe, complained in a letter to the Sakhalin Regional Execu-tive Committee (*Oblispolkom*) that they had been moved involuntarily, the *Oblispolkom* claimed otherwise. "People wanted to move to Nogliki immediately," they argued; there was little interest in traditional life, and the authors of the letter, "the majority of whom are elderly and illiterate," did not fully understand its contents. Chuner Taksami, the Leningrad ethnographer and initiator of the Venskoe letter, was chided for his "in-correct, subjective approach . . . which, advocating the preservation of 'northern peoples as children of nature,' was only representing obsolete customs, morals, and a way of life."[14] Northern peoples, long having achieved the stride across many Marxist modes of production, were not about to be left behind after such efforts. The resettlements marked the apogee of the progress narrative that effaced native distinctiveness be-yond the most ornamental purposes.

The committee's response coincided with the recasting of the broader Soviet nationality policy at the time, whereby Nivkhi were to have bloomed (*rastsveli*), drawn closer to Russian culture (*sblizilis'*), and finally merged with it (*slilis'*).[15] But the persistence of expressly Nivkh cultural forms (language, dress, and diet) plied at the contradictions of the official position: Traditional life was at once lauded (as a marker of the freedom of peoples) and suppressed (as a lingering resistance to abstract notions of Soviet homogeneity).

The resettlements, rather than representing a merger of collective interests, reduced the Nivkhi to second-class status. In the shuffle of kolkhoz reorganizations, Russians supplanted Nivkhi in the vast majority of skilled and administrative positions. In 1968, despite East's status as a Nivkh kolkhoz, only 19 percent of Nivkhi in the collective worked in skilled positions, and few were being trained for promotion.[16] Figures show that overall kolkhoz membership dropped sharply with the moves, while unemployment and underemployment in the Nivkh community increased markedly. Many who were unable to find work in the towns where they relocated lost their pensions and state benefits. The situation of one Nivkh woman who moved to Nekrasovka was typical of the descriptions of the resettlements.

> My parents didn't want to leave Romanovka and they stayed right up until 1971 or 1972. That was right up until they took the store away. My father was a party member and was told that he had to move or he would lose his card. Moving to Nekrasovka at first wasn't so bad, but it was obvious that there wasn't enough housing or work for everyone. That's when all the Russians stepped in to get the best jobs. The people who had it the worst were Nivkh women—most of them couldn't get any work at all. My mother was only six months short of finishing her thirty-five-year work term. When she couldn't find a job, she lost her pension.

One 1989 Sakhalin State Archive report looked back on the 1970s kolkhoz restructurings by noting that although "the concentration of the smaller national fishing kolkhozes led to a significant increase in kolkhoz membership," it was not from among the ranks of the Nivkhi. "The so-called national fishing kolkhozes have long since ceased being national [i.e., Nivkh]. Nivkh members of Red Dawn have never accounted for more than a third of the entire kolkhoz collective."[17]

Several years later the Soviet scholar Vladimir Boiko explained this failure of Nivkhi to rise within the ranks of their own kolkhozes as a casualty of their great leap forward.

> The poor work performance of the indigenous population in industrial production, without question, negatively affects supervisors' attitudes to sending native workers to be trained. . . . In the kolkhoz "East," where more than 30 percent of the working native population of the Nogliki district are employed, only six natives were sent for special training over the entire period of the Tenth Five-Year Plan. . . . The strict regimentation of the working day, unfamiliar working conditions, and the high intensity of industrial production do not correspond to the ethnopsychological makeup of the indigenous popu-

lation. . . . For Nivkhi, not having gone through the stage of the industrial revolution, this is particularly difficult.[18]

However, since the Nivkh character did not impede Nivkhi's successful management of kolkhozes either before or after World War II, we instead might consider the alternative explanation put forth by many Nivkhi. With the passing of a common goal, such as the war or postwar reconstruction, many Soviets saw the prosperity of the Far East as a source of transient wealth. New waves of workers continued to arrive as before, but few stayed longer than was required. *Vremenshchiki*, or temporary workers, flooded North Sakhalin and brought with them, as longer-time Nivkh and Russian residents insisted, a different moral ethic. Vasilii Mikhailovich, the retired Nivkh brigadier, recounted,

> The first Russians that came in the 1930s were so different from the Russians today. You know, a lot of them were Christians. Some were sent to Sakhalin as punishment for their beliefs. Others wanted to come to exert some kind of influence over Nivkhi. They would come and encourage us to grow potatoes, to work with machinery, that kind of thing. Those kind of people—you'll never find them again. You could leave money on a table and they would never take it. The only people that came in the 1960s were hooligans.

Two younger Nivkh brigadiers from Red Dawn added later,

> Before the resettlements, there was just less difference between Russians and Nivkhi. Later, it was a question of what people came for. The whole plan for the island shifted to oil development, and the oil workers never really cared what was going on. Sakhalin's fate!

The phenomenon of temporary workers was one that resonated across Siberia, and moved beyond the familiar genre of aboriginals mulling over lands lost. In the nostalgic prose of the Russian nationalist writer Valentin Rasputin, one can recognize any Sakhalin village in the days of Brezhnev. In Rasputin's short story, "The Fire," he writes,

> This was a bleak and untidy town, neither a city nor a village. It was more like a camp site, as if the residents, migrating from place to place, had stopped to wait out a storm and to rest up and had simply gotten stuck. . . . In the summer during bad weather the caterpillar tractors and timber trucks churned the mud into a black-sour-cream foam that got pushed to the sides in ponderous waves and that later dried in waves, turning into rock-hard ridges, which for the old folks became insurmountable hills. Every year the town council collected one ruble from each household for wooden sidewalks, and every year sidewalks were laid down; but spring would come, when people had to haul in firewood, and after logs had been dragged across them and rolled along them, all that would remain of the sidewalks were splinters. During the sum-

mer they never got around to putting in new ones—nobody felt like it in the summer; toward winter the "sidewalk" crew would make its appearance, the virgin boards would lie under the snow for three or four months scarcely touched by anyone's feet until February or March, and once again they'd perish senselessly under the treads of the caterpillars and the sheer weight of raw timber. And oftentimes people even used the remains of these little three-plank sidewalks as chopping blocks—they sawed and split wood on them.[19]

Some Nivkhi join with Rasputin in looking at the 1960s as the loss of real order and the need for a return to Stalinist values. But all Russians and Nivkhi I knew on North Sakhalin, regardless of political stripe, saw the Brezhnev era as a fundamental shift in the way state policy in general was implemented.

The Soviet state had long depended on ritual and spectacle for cultivating its collective identity, but for many the 1960s represented an absurd move into the realm of performance. It was the kind of shift that allowed for the best villages to be closed down in favor of the ones most conveniently situated for administrative purposes, and the kind of shift that saw the promotion of Nivkh kolkhozes where few Nivkhi found jobs. What is even more striking is that, as financial fortunes dwindled, self-congratulation from official circles mounted audibly. From any survey of the Sakhalin archives, one quickly sees that in the 1960s the documents dealing with northern native peoples themselves changed, as specificity gave way to effusive generalizations about northern accomplishments. A. I. Krushanov's 1985 *History of the Sakhalin Fishing Industry*, full of archival material on Nivkhi in the pre- and postwar periods, effectively grinds to a halt at 1961, when the documents drift into accounts of "further accelerated development," progress, and success. In the same period, lesser-known internal government documents began to cite the drops in investment for native education, housing, medical care, and professional development,[20] but the more common official narratives began with testimonies to how Nivkhi were buying more and more magazine subscriptions, thereby improving their lot.[21] At a formal level, Soviet linguists determined this manner of description in 1966 as the "official style," which was normally the jurisdiction of the media and schoolteachers. As Caroline Humphrey has noted,

> Before *glasnost'* all over the Soviet Union articles and letters ostensibly written by members of the public were rewritten by journalists in the appropriate style before publication. This was true even of the most humble newspapers. When Aleksei Losev was working on a local paper in a small town in north Sakhalin, it was his job to "organize" the reactions (*otkliki*) of the public to current political events. . . . In this style there is a limited range of adjectives and adverbs: success (*uspekh*) is creative (*tvorcheskii*), labor (*trud*) is also creative,

help (*pomoshch'*) is brotherly (*bratskaya*), participation (*uchastiye*) is active (*aktivnoye*), and so on. It is a truism to say that many political meetings carried out in this style were pure "performance." They achieved a change of state, for example the public "decision" to take some action, but this was irrespective of the attitudes of those attending. In many cases such meetings consisted entirely of incantations.[22]

It was by the same spirit of incantation that Rybnoe could produce detailed reports of meetings that never took place, attend to the burning of books only months after they had arrived at the village library, and formally disavow a closed neighboring town where a few still lived and to which everyone still retired on the weekends. It was perhaps by the same spirit of incantation that Il'ia Gurvich wrote in the wake of the Twenty-second Party Congress of 1961, "The path followed by peoples of the North fully bears out the position of the Program of the CPSU [Communist Party of the Soviet Union] that the nationality question in the Soviet Union, now behind us, has been successfully resolved."[23]

In this spirit the 1970 USSR census makers formally graduated Siberia's indigenous population to another rung, from "the small peoples" (*malye narody*) to "the nationalities of the North" (*narodnosti Severa*).[24] By definition, their being *narodnosti* meant that they had still not achieved the level of development characteristic of the larger, fully industrialized peoples of the Soviet Union,[25] but the diminutive implications of *malye* (meaning "numerically small," as in *malochislennye*, or just "small") and the relative position it suggested within the USSR's multiethnic union was jettisoned. The rise of the smaller Siberian groups up the conceptual ranks of the Marxist-Leninist scheme was one of many signals that the USSR had reached, in official parlance, a state of advanced socialism. At the very time when exceptional circumstances were ruling Nivkhi out of active participation in society, social planners called a halt to exceptional policies in their favor. In 1963, when the Russian Republic's Ministry of Education sent a letter to the Sakhalin *Oblispolkom* requesting that the committee outline its needs for native language education, Iuzhno-Sakhalinsk responded that native languages in the region were not studied due to a lack of interest.[26]

Despite the measures brought about under Brezhnev through Decree No. 300, the new kolkhoz East was in disarray. The medical clinic was not being funded, bath facilities were not functioning, and no work was being done to address growing rates of alcoholism and illiteracy.[27] Of particular consequence was the introduction of regulations governing the amount of salmon that Nivkhi were entitled to catch each year. Through the 1950s the Nivkh diet was still heavily dependent on salmon: Individuals consumed, on average, up to a thousand kilograms each year (much of it in dried form), an amount far beyond what local stores could afford. In 1962 an annual limit of two hundred kilograms was imposed, and in 1969, with concern for ever-weakening kolkhoz production, the limit was further reduced to sixty kilograms. Nivkhi's membership in the Soviet family of nations continued to underline the USSR's commitment to a diverse multinational environment, but the parameters of diversity were clearly being narrowed. After the resettlements, the reduction in fishing allowances turned out to be yet another reason for many Nivkhi, otherwise patriotic, to question their social contract.

Choosing the Past

> Before we lived in the swamps, and were unable to
> rise out, but today we stand with the mountains,
> and for that, Lenin, thank you!
> *(from the 1970 Festival of Northern Peoples,*
> *Nogliki)*

What made the resettlements of the 1960s so compelling was not only the attendant drop in the indigenous community's quality of life but the way the resettlements visually transformed the Sakhalin landscape. Coastlines once studded with villages every ten kilometers became littered with ghost towns.

The absurdity of the moves of the 1960s made even the harsher collectivization of the distant 1930s seem almost more favorable by comparison. With little economic rationale to explain the dramatic shifts, the explanations given were primarily cultural ones.

> The creation of concentrated villages in northern native areas goes hand in hand with the raising of [Siberian native peoples'] social and cultural potential, the creation of new forms of housing, and the mastery of nontraditional types of work: All this leads to a change in their ethnic self-consciousness. For these national minorities, life in multiethnic, multilingual villages and labor collectives is connected with the need for preserving their "ethnic identity," their roots and their cultural self-respect. In other words, the accelerated development of an international way of life and the transformation of traditional cultures into socialist ones sharpen rather than weaken the need for recognizing the diversity of national cultures.[28]

Rather than the resettlements strengthening and internationalizing, they produced a spirit of absence that was felt on economic, social, and personal levels. Rather than moving forward, they generated a retrospective force that pulled many back. The brigadier from Chaivo stayed behind when all of East was transferred to Nogliki. By 1970 he was the only one of seven hundred left, and to this day he visits Nogliki only a few months each year. Remaining behind in empty towns that no longer officially existed, he and others like him became icons of a "traditional" way of life that had become reified and reinforced by a policy expressly designed to diminish it. In creating a spatial dichotomy between past and present, the resettlements divided allegiances by obliging people to choose (and in most cases making the choice for them).

For the few who did stay behind in these villages and towns that no longer existed according to the centralized registers of the Sakhalin administration, their lives would take on a strange nether quality. In the 1960s the town of Romanovka had a population of little over five hundred, most of whom were employed by the kolkhoz Freedom. With dark soil and tall grasses fed by a river running through the village out to the Tatar Strait, Romanovka has little in common with the windswept Rybnovsk only twelve kilometers to the north along the island's northwestern shore. The state began the resettlement of residents from Romanovka to Nekrasovka in 1969, and the village was officially closed in 1972.

Reaching Romanovka some twenty years later in 1990 and 1992 required the same negotiation of back roads, sand dunes, and beaches during low tide as was necessary to reach Rybnoe and Rybnovsk. But in Romanovka, once the most prosperous village along the Rybnovsk shore, only fifteen houses remained. Four older Nivkh families lived in the village year round, and other Nivkhi like Kirill Taigun, who worked as Freedom's chairman before its closing, return in the spring and summer months only.

> We came to Romanovka in 1947 when Freedom moved from Vereshchagino. From 1962 to 1966 I was the kolkhoz chairman. What great land. Everyone had their own plots here and then they moved it all away. Before we used to have twelve horses and twenty-two cows in the village. There was a day care, a store, a bakery. We even had a poultry farm. My own dog sled had twelve dogs, and there were lots of other people who had sleds. We used the sleds often to cross over the strait since we used to get most of our goods from Nikolaevsk. It usually took about a week—three days there, one day in the town, and then three days back. That was when there was no limit to the amount of fish you could catch. You fulfilled the plan or you didn't. But you could fish as much as you liked.
>
> When they wanted to close the village, the adults had nowhere to go. Not everyone got jobs when they moved to Nekrasovka. A lot of us stayed. But then, slowly, bit by bit, they started to take the town away. So now this is like our *dacha*, our summer home. We moved out in 1972, but we always come back.

12. A dress made from salmon skin, as worn here by Zoia Agniun in the closed village of Romanovka in 1990, is a rare sight
on Sakhalin today.

Despite the obvious difficulties of living in Romanovka—no roads, no
electricity, no running water, and plagues of mosquitoes in the summer
months to rival the dark swarms recruited for insect repellent advertise-
ments—the village's enduring appeal was evident. Abundant quantities of
fish could be netted without difficulty along the river or off shore; the soil
was excellent for vegetable gardening; and perhaps best of all, there were
no public overseers. Among the older Nivkhi who remained for the better
part of the year were couples like the Agniuns, who had completed their
thirty-five-year terms of employment for pensions and spent their time

fishing, raising vegetables, and reading at night by candlelight in their cabin along the river. Two houses down, their neighbor Zoia Ivanovna, having lived through her childhood abduction, the epic journey to Moscow in 1937, and a life in the service of the state fisheries, spent most of the year in a tiny, spotless two-room house, drawing her own water and chopping her own wood, activities that, at age seventy-two, had made her a local folk icon. Closer to the shore, Grigorii Pakskun, at age seventy-seven, lived with his son's family who worked intermittently during the fish runs in Rybnovsk. And in the former office of the village soviet, Vasia and Lida Pogiun, also in their seventies, kept five dogs in a yard alongside a sled that had not been used in three years. This was the one group of people I met during my nine months on Sakhalin who freely communicated in the Nivkh language and led what best approximated a life resembling generations past.

The gray plaster walls were lined with coats, jackets, and rainwear for twenty, followed by a water dispenser for washing hands (*umylnitsa*), racks with dishes and cups for forty, five clocks, each proclaiming different times, and a portrait of Lenin entitled "October," portraying the Soviet grandfather at a Moscow conference pointing to the future, displayed alongside a calendar five years old.

While the insides of houses in Rybnoe and Rybnovsk differed in few fundamental ways from the interiors of those in Moscow or Leningrad, the lack of access and amenities in Romanovka precluded many of the more recent trappings of Soviet life. People's homes, instead, bore the marks of northern fishing cabins anywhere. During an afternoon of dining on sturgeon steaks and talking about fishing, the Pogiuns' home was stuffed to overflowing with the remnants of their lives thirty years earlier when they worked and lived in Romanovka full-time. In the three-meter-by-three-meter kitchen, the former reception area of the council office, jetsam covered every surface. In one corner was an ancient wood stove, rusting through cracked white paint and bearing a hammer and sickle on the oven door. In the opposite corner stood one narrow table, and the floor in-between was littered with old slippers, used sardine cans, wet logs, wood shavings, empty cigarette boxes, three axes, stove sweeps, four buckets, winter scarves, old pillows, heavy chain link soaked in oil, old glass vinegar bottles, five stools, an enormous pile of coats, and stacks of fishing gear in large boxes.

During the course of my first stay in 1990 I asked most of the Nivkhi I met, young and old, about their clan status and whether they still believed in any of the cosmological ideas discussed at such length in the works of Shternberg and his successors. Rarely did anyone under forty know their clan or remember the stuff of Nivkh legends. Among older Nivkhi, just as common was this response from a retired nurse in Okha:

"My clan? Oh, I always get confused. When people ask, I say Chaivingu. But that's not it. I forgot my clan. I used to be Chaivingu and then it changed when I got married. Cherzhengu? Chyozhengu? Koron? Yes, before it played an important role. The marriage rules were pretty strict." Vasia and Lida Pogiun were in fact the only Nivkhi I met during my research who said that their clans had played a role in their marrying. They were also among a small handful who had a vision of the Nivkh afterlife, or *Mlyvo* (Land of the Dead), where in a seeming play on the idealism of the October Revolution, all is inverted—the rich become poor and the poor become rich.[29] Lida explained that *Mlyvo* is by a town that once existed near the closed North Sakhalin village of Muzma.

> Once a man in Muzma noticed that one of his dogs was going away for long periods and returning full. He wanted to know where the dog was feeding, so one night he put the dog on a leash and was led to the mouth of a cave and down into its depths. The entrance was dark and the man was afraid, but he continued ahead and came upon an entire village bathed in light. He saw no residents but just racks and racks of gleaming dried fish, from which the dog began to eat. Wanting to bring back proof of his discovery, he wrapped up some of the fish in paper and returned to Muzma. When he unwrapped his parcel, the fish was rotten.

I asked if one could reach *Mlyvo* without being dead or if anyone still made the distinction between *Mlyvo* (the lower world) and *Tlyvo* (the upper world), but the real stuff of legends for Vasia and Lida and their other Nivkh guests lay elsewhere. If I really wanted to know about the Land of the Dead, they told me, I should find the 1989 article in *Komsomol'skaia Pravda* about the spirits who live on another planet and who caused the explosion of the space shuttle *Challenger* in 1986. Seizing upon this more solid piece of information, all present discussed the probability of alien influence in the shooting down of the Korean jetliner over Sakhalin in 1983, and the afternoon wound down.

Traditional life for most Nivkhi I knew was defined by a disparate constellation of elements—foodstuffs like cranberry potato purée (*mos'*) or the surprisingly tasty fish-skin custard (*muvi*); the remains of the Nivkh language, the setting of salmon out to dry each summer for a supply of *iukola* (dried fish), saving a dog sled for memories of years past, and an occasional seasonal tribute of tobacco and sweets to the gods of the sea and taiga who once played a more active role in people's lives. Older Nivkhi certainly had more access to these cultural resources, and the younger the Nivkhi, the less these factors resonated through their lives. "The other small farms, which were one by one being absorbed," wrote Caroline Humphrey in her work on the Buriats in the 1960s and 1970s, "are now being forgotten, and the younger generation which never knew

13. Younger families in search of quieter lives and richer land, such as the Firuns pictured here in Liugi in 1990, have remained behind in closed villages until their children reach school age.

them in life does not even know their names—a process not unlike the 'structural amnesia' observed in certain patrilineage systems."[30] But in the spirit of perestroika, the village resettlements of the 1960s and 1970s created a palpable focal point for a tradition that young and old could lay claim to. They also underlined the critical importance of place in memory itself. As in Frances Yates's classic book on Greek and Roman mnemonics, *The Art of Memory*, or Renato Rosaldo's ethnohistory, *Ilongot Headhunting*, place rises in importance as an architecture of memory among

Nivkhi displaced.[31] Villages like Romanovka on the western shore, and Pil'tun and Chaivo on the eastern shore became metaphors for a system not always working in their favor. Through the ruins, the villages increasingly became, for Nivkhi, what Tzvetan Todorov described as things and beings "present in absentia," pronounced by their absence, and pointing to the symbols of a life no longer extant.[32]

The Ambiguities of Stagnation

With the worsening ecological situation and growing bureaucratic regulations causing a drop in fish catches, the fortunes of both Red Dawn and East continued to decline through the 1970s and 1980s. Both kolkhozes have "national" status, meaning they receive special incentives and allowances as largely indigenous enterprises, but by 1982 Nivkhi comprised only 120 out of the 336 members of East and only 127 out of the 400 members of Red Dawn.[33] In 1980 a further decree, "On Measures for the Further Economic and Social Development of the Peoples of the North," was enacted by the Soviet Council of Ministers. The government spent enormous sums of money in the implementation of the decree—31.2 billion rubles by 1990, or 169,125 rubles for every indigenous representative in Siberia,[34] colossal amounts over a period when monthly salaries averaged 500 rubles. However, the Nivkh writer Vladimir Sangi, who helped draft the decree, noted ruefully that the funds intended for the cultural and economic development of the Nivkhi were spent by local authorities to purchase oil pipes, automobiles, thousands of pairs of plastic skis, typewriters, calculators, and compact toilets.[35]

By the late 1980s one retrospective assessment for Siberian peoples as a whole had little to say for the virtues of internationalization:

> The results of sixty years of development are not very comforting: From highly qualified reindeer herders, hunters, and fishermen, native northerners have been transformed into auxiliary workers, loaders, watchmen, and janitors.[36]
>
> This process of "lumpenization" of small peoples is looked upon by some "optimistic" experts as a "new progressive phenomenon—growth of the working class," while the profound social alienation, passivity, and pessimism engendered by this situation are regarded as "relics of the primitive patriarchal past."[37]

Public health statistics from recent years indicate the extent to which decades of required self-congratulation occluded considerable problems. As of 1988 the life expectancy of Siberian indigenous peoples was eighteen years lower than that of the USSR population as a whole—forty-five years for men and fifty-five years for women. Social problems such as alcoholism and suicide are four to five times as high as in the rest of the country, and few native communities have acquired the trappings of modern living: The housing base has changed little since the 1950s; only 3 percent of native homes have access to gas mains; 0.4 percent have running water; and only 0.1 percent are connected to district heating systems.[38] The venting of frustration over this state of affairs perhaps reached its formal climax at the first All-Union Congress of Northern Peoples held in Moscow in March 1990, when speaker after speaker mounted the podium to lash out at government mismanagement. Nikolai Solov'ev, one of the Sakhalin delegates, joined in the litany of lament by bemoaning decades of "shameless historians . . . discrimination and loss . . . government fictions . . . ecological disasters . . . and hypnotic blinders."[39]

While the spirit of disillusionment reigned throughout much of perestroika and its aftermath, it is nonetheless critical to bear in mind that Nivkh experience over the last seventy years does not render them passive, tragic figures. The Sakhalin Nivkhi with whom I worked were no more or less patriotic or resistant to Soviet ideology than were the Russians, Ukrainians, and Tatars around them. Indeed, in his research among the Evenki of the Podkamennaia Tunguska River Basin in central Siberia, Nikolai Ssorin-Chaikov has contended that Evenki in that area were even more patriotic than either the administrative staff of the local settlements or the Russian newcomers.

> Evenki tend to value administrative honors more than the Russians—medals and diplomas for the achievements in the building of socialism are kept in the forest among other precious things. . . . The most distinguished reindeer herders in the region, the restless and sincere defenders of the "socialist values" of *sovkhoz* organization, those who are usually invited to the regional administrative gatherings as tokens of "the progress of the Soviet minor nationalities," come from the families that suffered most during collectivization.[40]

In the 1920s, the Committee of the North sought to formulate a development strategy that reverberated between both the dominant perceptions of Siberian peoples—protecting their cultural integrity while preparing them for radical transformation. Nivkhi who look back on the period recall little hesitation about the new state of affairs.

> The prerevolutionary government wasn't interested in us the same way the Soviets were. When the Soviets came, the children started to study in schools. We got a hospital. Of course it was better than before. The first time I gave birth it was in a tent by myself, in keeping with Nivkh tradition. It was a frightening experience. Sometimes other women were with us but not always. One woman I knew gave birth alone in the winter and her legs became frostbitten. The Japanese doctor had to amputate.

The nascent educational system in particular was recalled again and again.

> We studied in Nivkh for two grades only, and then the readers ran out or something. We were pretty poor. For the first two years we had lessons from our primer and in mathematics. All in Nivkh. What a shame none of the textbooks are left. It was so easy to read the Latin letters. We missed our parents but it was fun to be with the other kids. We were all of different ages and we were pretty wild.

Those likeliest to have resisted the cultural program were the Nivkh shamans, but since Soviet power was not established on Sakhalin until 1925, there was little or no lag time between the point when shamans might have realized their potential threat to Soviet construction and the point when they became the subjects of concerted persecution toward the end of the decade. For the Nivkhi, the Stalinist period was undoubtedly the most turbulent of the century; however, as discussed in the previous chapter, the reign of terror was combined with the attractions of modernity. Given the weight of disorder and uncertainty during and after perestroika, one can see why many Nivkhi remember the Stalinist period for the seeming prosperity that followed in the wake of the purges. Indeed, after the mobilization of the female work force during World War II, almost the entire Nivkh population had been effectively integrated into the state economy.

It was with the controversial resettlements of the late 1960s that the two dominant depictions of Siberian peoples within Soviet policy—as timeless primitives and as model proletarians—were at their point of greatest tension. Traditional culture was unique and to be respected, but the celebration of Nivkh tradition could only be achieved in dialectical relation to Soviet modernity. The relocations were justified by this cultural dialectic, since, as noted above, "the accelerated development of an international way of life and the transformation of traditional cultures into socialist ones *sharpens* rather than weakens the need for recognizing the diversity of national cultures."[41] This kind of logic speaks to the Foucauldian vision of establishing identity through a heightened awareness of difference, though the nature of the difference in this context is negotiated by the state. With the same imperative by which the early Soviet reformers insisted on the primitivism of the prerevolutionary Nivkh past (at a time when many Nivkhi were widely involved in trade with their Japanese, Manchu, and Korean neighbors), the very notion of the traditional itself underwent a sort of collectivization in the 1960s. With the emphasis on internationalization, as Kerstin Kuoljok pointed out, "The cultural heritage of the peoples of the North is not something which belongs solely to the individual peoples." In an excerpt, she cites from Chuner Taksami,

14. Setting salmon out to dry into *iukola* has become common practice again, as here in Rybnovsk in 1990 amid the food shortages brought on by perestroika.

> The way of life which the Nivkhi share with other peoples, chiefly the Russians, appears clearly in the Nivkhi culture. Housing, clothing, food and other things are often borrowed from the Russians. But, at the same time, the Nivkhi have preserved the cultural elements which are of practical value. They then become the property of all the peoples with whom the Nivkhi live and work.[42]

Tradition in this sense is at its most malleable. David Anderson has also argued that ethnographic descriptions of Evenk reindeer herding tradition in southern Siberia in the 1970s and 1980s were often tailored to vindicate the Baikal-Amur railway project undertaken in the region at the time.[43]

The resettlements that originated in the 1960s may be roundly regretted today: In 1988 the otherwise pro-pan-Soviet Vladimir Boiko reported that more than half of all Sakhalin Nivkhi wanted to return to the closed village sites.[44] But not all Nivkhi, by any means, had to be coaxed into the new agrocenters, as two indicate here. One Nivkh woman in her forties told me: "My parents wanted to stay behind, but I didn't. Here we have running water and gas. It's the way they handled it afterward that started to cause problems." Her Nivkh neighbor, a pensioner, added:

"Sure I wanted to go. We got an apartment immediately, with a bathroom and a kitchen. I got a good job too. Today I would choose an old village over anything, but I didn't think twice about it then." During my first summer on Sakhalin in 1990, a letter to the editor of Nogliki's district newspaper, *Young Guard*, read, "Capitalist systems and imperialist systems are not created. They live that way because it is the most comfortable for the population. It is only in the Soviet Union that we 'create, render, fulfill, and implement' [*sozdaem, predotvoriaem, vypolniaem, ispolniaem*]." While historians like Hobsbawm and Ranger or anthropologists like Michael Taussig remind us that capitalist systems also create their own mythologies,[45] the deciding difference, as before, seems to be one of overt willfulness—the willfulness to fill every bookstore in the country with rows of texts on cultural construction; the willfulness to officially close down villages before the residents themselves leave.

The nostalgic process of remembrance that now reconfigures Nivkh experience may say as much about dissatisfaction with the present as it does about the past. The disintegration of the Soviet Union has been attended by widespread disillusionment, but for Nivkhi, this process has borne a double irony: As they come to more fully gauge the loss of their traditional culture, they also mark the loss of the pan-Soviet culture they traded theirs in for. In effect, this is the disintegration of *both* the mythic paradigms by which they have been cast. With a language largely forgotten,[46] a population dislocated, and an environment in ecologic ruin, few claims can be made for a romantic image of natives living out of time. But with all aspects of the Soviet past also under revisionist siege, it is no longer clear to Nivkh proletarians that their ambitious stride was worth the effort.

In the wake of this ideological reshuffling, Russian scholars have called for a development strategy for Siberian indigenous peoples based on "neotraditionalism."[47] The idea is a broad one, calling for a revival of the principles of native autonomy explored in the 1920s, an emphasis on traditional land use and economic development through smaller-scale, local initiatives. The approach is an important and useful one, but on North Sakhalin it begs a broader ontological question: After nearly seventy years of Soviet administration, what constitutes tradition?

Seven

Perestroika Revisited: On Dissolution and Disillusion

> The state must never take steps that can evoke an
> ironic attitude among its citizens.
> *(Fazil Iskander, 1989)*[1]

FROM THE TIME I left Sakhalin at the end of 1990 my next visit back to the Soviet Union was in November 1991, to Moscow. For November, Moscow was cold, wet, and dark, but the sense of gloom was further entrenched by the social disintegration that had worsened since the failed coup attempt the previous August. The coup plotters may have abandoned the stage as rapidly as they had seized it, but the defense of democracy so touted in the international press appeared to have been, at best, an accidental victory. Nor, as the credibility of the Soviet apparatus continued to crumble, could any Manichean dualisms be brought to bear on personal and political landscapes so compromised by participation in a system discredited by so many in such a wholesale manner. At this stage, the sense of tragedy and loss that had so dominated my previous stays only appeared to have deepened.

But with such a rapid unfolding of events over perestroika's brief tenure, each year was so greatly different from the next. The art of politics in 1985 was qualitatively different from what was possible in 1989. The year 1990 was qualitatively darker than 1989, and November 1991 seemed only darker still. When making my way back to Sakhalin for the second time, just seven months later in June 1992, not to the Soviet Union but to Russia, tragedy had mostly given way to nihilism and the gritty practicalities of living by an old system under a new name.

Sakhalin may have once inspired dread in the heart of every Russian, but its modern threat to most of Russian humanity of the day lay in the nine-hour Aeroflot flight from Moscow. I recount one flight here for another reading of perestroika: For if we rest at the level of policy developments—new budget measures that led to new elections that led to new politicians—it is easy to miss the stunning sense of mayhem and the absurd that flourished in the growing anarchy.

While hunting down tickets for my first visit in 1990, I regularly joined the early morning crush outside Aeroflot's offices in Moscow on Ulitsa Petrovka at 7:00 A.M., and usually passed a day waiting in line in an airless second-floor chamber filled with resident black-marketeers and foreigners emulating the lesser of Russian queuing techniques. In 1992 the crowds appeared to have shifted out of doors, with Ulitsa Petrovka jammed by crowds of people hawking their possessions for cash. In the back alley courtyard of Aeroflot, by contrast, all appearances suggested they had closed down. Instead of finding fifty people clamoring at the door, about to crush through the glass, only white poplar seeds floated about the empty yard. Climbing to the second floor, I walked into the same hall where I had often been before, and found not one hundred people, but one. Assuming to have come upon the wrong room, and waiting for an ever irate clerk to raise his voice to this effect, I ventured to an open wicket with a sense of cognitive dissonance so fundamental as to feel almost queasy. Ten minutes later I had a ticket. That I had just paid nine hundred dollars, rather than the fifteen dollars I had paid two years earlier, seemed hardly noticeable under the otherwise otherworldly circumstances. That prices had gone up sixtyfold was also not dissimilar to the hyperinflation beginning to plague more essential ventures.

Several days later, with Aeroflot functioning on little gasoline and fewer scheduled flights, the plane to Iuzhno-Sakhalinsk took off after hours of delay on the ground. The cabin was stuffed to overflowing, with baggage in the aisles and spilling off open racks overhead, as no one would trust the airline's baggage handlers not to steal their possessions. The passenger seated behind me removed her socks and wedged a pungent corny foot between the wall and my elbow. The normal respite, a walk to the back of the plane, was out of the question, since the aisle was clogged further by drunken passengers in the process of getting still drunker from the bottles they had brought with them. The bathroom floors were soaked with water and urine, rank with ammonia that had been splattered about indiscriminately. Lunch, rock-hard chicken with hair still on the skin, was impervious to knife and fork. Sticky soda was served in unwashed plastic cups. This was the Aeroflot I had known and loved.

After eight hours of the flight, pinned to the wall against my neighbor's foot, the stewardess announced with a studied abruptness that fog prevented our landing on Sakhalin and that the flight would be diverted temporarily to Khabarovsk, the large metropolis of the Russian Far East. An already boisterous cabin turned to organized revolt: The passenger collective rancorously agreed that this was an excuse for the Khabarovsk-based crew to go home early, and a shower of raucous shouting ensued. "You bastards! We paid for this flight! We know what you're doing! Charlatans! Fog—tell us another one! Kill the pilot!" The fracas was led by the largest fellow on the plane who, after having gone to the front to threaten the crew, acted as incendiary for the remaining fifty minutes of shouting, laughing, and slander. The passengers around me, with whom I had exchanged only predictable conversations at the start of the flight, animatedly explained that this, in the age of a new independent Aeroflot, had become standard fare. And so upon landing, with revolt having led to resignation, the plane finally came to a stop along the runway, and we waited for the now wholly slandered crew to usher us off the plane. Some ten minutes passed when the same self-appointed passenger-thug went to investigate. In the rear of the plane could be heard only his outraged announcement. "They're gone!" he cried. And indeed, the entire crew of pilots and attendants had escaped by a rope ladder through a baggage hatch at the front of the plane, nary to appear again.

Some twelve hours later, after further passenger protests had required the arrival of airport guards with rifles (to disband the group of passengers organizing a sit-in on the tarmac), after the emptying of the plane, after the reloading of the plane, further threats to Aeroflot officials, and after the discovery upon final arrival that the few hundred dollars worth of random electronics, clothing, and personal effects taken from my checked suitcase would be reimbursed at the rate of fifteen cents a kilogram, a familiar face from the Sakhalin Aeroflot ground crew looked at me wryly. "Bruce," she said, trying not to sound too patronizing, "You didn't really believe that fog business, did you?"

After two days in the local capital of the southern end of the island, Iuzhno-Sakhalinsk showed its own kinds of change. Sakhalin had been obliged by a UN declaration in 1991 to rescind its status as a closed border zone, which once had meant that even Soviet citizens had to obtain special visas to go there. But the two main city streets still intersected at the corners of Lenin and Communist Prospects, while the statue of the bolshevik leader still presided over the main square. City bus fares had gone up fifteen times what they had been; the portraits of Marx, Engels, and Lenin at the corner of Communist and Peace Prospects had been replaced by a billboard for the Baltic Bank; the former East Hotel was now the International Lada Business Center, and, at the behest of the Baha'i evangelist cum shipping magnate who had been among the first of foreign businessmen to venture into the Sakhalin market, the front pages of the main newspaper *Soviet Sakhalin* now carried inspirational axioms from the Baha'i leader, Baha'u'llah. Valentin Fedorov, the island's relentlessly self-promoting governor who had come to power on a well-publicized privatization platform, had secured a multimillion dollar oil development scheme for North Sakhalin, but as in the rest of the country, lesser entrepreneurship was limited almost exclusively to mafia-run kiosks proffering chocolate and alcohol. During a period when average monthly salaries were 3,000 rubles (up from 300 two years ago), would-be entrepreneurs, wanting to establish their own bakeries, bookstores, and art studios, were told by the island government that bribes started at 500,000 rubles.[2] While newspapers touted the opening of a new hard currency café in the city, it was more astonishing that more than half the rubles cafeterias had closed for lack of patrons able to afford the prices. The Sakhalin Regional Museum, which had generously organized my stay the first time around, was now continuing to operate only by paying its researchers the most nominal of salaries.

On North Sakhalin the financial strains were exacerbated by almost complete deficits of available cash in the public sector. In the Nogliki and Okha areas, checkbooks had been issued for the first time ever, but these had run out. To cash a check required a special identification card, and these had run out as well. Since few stores had any cash, no change could be given, and credit was prohibited by state law. People either bought in bulk or, out of exasperation, disbursed entire check sums on trifles. Worse still, since checks could only be guaranteed in the districts that printed them, one could not take one's check to Iuzhno-Sakhalinsk where stores had cash and did give change. For the same reasons, most people had not received their salaries for at least two months, while in the most extreme example, men on the fishing brigade in Rybnovsk had received no salaries for ten months. Artifacts of the first humanitarian aid programs to the former USSR were on sale on street corners everywhere. Western European and North American relief agencies had been diligently sending food baskets to Sakhalin pensioners and veterans, despite their being no signs of any actual privation or want of food, just higher prices.

All these changes had affected the lives of the people I knew on Sakhalin across the board. But it was only when I returned to Rybnoe that I was able to put the developments in a more familiar context. In this respect, for Rybnoe, less perhaps had changed, rather than more. Granted, in place of the hammer and sickle, a new Russian tricolor flag flew over the office of the village council, and two new state housing bungalows, which had been four years in the making, were finally completed. But around the kolkhoz, inspirational maxims from "The Moral Code of the Soviet Citizen" still hung from the walls of the workplace: "Your Honor Is the Honor of the Collective!" "Soviet Means Outstanding!" "The Conscience of the Worker Is Greater Than Any Supervisor!" Rybnoe fishermen and fisherwomen, who once passed their evenings glued to the Brazilian serial "Slave Girl Izaura" and the Czech melodrama "Suburban Hospital," had by now made their way through the first 50 episodes of the 250-installment Mexican soap opera, "The Rich Cry Too," and had just embarked on the beginning of five years' worth of the American daytime drama, "Santa Barbara." It was one of the first times such lengthy serials had been shown on television, and many wanted to know why there was no end to the plots. Men in the salting section at the kolkhoz discussed "Santa Barbara" with equal vigor as the women in the cleaning section, and within a few days I was happy to join in these evening viewing rituals.

But what in the last two years had happened to the kolkhoz? On the eve of my departure in 1990, fishery meetings were charged with the invective of independence, yet it soon appeared that, as elsewhere in the country, brief reforms had given way to the inertia of the past. Officially Rybnoe did separate from Red Dawn. Now, rather than being "*Rybabaza 'Rybnoe' Rybnovskogo Rybkombinata Oblrybakkolkhozsoiuza*," it was now just "*Rybabaza 'Rybnoe.'*" Federal laws still prohibited the fishery from selling its fish to whomever it liked, and the lack of modern equipment made visiting Japanese businessmen cringe from shock. So relations essentially continued as before, with Rybnoe processing the fish that Red Dawn brought in. Administratively the fishery now had more latitude in making its own decisions, but the same transient administrators, having come to Sakhalin to make money and prone to abuses of power, still ran the day-to-day affairs. Rybnoe's 1990 director had since relocated to the fishery in Rybnovsk where he was being investigated for fraud. His replacement in Rybnoe, who had previously led the fight for independence, became cowed by his new responsibilities and left town after only a few months. For the first time in several years, both fisheries were unprepared for the season's most important fish run when the summer began.

I had greater hopes for the mostly Nivkh fishing brigade in neighboring Rybnovsk. Some thirty men from Nekrasovka had been living one hundred kilometers down the coast in Rybnovsk in a dormitory during the fishing seasons of the last number of years, and in 1990 plans were finally laid to have them form their own fishery. They were led by one of the few Nivkh men who had a handle on the art of administration, and they were one of Red Dawn's most efficient units. To start their own fishery they would have had to purchase their own boats, their own processing equipment, and other necessities. But in the end the greatest obstacle was the men themselves, who, despite having lived apart from their families six months out of the year for several years running, were unwilling to give up apartments in Nekrasovka for life on the Rybnovsk shore without running water. Tolia Ngavan, the brigade leader, was considering giving it all up and moving his family back to the abandoned village of his youth to live more quietly.

Nonetheless the kolkhoz did show new, unexpected signs of life. In Rybnoe a handful of men and women who once resembled the walking dead were now miraculously revived by the new shortages of alcohol. With residents out of pocket, and local suppliers no longer obliged to ship beer, wine, and vodka to the village store, old habits were hard to maintain.

The village soviet was now simply known as the village administration, and here too the changes had mostly to do with the dispensing of formalities. Where portraits of Lenin and Gorbachev once hung on the walls of the council office, Gorbachev had been happily jettisoned and Lenin alone now presided. The village council chairman and the village secretary were no longer obliged to preside over the burning of censored books in the library, and once familiar institutions such as the Women's Soviet (to ensure cleanliness in the home) and the Voluntary Friendship Society (to monitor public behavior) were done away with. But as the village chairman intoned, the sense of open-endedness was at times illusory.

> Our job is to look out the window and make sure that people are observing the laws of the region and of the country. But what are we supposed to do? We still don't have a constitution. We have an old constitution for a country that doesn't exist any more. So what has changed? Nothing has changed. Nothing will change until we have private property, and we have nothing of the sort right now.

As elsewhere in the country, the new spirit of democracy occasionally meant dispensing with governance altogether. Where the village soviet once administered monthly meetings of an elected town council, plans for 1992 sessions had been scrapped. "The town is about the size of your finger, so why bother meeting?" the village chairman said. "You see people every day. You already know what they think."

It was the village store, perhaps, that showed the greatest marks from two years of upheaval. Once the best-stocked store I had seen anywhere in Moscow, St. Petersburg, or Sakhalin, it had now joined the ranks of the disemboweled. Formally, the store became more independent under the new local administrations. Where it once routinely sold whatever was shipped to it and returned all the profits to the central depot in Rybnovsk, it was now affiliated with the Commercial Section of the district government in Okha. The director could order what she wanted and keep the profits, but she was now obliged to pay taxes and maintain the building.

On the day I went in with my notebook to ask about price changes, the store's blue-haired Ossetian director was in the midst of an animated conversation over events transpiring on "The Rich Cry Too." I asked her if we could go through the prices of what was in the store and the list of what had since become unavailable. We started at one end of the horseshoe-shaped counter and spent half an hour going from one near-empty glass case to another. "Over here is where we used to keep the tools," she began. "The locks, the hammers, the glue, the paint, the nails, the bolts and screws, the keys and hooks." She effortlessly delivered her list with the same tired voice that older Nivkh women would use to tell me about all the different kinds of flowers and edible berries that no longer grew on the island. "We used to have the winter coats behind you. Two years ago they were 600 rubles each. Then they went up to 15,000 so we had to send them back. And up top behind me is where we used to keep all the toys. Do you remember all the toys?" I did remember all the toys, which had made such an impression on me before, as well as the electric kettles, the irons, the crystal decanters, and the candles that came in different colors. So too did the three other people in the store who had been standing in the corner talking and who came over to join in. "Over here were the pens and schoolbooks," another shopkeeper laughed. "Look at that soup pot. Two years ago you could get one for 8 rubles. Now its 702!" What had begun as a solemn marking of absent goods and mordant prices had now become a boisterous tour. The village baker joined in. "Look at that rubber raft. Volodia bought one when they cost 95 rubles," she chortled. "How much is it now?" "5,370!" they wheezed breathlessly. The two shopkeepers were now splitting their sides. By the middle case in the store, everyone was talking animatedly at the same time. "Refrigerators! Over 20,000 rubles! Who would have guessed!" "Do you remember that toothpaste we used to have? Look, we still have an empty box!" "Ginger cookies—up fifty times what they were!" For the women in the store who each earned no more than 3,000 or 4,000 rubles a month at the time, the prices were indeed cause for either laughter or grief, and genuine mirth over what had happened to their salaries prevailed for the moment. But as the spectators peeled away, and our excursion from case to case wound its way down, my guide resumed a more funereal tone. "We kept the candy jars but left them empty. Maybe that's just as well. The plastic chandeliers no one bought anyway. This is where we used to keep the light bulbs. Now I dare you—you try to find one light bulb anywhere on this island, and I'll buy it from you."

On expressly Nivkh fronts, some substantial changes had been made in the way people could regain their former homes. Aided by a decree from Yeltsin, Sakhalin had embarked on a system of clan plots for Nivkhi, whereby Nivkh families could return to areas where they once lived to start up their own fishing and processing enterprises.[3] The move was a far cry from proposals in 1990 to return almost a third of Sakhalin to its circa 1850 status as largely Nivkh territory, but the idea of clan enterprises had caught on. The average allotment was twenty square hectares. Originally they were intended to be given in perpetuity as private property, but reluctant local officials intervened and leased them on time-limited arrangements. By August 1992 thirty-six plots had been claimed.[4] Some families had returned to the abandoned village sites of their youth and looked upon the plots as subsistence operations for their families. Others sought formal sponsors such as the Sakhalin Geological Trust to make bigger profits. In the latter cases, some had taken out colossal loans of up to 200,000 rubles, only to discover by the time the money was disbursed that it was no longer worth as much as they needed. But the enterprises nonetheless had drawn Nivkh men and women into a form of independent activity they had not known since before World War II. Nivkh friends in Okha, in whose homes I had once spent long quiet evenings, now stepped up the usual barter trading into a frenzy of exchange: Twenty kilos of fish for two crates of beer, two sacks of sugar for ten sacks of salt, one ton of gasoline for fifty kilograms of mutton . . . cars for apartments, refrigerators for motorcycles, a case of vodka for telephone installation . . . and on and on. At a time when money did not necessarily make someone rich, exchange could.[5]

The new flurry of activity was an improvement over the first efforts in 1989 and 1990 to start the umbrella Nivkh cooperative known as *Ykh-Mif*, or "Our Land." The idea was to gather together Nivkhi who knew the land well in order to collect and market the island's fruits, which had almost never been available in stores. But it had not gone well. Only three years after its founding in 1988 did *Ykh-Mif* finally receive permission to formally exist, but by then the dissolution of the country and the talk of clan plots had altered the terms of debate. The Nivkh representative for native affairs in the Okha district administration summed up how her work had changed when we saw each other again two summers later.

AN: Clan plots, some of the first in Russia, have made a big difference. We didn't pay much attention a few years ago, especially because we figured that no one would be interested, that people were already too Russified. But this year, we figured, things have already gotten so bad, why not try? We have nothing to lose. The first plot was given to Valia Poliakova in Chingai, then a few more, then a few more, then a total wave. And the best part is that they have attracted the young people, young people from Red Dawn and so on. I honestly didn't think that much could come of it at the start, but I have been totally surprised.

It means that you end up having some way to battle with the problem of passivity. [Here, she named five young Nivkh families in Nekrasovka]—they all moved back to their native areas, and I can't tell you what that means. You want to help them with all your strength. But what are you supposed to do? Business has never been our specialty.

No one has any money and everyone needs everything. They need boats, they need snowmobiles, they need fuel, they need construction materials for housing . . . the list is endless. People are ready to relocate their entire families back into the middle of nowhere, back to where they were living thirty years ago, and we are completely unable to help them. So we now have the idea of trying to revive a few of these villages that used to exist. Obviously we are talking about the smallest, most incremental changes. But look at Valia in Chingai—they built their own house, they are sleeping on Nivkh-style benches, they are using seal fat for their lamps instead of kerosene. They're not living that way because it's tradition, they're living that way because, as the rest of the island collapses around them, this is the only alternative left!

Goskomsever [the newly formed State Committee for Northern Development] has made a few gestures in our direction, but we are talking about kopecks. Everyone is completely on his own. And we are all without any experience in enterprise. So now we have the idea of trying to revive Romanovka. But who knows. It is a battle in and of itself just to get permission to trap a bear. Clan plots got permission to catch only two tons of salmon this spring alone—this is nothing, and there is nothing left for the fall. This is far from enough. This is not enough. We are encouraging people with one hand and setting them back with the other.

BG: What about the fact that all the Nivkh activists are women? Do you think there's a reason for this?

AN: With the clan plots, there are more young men involved and I can't tell you how good this is. This is extremely important. They are great fellows. Before they spent all their time drinking, and now they are actually doing something. Our hunters, on the other hand, have all drunk themselves into the grave. Hunting is supposed to be a Nivkh tradition, but today you will find only one or two who still know how to set out after an animal properly. There are no real Nivkh hunters left, but suddenly the young people are starting to set old-style traps again, they're starting to ask for hunting licenses again. Why? Because it's useful for them.

BG: But what happened to the men of your generation?

AN: This is the real tragedy. They drank themselves away. Drank themselves away [*spilis'*]. Look at the women around you. Look at L——, she's alone. Look at M——, she's alone. Look at O——, she's alone. These women have no one to spend their lives with. Either the men killed themselves, or they drowned in alcohol—they felt they had no other way out of their problems, and their loss is something we still feel every day. They drank themselves to death because they couldn't see any role for themselves in the world the way they had come to know it—instead of working as fishermen or hunters, they were given jobs of the lowest sort. This is a tragedy for all of us.

Those of us who do things, I mean, for other Nivkhi—today we're not ready at all, because there is no one left to do our work when we leave off. Sure there are younger Nivkhi, but we realize now that we haven't done anything to prepare them to take on the kind of work I'm doing for native affairs in the city council, or that Rima Khailova has been doing on the Nivkh-language newspaper, the kind of cultural work that Zoia Ivanovna Liutova has been doing in the library, and so on. We ourselves are somewhat guilty of this, for not having trained our successors.

In a sense we all went through the same kind of system, we were all raised in *internaty* [state boarding schools]. But when my generation went through these schools, we were constantly working—we were chopping wood, we were hauling water, we were made to look after the younger children—it was a completely different mind set. The generation below us, they went through boarding school in a completely different age, politically and economically, and like it or not, we can't depend on them now. They were raised always to have other people do things for them. In the next ten years we should all be starting on our pensions and who is left to take up our work?

BG: *Internaty*—it's common today to portray them as something out of Dickens, and it's not hard to imagine. But a lot of the time, people speak of them with nostalgia. Of all those wonderful years . . .

AN: The ones that are smiling are from my generation. Those are my friends, and that's because when we went through the *internaty*, it was a real collective. We collected berries together, we all lived as one big family. We planted potatoes together, we chopped wood together, we caught fish together, we all depended on one another and we all helped one another. We did it for ourselves and we did it for one another. And it was, in its own strange way, fun. But for children who went through them in the last twenty years it was a different story. Everything was ready for them. Everything was given to them. The government fed them and clothed them and bought them shoes and did their laundry. That's all very well, and even good in a sense, maybe that's the way life should be. But that's when the dark side of the state boarding school system came out. It produced a whole generation of young people completely unable and uninterested in taking care of themselves. It is an entire generation that was raised apart from their parents, and of course in the end the result was unfortunate. The language, the culture—everything fell by the wayside. Moreover, it gave rise to a real cynicism.

For all the efforts to have our young people get a good education in colleges and institutes around the country, just as before most of the Nivkh youth are abandoning their studies to just stand in place, to remain on Sakhalin. You might think this is nice, that they want to stay on the island, but when you look at the level of education around us and see the want of leadership, you see that this is really a problem. Even if we were able to train just one person for each of our jobs, that would be something. That would be a lot. Yet they themselves don't really want to. They've gotten used to having other people do everything for them. That's the problem.

It's not even on the regional level or the district level, but on the village level. For example, Zoia Ivanovna Liutova has left the library in Nekrasovka and that's it. That's the end. There is no one that can or wants to take her place. She used to lead the Nivkh-language circles and organize Nivkhi when we all needed to meet. And you immediately feel her absence because of all that she used to do. There are all kinds of examples like that. Or Liudmila Kravchuk, who used to work in the village soviet and who now has left for Schmidt to run her own clan plot up in Muzma. She knew all the local Nivkhi in her town and she constantly helped me. I mean, I know people of my own generation, but I don't know the lives and details of the younger generation. I could phone her at any time and ask her what was going on, which families needed assistance for the season, and so on. She was my right hand, and now she's gone. But most important, I can't think of a single Nivkh to call and get the same advice from.

BG: Let's move over to utopia. If you had a great deal of money, how would you get down to work?

AN: If we had a great deal of money [chortles], we would rebuild the infrastructure for the town of Romanovka, so that people would be able to move there and feel themselves at home. We would resurrect places like Chingai, Uspenovka. . . . We would help unite a few of the clan plots so they could form a real fishery of their own. People would be "occupied," but occupied in the best sense of the word; people would be doing what they wanted to be doing. . . . But it's not really about money anyway. Everywhere I go people ask me, "Why is *Goskomsever* taking so long? Why haven't they subsidized us yet?" And I tell people, forget about *Goskomsever*, forget about everyone else, just start working. Two tons of salmon is nothing, I realize, but catch it anyway. Collect mushrooms, collect fiddleheads, collect wild onions, collect berries— do everything you can to at least feed your own family and then start thinking about getting ahead. To do that today is already a big accomplishment.

To accomplish anything at the time was indeed an achievement since everywhere were signs of disintegration and few signs of rebuilding. The sense of social confusion was palpable. Over lunch one day with Russian friends from my first stay, the director of the bookstore in Okha said that her store would probably close because of lack of funds. Her husband, a reporter for the *Sakhalin Oil Worker*, added, "I'm a correspondent. I've worked here for years. I'm supposed to write about the economy, and I swear, I don't have the slightest idea what is going on! Not the slightest!" On another day, with another reporter from a smaller rival paper, *Free Sakhalin*, our conversation was interrupted by a caller with a lead for a story. Three hundred kilograms of fresh pork, a rare and outrageously expensive commodity, had been found in a garbage dump out by the airport. The reporter hung up the phone and poured some more tea. "Aren't you going to go and find out about it?" I asked. "No," he said, "This kind of stuff happens all the time." I offered my theory that the local mafia probably wanted to keep prices up by imposing scarcity.

"Maybe," the reporter said. "Or maybe the people who were supposed to sell it just didn't feel like it."

At a dinner before I left to return to the southern end of the island, I sat with one of the Nivkh men who had always been among the staunch-est supporters of the Soviet system I had known. We sat with his children around a table in the living room adorned with miniature busts of Lenin and politically inspired greeting cards. He raised his vodka glass for a baleful toast, "No one believes in anything. You can't trust anyone. Nothing is interesting. So eat. Food is our only insurance."

Eight

Conclusions: The Subjects Presumed to Know

> Among the group of strange folk squatted on the beach by the fading light of day was a particularly intelligent [Nivkh] elder, who had evidently seen more of the Russians than any of the others. He had overheard the first question which I had put to the [shaman] about the home of his forefathers, and in an impressive way he exclaimed . . . "How can you expect me to know?"
>
> *(Charles Hawes,* In the Uttermost East, *1904)*[1]

> I said to my nun, "What does the Church say about heaven today? Is it still the old heaven, like that, in the sky?"
> She turned to glance at the picture.
> "Do you think we are stupid?" she said.
> I was surprised by the force of her reply.
> "But you're a nun. Nuns believe these things. When we see a nun, it cheers us up, it's cute and amusing, being reminded that someone still believes in angels, in saints, all the traditional things."
> "You would have a head so dumb to believe this?"
> "It's not what I believe that counts. It's what you believe."
> "This is true," she said. "The nonbelievers need the believers."
>
> *(Don DeLillo,* White Noise*)*[2]

INDIGENOUS PEOPLES, almost by modern definition, rest at the periphery of other people's social orders. They are bearers not of knowledge but wisdom; they are not old but elders. We have come to expect this from them. But in the aftermath of events such as the collapse of the USSR, being positioned on the periphery can sometimes have its advantages. Given the legacy of a Soviet system that promoted the Nivkh language and then repressed it, that gathered Nivkhi into kolkhozes and then presided over widespread job and housing discrimination, and that has generally taken a dim view of its own past, Sakhalin residents are increasingly touting Nivkhi as the only group on the island who survived the Soviet period with their integrity intact. The noble savage reappears. In 1990, when the Sakhalin government was considering a quixotic project to transfer advisory control of almost half of North Sakhalin into Nivkh hands (then known as *prioritetnoe prirodopol'zovanie*, or priority land use),[3] the idea drew widespread support from Russian environmentalists. The plan was not without its complications. Many people objected that the transfer of so much land to such a small group transgressed the notion that all citizens were equal in the eyes of the state. When I asked some of the Russian proponents about their active endorsement of the Nivkh stewardships, a common answer was, "Everyone knows that the Nivkhi will be more protective of the land than other people. It's in their tradition." While their response walked a fine line between philanthropy and public relations, clearly the idea that Nivkhi were unfairly severed from the land and deserved recompense was useful from the point of view of ecology. Cloaking the environment in the rhetoric of the noble savage protects it from savagery of a more civilized nature.

This was one appropriation of Nivkh identity by outsiders that many Nivkhi seemed to endorse. It also took root in the first of the two myths about Siberian indigenous peoples that I offered at the outset—the vision of timeless tradition, whereby Nivkhi have essentially lived apart from the flow of historical events around them. In the post-Soviet era it might be seen as an affirmative gesture, conferring faultlessness on Nivkhi in a society obsessed, for the time, with the vectors of blame. But it overlooks the crucial fact that Nivkhi have changed greatly with the dramatic history in which they took part. The presumption of Nivkh innocence is an idealism on the upswing on Sakhalin, but ironically it refuses recognition of the very coevalness of Nivkhi—the at least formal recognition of Nivkhi as equals—which was one of the few dividends of the Stalinist vision of Nivkhi as instant moderns. In the rhetoric of the environmentalists, Nivkhi are, like Jacques Lacan's image of *le sujet supposé savoir*, "the subjects presumed to know," presumed to be the bearers of values no longer appreciated in the world of the disenchanted.

The second central narrative, the myth that Siberian indigenous peoples were making a stride across a thousand years, was not only a rhetorical device for including them in a program of rapid modernization, it projected an aura of success for the cultural agenda of a country which, by definition, had been experimental. Since Siberian peoples were considered to be a blank slate on which to inscribe a new Soviet identity, their experience perforce was to have been one of the most lucid markers of the new state culture. In return for their great leap forward, Siberian indigenous peoples were granted a vision of coevalness that was rare for an otherwise largely colonial relationship. It was that vision of coevalness which was essential for many Nivkhi in seeing themselves as participants in the Sovietization movement.

Against the rhetoric of their heroic leap from cave life to communism, the Nivkh denial of culture, the professed "culturelessness" that was so regnant in 1990 and to a lesser extent in 1992, came as the ultimate revenge against a state that defined them so capriciously for so many decades. This was the very inversion of the triumphant stride, not one step forward but two steps back. After decades of dramatic reification of the idea of culture itself, of having given up a "traditional" culture so as to build a "modern" one, these denials of culture were the reciprocal responses: We are the truest bearers of your ethnicity, and look what happened. With little to work with but their pasts, Nivkhi are discovering symbolic capital amid the ruins of both these myths.

These kinds of inversions would appear to be strategic, since, as the preceding chapters have tried to demonstrate, both polar visions of Siberian indigenous peoples had their dark sides. These were state policies that had trenchant consequences for the peoples they designated and redesignated in turn with each new political generation. When idealized versions of traditional life were invoked, as we saw at the outset of the Soviet period in the 1920s, the resulting social policies were oriented to self-government and the creation of new hybrid social forms. When idealized versions of radical transformation were hegemonic from the Stalinist period through to Brezhnev, the policy of Soviet cultural construction hinged on a willed negation of the past. The myth of childlike purity also fed into the charge for change under Stalin, but the political consequences in this event were just as detrimental: If Nivkhi were children of nature, their past need be forgotten; if they were on the road to building socialism, their past again need be forgotten; if they were part of the natural landscape, they did not require attention; if they were part of the cultural landscape, they were already attended to. With a future predetermined and the past redetermined, the stride across a thousand years heeded everything but the present.

With the collapse of the USSR, these dialectics were for once at a standstill. Neither innocents nor moderns, neither of nature nor culture, most Nivkhi I knew were culling through their own personal and collective pasts for moments of redemption. The Sakhalin Island of Nivkh history, littered with ghost towns, suffered no shortage of ruins either literal or metaphoric—Nivkh ruins, Russian ruins, Korean ruins, Japanese ruins, ruins of culture and ruins of time, ruins of politics and ruined lands, ruined individuals. Yet, to return to Walter Benjamin's reflections on Trauerspiels, the Nivkh narratives were more about compromise and contradictory allegiances than revisionist heroics. Emblematic of the time was a loyalty to the Soviet system increasingly confronted by its debasing absurdities; a respect for familiar Soviet icons countered by the headiness of change; the ready dismissal of the centralized economy countered by a deep distrust of private property; and the eagerness to jettison a discredited past without at the same time discounting it. These were points of tension set before Nivkhi and Russians alike.

Throughout the Soviet period, at the level of public political discourse, there was a strong and conscious reification of the opposition between the traditional and the modern, the local and the federal, Nivkh and Soviet. These were reified if not buttressed in ironic ways by a Soviet nationality policy that expressly sought to collapse these oppositions, emphasizing the dialectical negotiations of the traditional and the modern in the pursuit of creating the pan-Soviet nation. Political dissent also fed these polarities, since opposition to the state almost inevitably found expression by juxtaposing any nationality to the Soviet center. With a tradition in the West of Soviet nationality studies that emphasize political factors over social or cultural ones, these public discourses are the ones most of us know best.

However, one gets a different impression at the level of the lived experience of these discourses, where such kinds of oppositions are harder to distinguish because of the ways in which they were so mutually manifested. Most Nivkhi I knew thought of themselves as Soviets first and Nivkhi second; a good number of others, especially younger people, thought of themselves as Soviets only. It was at this level that one had to sort through the seeming contradictions of dwelling on the loss of family members during Stalin's purges and then praising Stalin for his firm hand, of Nivkhi who had lost their homes or pensions during the resettlements and yet so vigorously opposed the loosening of state control under perestroika. With dialectics wrought still, and uncertainty so regnant, the Manichean dualisms that for so long held sway over Nivkh identity lost their currency.

Had I remained on Sakhalin only through the first month, when the Nivkh assertions of having been left in ruins were at their most earnest, my impression of Nivkh life and Nivkh history would likely have been confined to the level of public discourse at which their discontent was being presented. The spirit of loss was not hard to see in the Nivkh setting, but while this is true, it is a partial truth. In their narratives, Nivkhi did not see themselves as passive or tragic figures—disgruntled, yes, in mourning, yes, perhaps now for the first time independently politicized, yes, but tragic, no. Like the rest of the nation being transformed around them, they felt they had followed a path that did not take them where they wanted.

What makes the historical trajectory of Nivkhi in the twentieth century so remarkable is the dramatic roller coaster of policy shifts that continually transformed it. From one political generation to the next, between the imperial and Soviet systems as well as within the Soviet frame, each new wave rested on the partial reworking of the past. The negation of the past may be germane to modernity itself, as Freud and Nietzsche have both argued.[4] Yet the Soviet materials here present a case in the extreme, since the dramatic policy shifts also meant the systematic elision of documents, ideas, and persons from previous periods on which each step forward was predicated. By destabilizing the physical bases for knowing the past in such a fundamental way, the state had a far greater capacity for managing the identities of each of the nationalities under its aegis, the smaller ones in particular. The same talent for identity management also left the state's constituents with an extraordinarily reified sense of culture as an object to be constructed, reconstructed, and dismantled at will, "created, rendered, fulfilled, and implemented."

Amid all these shifts, what then became of Nivkh notions of the authentic? When I arrived on Sakhalin in the spring of 1990, many Nivkhi I met had photographs and slides to show from the shooting of a film the previous summer on Sakhalin's northern Schmidt peninsula. The film was based on the writer Chingiz Aitmatov's short story, "Spotted Dog Running along the Seashore."[5] The screenplay was a Paleoasiatic *Bildungsroman* set amid the timeless life of Nivkh fishermen who lived in tents, wore fish-skin garments, and communicated in a mysterious language germane to the austere northern landscapes. Although professional Kazakh actors portrayed the lovelorn Nivkh leads, a great number of Nivkhi took part in the project. The northern village of Nyvrovo, closed down during the 1960s, served as the main locale for filming. Special sets re-created traditional Nivkh life, including a bear that served as the focal point for many of the film's affinity-with-nature scenes. Despite the usual shortcuts in accuracy, where at times almost any ethnic-looking setting or costume or language sufficed for the film's purposes, it was an important time for many Nivkhi, young and old, to reconnect with an imagined past. The photographs from the shooting showed an almost jamboree-like atmosphere. It was a few years after this, toward the end of my second stay on Sakhalin, that I asked the film's main Nivkh consultant what kind of film she would have preferred to make had the decision been hers.

> **GD**: When we had the filming on Schmidt, I gathered together all the Nivkhi I could find, especially the ones that everyone thinks of as no-goods and parasites [*tuneiadtsy*]. When we were all out on the tundra together, you can't imagine how they came to life! If I had my way, I would have made a film just about them. They were wonderful.

People call them lazy, but it's not laziness. I mean, you go and try to catch a bear, hunt him and kill him, by yourself. That's not laziness. It is the internal psychology of the Nivkh. He isn't afraid of going to hunt a bear by himself. He knows deep down that he will catch him. Or if he goes fishing, he wouldn't do what we do today. He wouldn't say—let's go fishing tomorrow. He wouldn't get up at 8:00 in the morning and stay until 8:00 at night and freeze all day just because it's convenient, like in the kolkhoz. A real Nivkh wouldn't do that. A real Nivkh would already know the ecological calendar, the local conditions. He knows the meaning of all the natural signs . . . the direction of the wind, the direction of the water. He doesn't need to plan anything, he just bears these things in mind and one day he'll say, "I'm going fishing now." And at 4:00 o'clock in the afternoon he'll go and catch fish. The rest of the time he'll sleep, daydream, do nothing . . . because he already knows precisely what to do and when to do it. That's a real Nivkh. To Russians this is laziness and to me this is the height of living [*vostorg*]. I don't know how else to describe it.

BG: What about someone like K——? He still hunts and fishes privately for the former party leaders. How does he get around the system?

GD: He's already worked his required thirty years, but he's too young to be on a pension. He worked from age fifteen and finished at forty-five. He didn't have the right to get another job because he already worked his limit, but he isn't fifty-five yet and so can't get his pension. So he works on the side until he can start receiving his pension. He works for himself. He wanders around the forest. He sleeps a lot. He goes fishing. He decides he wants a boat and makes one himself. He makes his own nets. Imagine! People call him lazy and he is nothing of the sort. Who could be more energetic? This is the Nivkh way of thinking. He knows what he wants and he goes his own way quietly. He's not interested in being rich. He doesn't dream of having a table laden with wine and *kolbasa*. He wants to eat fish, so he goes and catches some. He has fresh fish all year long. If he catches a bear, then they have bear meat. If he catches a deer, they have deer meat. If he catches a seal, they have seal meat. It's all illegal of course, but that's another matter. People like him never go hungry. If I had my way, he's the kind of person I would make a film about. Why? Because he's a normal person.

BG: D—— reminded me of the same type, though he wasn't quite as sociable.

GD: There are times when he's supposed to go to his Soviet work, but everything inside him tells him he should go fishing instead. He even told me once, it's like a pathology—he has to go fishing. Then it subsides and he goes back to his Soviet job. It seems to me that that's how it should be for everyone. For me it's a mix of both—part of me is very Nivkh and part of me is more modern. I want to have a nice apartment, I want to be able to move around and see things, I want to have different kinds of food on the table, and for that I have to have money. For that I have to go to work.

BG: I get kind of depressed when I see films like O——'s about how Baba Nastia makes robes from fish skin. On the one hand it's genuine art, and it's interesting to see. But it gets passed off as "daily life" when, in fact, Baba Nastia makes robes from fish skin only if she needs something to wear for a funeral, or if an ethnographer comes and asks her to.

GD: What you have to do is kind of play a trick on the viewer. Give them the stereotype they think they already know, give them the lazy native, and then shift the ground out from under them.

BG: When I was at the Rybnoe centennial two years ago, I remember when Baba Olia got up on stage. It was so quiet. And also kind of depressing because the dance was all about shamans in the forest but there were neither shamans nor, for that matter, many forests left in real life. Then a folklore ensemble of Russian women got up on stage and started stomping and yipping—it was really almost a violent performance. To compare Baba Olia with the women on the stage was incredible. When I went home that night I was going to write about it and thought, "So, you know, the Russians are well, Russians, and the Nivkhi are . . . well, kinder." Kinder! I know lots of Nivkhi that are not so kind. I had returned full circle to the nineteenth century!

GD: The Russians will never understand that though. The Russians look at their own art and they are delighted. They look up at a Nivkh woman singing and all they see is some drunk up on stage. It's the same thing when *Spotted Dog* won first prize at the Moscow Film Festival this year. Oleg Iankovskii, the festival organizer, said, "Why would they want to give a prize to a film like that?" For me, that said it all.

To think of Sakhalin at both ends of the Soviet period, at the turn of the twentieth century and now at its close, there are signs that the former cosmopolitanism of the island is resurgent. With the return of Japanese fishing interests, American oil developers, New Zealand peat brokers, German manufacturers, Baha'i evangelists, and Mexican soap operas, and with an indigenous population increasingly aware of the political rights and hazards of what being "indigenous" means elsewhere, the face of the island is poised for change. But with no food in the stores, no cash in the tills, and life in a society where even the highest echelons of power are unsure of what is transpiring, the new Old World is still working on its appeal. For the time being, Nivkhi who have the personal resources to retreat to the hills, live without electricity, and dry fish properly enough to store it for the winter are arguably among the few citizens of Sakhalin Island who are finding peace of mind.

In the wake of the Soviet period, many Nivkhi are looking ahead, mindful of the past and wary of the present. But in contrast to the six political generations before them, there is no call to negate the past by superimposing the future. The past is now an open field, albeit one in ruins. For Nivkhi tied to their kolkhoz lives in Rybnoe and Rybnovsk, or remaining in their Soviet housing blocks in Nogliki or Okha, for whom the hermitic life is out of reach, there is at least one consolation in the emergent present—living among and with the ruins of the old order, rather than actively forgetting them.

Appendix _____

"A Recently Discovered Case of Group Marriage"

Frederick Engels[1]

Since it has recently become fashionable among certain rationalistic ethnographers to deny the existence of group marriage, the following report is of interest; I translate it from the *Russkiye Vyedomosti*, Moscow, October 14, 1892 (Old Style). Not only group marriage, i.e., the right of mutual sexual intercourse between a number of men and a number of women, is expressly affirmed to be in full force, but a form of group marriage which closely follows the punaluan marriage of the Hawaiians, the most developed and classic phase of group marriage. While the typical punaluan family consists of a number of brothers (own and collateral) who are married to a number of own and collateral sisters, we here find on the island of Sakhalin that a man is married to all the wives of his brothers and to all the sisters of his wife, which means, seen from the woman's side, that his wife may freely practice sexual intercourse with the brothers of her husband and the husbands of her sisters. It therefore differs from the typical form of punaluan marriage only in the fact that the brothers of the husband and the husbands of the sisters are not necessarily the same persons.

It should further be observed that this report again confirms what I said in *The Origin of the Family*, 4th edition: group marriage does not look at all like what our brother-obsessed philistine imagines; the partners in group marriage do not lead in public the same kind of lascivious life as he practices in secret, but that this form of marriage, at least in the instances still known to occur today, differs in practice from a loose pairing marriage or from polygamy only in the fact that custom permits sexual intercourse in a number of cases where otherwise it would be severely punished. That the actual exercise of these rights is gradually dying out only proves that this form of marriage is itself destined to die out, which is further confirmed by its infrequency.

The whole description, moreover, is interesting because it again demonstrates the similarity, even the identity in their main characteristics, of the social institutions of primitive peoples at approximately the same stage of development. Most of what the report states about these Mongoloids on the island of Sakhalin also holds for the Dravidian tribes of

India, the South Sea Islanders at the time of their discovery, and the American Indians. The report runs:

"At the session of October 10 (Old Style; October 22, New Style) of the Anthropological Section of the Society of the Friends of Natural Science, N. A. Yanchuk read an interesting communication from Mr. [Lev J.] Sternberg on the Gilyaks, a little-studied tribe on the island of Sakhalin, who are at the cultural level of savagery. The Gilyaks are acquainted neither with the agriculture nor with pottery; they procure their food chiefly by hunting and fishing; they warm water in wooden vessels by throwing in heated stones, etc. Of particular interest are their institutions relating to the family and to the gens. The Gilyak addresses as father, not only his own natural father, but also all the brothers of his father; all the wives of these brothers, as well as all the sisters of his mother, he addresses as his mothers; the children of all these 'fathers' and 'mothers' he addresses as his brothers and sisters. This system of address also exists, as is well known, among the Iroquois and other Indian tribes of North America, as also among some tribes of India. But whereas in these cases it has long since ceased to correspond to the actual conditions, among the Gilyaks it serves to designate *a state still valid today*. To this day *every Gilyak has the rights of a husband in regard to the wives of his brothers and to the sisters of his wife*; at any rate, the exercise of these rights is not regarded as impermissible. These survivals of group marriage on the basis of the gens are reminiscent of the well-known punaluan marriage which still existed in the Sandwich Islands in the first half of this century. Family and gens relations of this type form the basis of the whole gentile order and social constitution of the Gilyaks.

"The gens of a Gilyak consists of all—nearer and more remote, real and nominal—brothers of his father, of their fathers and mothers (?), of the children of his brothers, and of his own children. One can readily understand that a gens so constituted may comprise an enormous number of people. Life within the gens proceeds according to the following principles. Marriage within the gens is unconditionally prohibited. When a Gilyak dies, his wife passes by decision of the gens to one of his brothers, own or nominal. The gens provides for the maintenance of all its members who are unable to work. 'We have no poor,' said a Gilyak to the writer. 'Whoever is in need, is fed by the *khal* [gens].' The members of the gens are further united by common sacrificial ceremonies and festivals, a common burial place, etc.

"The gens guarantees the life and security of its members against attacks by non-gentiles; the means of repression used is blood revenge, though under Russian rule the practice has very much declined. Women are completely excepted from gentile blood revenge. In some very rare cases the gens adopts members of other gentes. It is a general rule that the property of a deceased member may not pass out of the gens; in this respect the famous provision of the Twelve Tables holds literally among the Gilyaks: *si nous heredes non hablet, gentiles familiam habento*—if he has no heirs of his own, the members of the gens shall inherit. No important event takes place in the life of a Gilyak without participation by the gens. Not very long ago, about one or two generations, the oldest gentile member was the head of the community, the *starosta* of the gens; today the functions of the chief elder of the gens are restricted almost solely to presiding over religious ceremonies. The gentes are often dispersed among widely distant places, but even when separated the members of a gens still remember one another and continue to give one another hospitality, and to provide mutual assistance and protection, etc. Except under the most extreme necessity, the Gilyak never leaves the fellow members of his gens or the graves of his gens. Gentile society has impressed a very definite stamp on the whole mental life of the Gilyaks, on their character, their customs and institutions. The habit of common discussion and decision on all matters, the necessity of continually taking an active part in all questions affecting the members of the gens, the solidarity of blood revenge, the fact of being compelled and accustomed to live together with ten or more like himself in great tents (*yurtas*), and, in short, to be always with other people—all this has given the Gilyak a sociable and open character. The Gilyak is extraordinarily hospitable; he loves to entertain guests and to come himself as a guest. This admirable habit of hospitality is especially prominent in times of distress. In a bad year, when a Gilyak has nothing for himself or for his dogs to eat, he does not stretch out his hand for alms, but confidently seeks hospitality, and is fed, often for a considerable time.

"Among the Gilyaks of Sakhalin crimes from motives of personal gain practically never occur. The Gilyak keeps his valuables in a storehouse, which is never locked. He has such a keen sense of shame that if he is convicted of a disgraceful act, he immediately goes into the forest and hangs himself. Murder is very rare, and is hardly ever committed except in anger, never from intentions of gain. In his dealings with other people, the Gilyak shows himself honest, reliable, and conscientious.

"Despite their long subjection to the Manchurians, now become Chinese, and despite the corrupting influence of the settlement of the Amur district, the Gilyaks still preserve in their moral character many of the virtues of the primitive tribe. But the fate awaiting their social order cannot be averted. One or two more generations, and the Gilyaks on the mainland will have been completely Russianized, and together with the benefits of culture they will also acquire its defects. The Gilyaks on the island of Sakhalin, being more or less remote from the centers of Russian settlement, have some prospect of preserving their way of life unspoiled rather longer. But among them, too, the influence of their Russian neighbors is beginning to make itself felt. The Gilyaks come into the villages to trade, they go to Nikolaievsk to look for work; and every Gilyak who returns from such work to his home brings with him the same atmosphere which the Russian worker takes back from the town into his village. And at the same time, working in the town, with its chances and changes of fortune, destroys more and more that primitive equality which is such a prominent feature of the artlessly simple economic life of these peoples.

"Mr. Sternberg's article, which also contains information about their religious views and customs and their legal institutions, will appear unabridged in the *Etnografitcheskoye Obozrenie* (Ethnographical Review)."

Notes

Preface

1. Brackette Williams, "A Class Act: Anthropology and the Race to Nation across Ethnic Terrain," *Annual Review of Anthropology* 18 (1989): 401–444.

Chapter One
Introduction

1. Valentin Petrovich Kataev, *Time, Forward!*, trans. Charles Malamuth (New York: Farrar and Rinehart, 1933), 11, 12.

2. Joseph Stalin in Kataev, *Time, Forward!*, 12.

3. For a recent survey of early Soviet cultural experiments, see Abbott Gleason et al., eds., *Bolshevik Culture: Experiment and Order in the Russian Revolution* (Bloomington: Indiana University Press, 1985), and Richard Stites, *Revolutionary Dreams: Utopian Vision and Experimental Life in the Russian Revolution* (New York: Oxford University Press, 1989). I follow Marshall Berman's distinctions between modernity (as a historical period), modernism (as an ideology befitting the period), and modernization (as the primarily political and economic consequences of the ideology), from *All That Is Solid Melts into Air* (New York: Penguin, 1988), 15–17.

4. S. Frederick Starr, *Red and Hot: The Fate of Jazz in the Soviet Union* (New York: Limelight, 1985), 6.

5. The German ethnographer Leopold von Schrenk initially conducted a lengthy survey of Nivkh life for the Imperial Academy of Sciences in 1859. He was followed by Lev Shternberg who spent eight years as prisoner cum ethnographer in exile on Sakhalin from 1880–88. The Polish scholar Bronislaw Pil'sudskii (older brother of the Polish leader Iuzef) later joined Shternberg in exile on Sakhalin. At the outset of the Soviet period one of Shternberg's graduate students, Erukhim Kreinovich, began what would become decades of research on Nivkh life; while in the 1960s, 1970s, and 1980s, considerable contributions have been made by Anna Smoliak, the Nivkh ethnographer Chuner Taksami, and the collective of the Sakhalin Regional Museum. In the English language, Lydia Black put the nineteenth-century materials to excellent use in her monographs on Nivkh social organization and symbol systems. The Nivkh language has been the subject of many studies, including those by Robert Austerlitz, Roman Jakobson, Claude Levi-Strauss, Galina Otaina, and Vladimir Panfilov.

6. Alexander Shtromas, "Dissent, Nationalism and the Soviet Future," *Studies in Comparative Communism* 20 (1987): 280.

7. Mark Bassin, "Expansion and colonialism on the eastern frontier: Views of Siberia and the Far East in pre-Petrine Russia," *Journal of Historical Geography* 14 (1988): 16.

8. Charles H. Hawes, *In the Uttermost East* (London: Harper and Brothers, 1904), vii.

9. Vito Sansone, *Siberia—Epic of the Century* (Moscow: Progress, 1980), 153.

10. Marcel Detienne, *The Creation of Mythology* (Chicago: University of Chicago Press, 1986), 14.

11. Sansone, *Siberia*, 12.

12. Catherine Lutz and Jane L. Collins, *Reading National Geographic* (Chicago: University of Chicago Press, 1993), 104.

13. Aleksandr Ivanovich Pika, "Malye narody Severa: iz pervobytnogo kommunizma v real'nyi sotsializm," in *Perestroika, Glasnost', Demokratiia, Sotsializm: v chelovecheskom izmerenii* (Moscow: Progress, 1989), 308.

14. Anatolii Panteleevich Derevianko and Vladimir Ivanovich Boiko, "Puti kul'turnogo razvitiia Sibiri," in Vladimir Ivanovich Boiko, ed., *Kul'tura narodnostei Severa: traditsii i sovremennost'* (Novosibirsk: Nauka, 1986), 7–8.

15. Ibid.

16. Vladimir Ivanovich Boiko, ed., *Nivkhi Sakhalina: Sovremennoe sotsial'no-ekonomicheskoe razvitie* (Novosibirsk: Nauka, 1988), 7.

17. Ibid.

18. David A. Anderson, "Turning Hunters into Herders: A Critical Examination of Soviet Development Policy among the Evenki of Southeastern Siberia" *Arctic* 44, no. 1 (1991): 18.

19. Boiko, *Nivkhi Sakhalina*, 16.

20. By equating ethnicity with nationality, the Soviet state defined itself as "multinational" in the sense of having many ethnic groups under its banner. According to the principles of historical materialism, groups could be referred to as a *plemia* (tribe), defined as an endogamous unit consisting of exogamous clans and having poorly developed productive forces; as a *narodnost'*, an intermediate group that arose when tribes and clans amalgamated; or as a *natsiia* (nation), which required a territorial, cultural, and linguistic community, in addition to a comprehensive economic system. After the revolution, many Siberian native groups found themselves at one of these stages or between the first two, depending on the criteria used by a given scholar. (See, for example, Kerstin Eidlitz Kuoljok, *The Revolution in the North: Soviet Ethnography and Nationality Policy* [Stockholm: Almqvist and Wiksell, 1985], 22–23). However, all citizens were also grouped according to *natsional'nost*, for which Teodor Shanin has pointed out there is no adequate translation ("Soviet Theories of Ethnicity: The Case of a Missing Term," *New Left Review*, no. 158 (1986): 113–122). Given its colloquial usage, the closest translation might be "ethnicity," but I follow the customary use of "nationality" to retain the formal implications of the state policies.

21. John Comaroff, "Humanity, Ethnicity, Nationality: Conceptual and Comparative Perspectives on the USSR," *Theory and Society* 20, no. 5 (1991): 675.

22. Patricia Seed, "Poststructuralism in Postcolonial History," *Maryland Historian* 24, no. 1 (1993), 10–11.

23. Elizabeth Colson, *The Makah Indians: A Study of an Indian Tribe in Modern American Society* (Manchester: University Press, 1953), 172.

24. Marilyn Strathern, *The Gender of the Gift* (Berkeley: University of California Press, 1988), 1–21, esp. 16–17.

25. Debbora Battaglia, "At Play in the Fields (and Borders) of the Imaginary: Melanesian Transformations of Forgetting," *Cultural Anthropology* 8, no. 4 (1993): 430.

26. For the role of internal passports in creating a Soviet identity, see Victor Zaslavsky and Yuri Luryi, "The Passport System in the USSR and Changes in Soviet Society," *Soviet Union/Union Sovietique*, pt. 2 (1979): 137–153; Rasma Karklins, *Ethnic Relations in the USSR* (Boston: Allen and Unwin, 1986), 31; and Teresa Rakowska-Harmstone, "Minority Nationalism Today: An Overview," in Robert Conquest, ed., *The Last Empire: Nationality and the Soviet Future* (Stanford: Hoover Institution Press, 1986), 252.

27. Virginia Dominguez, *People as Subject, People as Object: Selfhood and Peoplehood in Contemporary Israel* (Madison: University of Wisconsin Press, 1989); Richard Handler, *Nationalism and the Politics of Culture in Quebec* (Madison: University of Wisconsin Press, 1988).

28. Lydia Black, "Relative Status of Wife Givers and Wife Takers in Gilyak Society," *American Anthropologist* 74, no. 5 (1972): 1244.

29. Walter Benjamin, *The Origin of German Tragic Drama* (London: Verso, 1990).

Chapter Two
Rybnoe Reconstructed

1. Benjamin, *The Origin of German Tragic Drama*, 177–178.

2. At the turn of the century the island's indigenous population consisted mainly of Nivkhi (Giliaks), Oroki, and Evenki (Tungus) on the northern half, and Ainu on the southern half, though all four groups traveled the island widely. The Ainu were relocated to Japan in 1945, after forty years of Japanese rule on the southern half of Sakhalin came to an end. As of 1989 the largest indigenous groups on Sakhalin included 2,008 Nivkhi, 129 Oroki, and 188 Evenki (from Goskomstat SSSR, *Raspredelenie naseleniia po natsional'nosti, rodnomu iazyku i vtoromu iazyku narodov SSSR po Sakhalinskoi Oblasti, Tom I* [Iuzhno-Sakhalinsk, 1990], 5–7).

3. *Tsentral'nyi Gosudarstvennyi Arkhiv RSFSR Dal'nego Vostoka* (Tomsk) [hereafter *TsGADV*], f. 702, o. 2, d. 117, "O lovke ryby na Severe Sakhalina," ll. 2–61; N. A. Troitskaia, "Russkaia burzhuaziia na Ostrove Sakhalin, materialy k biografiiam," *Kraevedcheskii Biulleten'*, no. 1 (1991): 10.

4. *TsGADV*, f. 1133, o. 1, d. 1511, "O prestupleniiakh i prostupkakh inorodtsev" (1896–98), ll. 16–25, esp. 17o.

5. *Gosudarstvennyi Arkhiv Sakhalinskoi Oblasti* (Iuzhno-Sakhalinsk) [hereafter *GASO*], f. 53, o. 1, d. 1497 "Ob utochnenii perechnia perspektivnykh, ogranichennogo razvitiia i neperspektivnykh naselennykh punktov oblasti" (1982), ll. 54–56, 64–73.

6. "Ispolnitel'nyi komitet Liuginskogo sel'skogo soveta narodnykh deputatov: Protokoly, sessii, resheniia priniatye sessiiami i materialy k nim za 1989 g.; Protokoly zasedanii ispolkoma i materialy k nim za 1989 g." (Unpublished government report).

Chapter Three
Nivkhi before the Soviets

1. Shternberg in Lydia Black, "The Nivkh (Gilyak) of Sakhalin and the Lower Amur," *Arctic Anthropology* 10, no. 1 (1973): 32.

2. For English-language surveys of the ethnographic and linguistic classifications, see Marjorie Mandelstam Balzer, "Peoples of Siberia," in Stephen M. Horak, ed., *Guide to the Study of Soviet Nationalities: The Non-Russian Peoples of the USSR* (Littleton, Colo.: Libraries Unlimited, 1982), 239–252; Bernard Comrie, *The Languages of the Soviet Union* (New York: Cambridge University Press, 1981); M. G. Levin and Leonid Pavlovich Potapov, eds., *The Peoples of Siberia* (Chicago: University of Chicago Press, 1964); Ronald Wixman, *The Peoples of the USSR* (Armonk, N.Y.: M. E. Sharpe, 1988).

3. James Forsyth, "The Siberian Native Peoples before and after the Russian Conquest," in Alan Wood, ed., *The History of Siberia: From Russian Conquest to Revolution* (London: Routledge, 1991), 75.

4. These are *Goskomstat RSFSR* figures from the 1989 census as noted in Zoia Petrovna Sokolova, "*Narody Severa SSSR: Proshloe, nastoiashchee i budushchee,*" *Sovetskaia Etnografiia*, no. 6 (1990): 31. These twenty-six groups comprise the 184,478 "peoples of the North" as of 1989. I rest with these figures here for purposes of approximation, though numerous discrepancies abound. Heonik Kwon charts the flux of Orok (also known as Orochon or Ul'ta) demographic figures in his doctoral dissertation, "Maps and Actions: Nomadic and Sedentary Space in a Siberian Reindeer Farm," Department of Social Anthropology, University of Cambridge, 1993, 5–8. *Goskomstat* lists 1,511 Chuvantsy in the census, based on self-definition during polling, although others contend that the assimilation of the Chuvantsy by Russians and Chukchi at the start of the century leave them more closely affiliated to the Iukagiry. See, for example, Juha Janhunen, "Ethnic Death and Survival in the Soviet North," *Journal de la Société Finno-ougrienne* 83 (1991): 111–122.

5. Western scholars and nineteenth-century Russian scholars have generally referred to the entire territory east of the Urals as Siberia. However, within modern Russia, the contemporary usage distinguishes between West Siberia, East Siberia, and the Far East. I use "Siberia" here for the purpose of evoking its history of representation, but for contemporary purposes Sakhalin rests within the Russian Far East proper.

6. For a broader treatment of Siberia in the Russian imaginary, see Galya Diment and Yuri Slezkine, eds., *Between Heaven and Hell: The Myth of Siberia in Russian Culture* (New York: St. Martin's, 1993).

7. Yuri Slezkine, "Russia's Small Peoples: The Policies and Attitudes toward the Native Northerners, 17th c.–1938," Ph.D. dissertation, Department of History, University of Texas at Austin, May 1989, 16.

8. For more on the prerevolutionary fur trade in Siberia, see Bassin, "Expansion," 3–21; Basil Dmytryshyn et al., *Russia's Conquest of Siberia, 1558–1700, a Documentary Record* (Portland: Western Imprints, 1985); Raymond Fisher, *The Russian Fur Trade, 1500–1700* (Berkeley: University of California, 1943); George Lantzeff, *Siberia in the Seventeenth Century: A Study of the Colonial Administration* (Berkeley: University of California, 1943).

9. Vasilevich in Slezkine, "Russia's Small Peoples," 28.

10. Mark Bassin, "Inventing Siberia: Visions of the Russian East in the Early Nineteenth Century," *American Historical Review* (June 1991): 768.

11. Marc Raeff, *Siberia and the Reforms of 1822* (Seattle: University of Washington Press, 1956), 6. See also Bassin, "Inventing Siberia," 770.

12. Slezkine, "Russia's Small Peoples," 116.

13. Ibid., 84.

14. For a longer discussion of the Speranskii reforms, see Raeff, *Siberia and the Reforms*; Slezkine, "Russia's Small Peoples," 124–146.

15. Quoted in Bassin, "Inventing Siberia," 776.

16. Quoted in ibid., 787 [italics in the original].

17. *Sibiriak* is a Russian term denoting a person of Russian-Siberian identity; see, for example, Marie A. Czaplicka, *My Siberian Year* (London: Mills and Boon, n.d.), 242–244. Iadrintsev is quoted in Boris Chichlo, "La Collectivisation en Sibérie: un problème de nationalités," in *L'expérience soviétique et le problème national dans le monde, 1920–1939*, vol. 1 (Paris: CNRS, 1978), 282.

18. Alan Wood, "Siberian Exile in the Eighteenth Century," *Siberica* 1, no. 1 (1990): 45, 57.

19. Bassin, "Inventing Siberia," 774.

20. James Forsyth, *A History of the Peoples of Siberia: Russia's North Asian Colony, 1581–1990* (Cambridge: Cambridge University Press, 1992), 191.

21. A. A. Panov, *Sakhalin kak koloniia* (Moscow: I. D. Sykin, 1905), 1.

22. Hawes, *In the Uttermost East*, 269.

23. John J. Stephan, *Sakhalin: A History* (Oxford: Clarendon, 1971), 68.

24. Hawes, *In the Uttermost East*, 337.

25. A. Ermakov, "Dva goda na Sakhalinskoi katorge" (*GASO: Fond Ryzhkova*), 3.

26. B. Douglas Howard, *Life with Trans-Siberian Savages* (London: Longmans, Green, 1893), 5.

27. James McConkey, *To a Distant Island* (New York: Dutton, 1986), 154.

28. See, for example, Harry DeWindt, *The New Siberia* (London: Chapman and Hall, 1896); Vlas Mikhailovich Doroshevich, *Sakhalin: Katorga* (Moscow: I. D. Shchukin, 1903); Hawes, *In the Uttermost East*; Paul Labbé, *Ostrov Sakhalin: putevye vpechatleniia* (Moscow: M. V. Kliukin, 1903); Nikolai Iakovlevich Novembergskii, *Ostrov Sakhalin* (St. Petersburg: Dom Prizreniia Maloletnykh Bednykh, 1903).

29. These three Chekhov quotations are from McConkey, *To a Distant Island*, 15.

30. Cathy Popkin, "Chekhov as Ethnographer: Epistemological Crisis on Sakhalin Island," *Slavic Review* 51, no. 1 (1992): 36. Page references in parentheses are from Anton Chekhov, *Ostrov Sakhalin: (Iz putevykh zapisok), Polnoe*

sobranie sochinenii i pisem, Sochineniia, vols. 14–15 (Moscow: Nauka, 1978). The English edition has been published in two separate editions under the titles, *The Island: A Journey to Sakhalin*, trans. Luba and Michael Terpak (New York: Washington Square Press, 1967), and *A Journey to Sakhalin*, trans. Brian Reeve (Cambridge: Ian Faulkner, 1993).

31. Quoted in McConkey, *To a Distant Island*, 119.

32. Quoted in Robert Payne, "Introduction," in Chekhov, *The Island*, xxi.

33. Quoted in McConkey, *To a Distant Island*, 141.

34. Popkin, "Chekhov as Ethnographer," 44.

35. Ibid., 42.

36. Ibid., 47.

37. Chekhov, *The Island*, 146.

38. Popkin, "Chekhov as Ethnographer," 47. See also Joseph L. Conrad, "Anton Chekhov's Views of the Ainu and Giljak Minorities on Sakhalin Island," in Rolf-Dieter Kluge, ed., *Anton P. Cechov: Werk und Wirkung*, vol. 1 (Wiesbaden: Otto Harrassowitz, 1990), 433–443.

39. Howard, *Life with Trans-Siberian Savages*, 21.

40. Ibid., 37, 59, 63.

41. Paul Labbé, *Ostrov Sakhalin*, 228.

42. de Windt, *The New Siberia*, 112–113.

43. Hawes, *In the Uttermost East*, 274.

44. Ibid., 355.

45. Ol'ga Alekseevna Shubina, "Sovremennoe sostoianie arkheologicheskoi izuchennosti Sakhalina i zadachi sakhalinskoi arkheologii," *Kraevedcheskii Biulleten'*, no. 4 (1990): 106–119. The Northern Neolithic culture suggested a sedentary way of life distinguished by land hunting, river fishing, sea mammal hunting, and gathering in the taiga—all of which closely resembled early accounts of Nivkh life. The housing structures from the Neolithic period were also quite similar to those of nineteenth-century Nivkhi.

46. Erukhim Abramovich Kreinovich, *Nivkhgu* (Moscow: Nauka, 1973), 21–22; Leopold von Schrenk, *Ob inorodtsakh Amurskago kraiia* (St. Petersburg: Izdanie Imperatorskoi Akademii Nauk, 1883), vol. 1, chap. 2; Lev Iakovlevich Shternberg, *Giliaki, orochi, gol'dy, negidal'tsy, ainy* (Khabarovsk: Dal'nevostochnoe knizhnoe izdatelstvo, 1933), 15–21; Anna Vasil'evna Smoliak, *Etnicheskie protsessy u narodov Nizhnego Amura i Sakhalina* (Moscow: Nauka, 1975), 16–18; Chuner Mikhailovich Taksami, *Osnovnye problemy etnografii i istorii Nivkhov* (Leningrad: Nauka, 1975), 191–200; Taksami, "Problèmes de l'ethnogenèse des Nivkhes," *Inter-Nord* 15 (1978): 65–78; Taksami, "Problemy etnogeneza nivkhov," in Il'ia Samoilovich Gurvich, ed., *Etnogenez narodov severa* (Moscow: Nauka, 1980), 196–211.

47. Stephan, *Sakhalin*, chap. 2.

48. Ibid., 22–24.

49. John A. Harrison, trans., "*Kito Yezo Zusetsu* or a Description of the Island of Northern Yezo by Mamiya Rinsō," *Proceedings of the American Philosophical Society* 99, no. 2 (1955): 111–113.

50. Harrison, "*Kito Yezo Zusetsu*," 115.

51. Ibid., 107.

52. *TsGADV*, f. 1133, o. 1, d. 2031 (1900), l. 11.

53. See Tjeerd de Graaf, "Dutch Encounters with Sakhalin and the Ainu People," Contribution to the Pil'sudskii Conference, Iuzhno-Sakhalinsk, November 1991 [Manuscript]; Stephan, *Sakhalin*, chap. 3.

54. von Schrenk, *Ob inorodtsakh Amurskago kraiia*, vol. 1 (1883): 3; vol. 3 (1903): 277.

55. Petr Aleksandrovich Tikhmenev, *Istoricheskoe obozrenie obrazovaniia rossiisko-amerikanskoi kompanii i deistvii ee do nastoiashchego vremeni*, vol. 2 (St. Petersburg: Eduard Veimar, 1863), 128.

56. Schrenk's Russian transliteration of *dzhangin'* somewhat obscures the Chinese provenance of the word, which may have been a version of what is now romanized as *zhangren* (Pinyin system of transliteration) or *chang-jen* (Wade-Giles system), which would be a traditional address along the lines of "my elder" but not indicative of an official status; *zhangguan* (Pinyin) or *chang-kuan* (Wade-Giles) may have been closer to an address to an official of rank. I am grateful to Alan Berkowitz for sifting through these variants.

57. von Schrenk, *Ob inorodtsakh Amurskago kraiia*, vol. 3 (1903): 34–41.

58. See, for example, Nina Ivanovna Gagen-Torn, *Lev Iakovlevich Shternberg* (Moscow: Nauka, 1975), 28–30.

59. Lev Shternberg, *The Social Organization of the Gilyak* [Translation manuscript] (New York: Archives of the Department of Anthropology, American Museum of Natural History [hereafter AMNH], n.d.), 1.

60. Shternberg, *Social Organization*, 5; Shternberg, *Giliaki*, 22, 23.

61. Smoliak, *Etnicheskie protsessy*, 161–182; Smoliak, "Zametki po etnografii nivkhov Amurskogo Limana," in *Trudy Instituta Etnografii*, no. 56 (1960): 96–98.

62. Shternberg, *Giliaki*, 27.

63. Shternberg, *Giliaki*, 49–79.

64. For example, please see the authors listed in chapter 1, note 5.

65. Ia. P. Al'kor [Koshkin], "Predislovie," in Shternberg, *Giliaki*, xxxvi.

66. Gagen-Torn, *Shternberg*, 57–58; Shternberg, "*Dnevnik*," in *Peterburgskii Filial Arkhiva Akademii Nauk Russkoi Federatsii* [hereafter *PF AAN RF*] f. 282, o. 1, d. 190, l. 59.

67. Frederick Engels, *The Origin of the Family, Private Property, and the State: In Light of the Researches of Lewis H. Morgan* (New York: International Publishers, 1972), 119, 128.

68. Ibid., 144.

69. Shternberg's cardinal writings on Nivkh kinship are in *Giliaki*, 30–45, 81–246, and *Sem'ia i rod u narodov Severo-Vostochnoi Azii* (Leningrad: Institut Narodov Severa, 1933), passim; the clearest summaries in English are in Lydia Black, "Dogs, Bears, and Killer Whales: An Analysis of the Nivkh Symbolic System," Ph.D. dissertation, Department of Anthropology, University of Massachusetts, Amherst, 1973, chap. 4, and Black, "Wife Givers and Wife Takers," 1244–1248. An excellent Russian review is Smoliak, *Etnicheskie protsessy*, 76–88, 150–167, and 222.

70. Black, "Dogs, Bears, and Killer Whales," 34.

71. Shternberg, *Giliaki*, 169, and *Social Organization*, chap. 6. Portions of this material are in English translation in Chester Chard, "Sternberg's Materials on the Sexual Life of the Gilyak" *Anthropological Papers of the University of Alaska* 10, no. 1 (1961): 13–23.

72. *Russkie Vedomosti*, 14 October 1892. Reprinted in German in *Die Neue Zeit* 11, no. 12 (1892), Band 2, 373–375, and in English in Engels, *Origin*, 238–241.

73. Engels, *Origin*, 78.

74. Ibid., 239.

75. Shternberg, *Giliaki*, 110, 113. In *Social Organization*, Shternberg wrote, "Contrary to the old view that the life of primitive man is largely communistic, we find now the primitive household, at least in providing shelter, and the preparation of food and clothing, in the main, individual" (AMNH, 71). Shternberg's writings on property among the Nivkhi are widely disputed in Kreinovich, "Perezhitki rodovoi sobstvennosti i gruppovogo braka u giliakov," *Trudy Instituta Antropologii, Arkheologii i Etnografii* 4 (1936): 711–754; Smoliak, *Etnicheskie protsessy*; and Taksami, *Osnovnye problemy*.

76. Shternberg in Smoliak, *Etnicheskie protsessy*, 86.

77. Smoliak, in ibid.; Taksami, *Osnovnye problemy*, 86, 110.

78. From Al'kor in Shternberg, *Giliaki*, xxi.

79. Provisional currency coupons had been issued in the name of Aleksandr Vasil'evich Kolchak (1874–1920), the Russian admiral and explorer who became war minister in the antibolshevik government that formed in Siberia after the October Revolution in 1917.

80. Slezkine, "Russia's Small Peoples," 248.

81. *TsGADV*, f. 702, o. 3, d. 310 (1911), l. 293.

82. *TsGADV*, f. 702, o. 1, d. 645 (1909), l. 4.

83. *Gosudarstvennyi arkhiv Irkutskoi oblasti*, f. 24, o. 10, d. 1659, ll. 5–23. I am grateful to Galina Dem'ianovna Lok for these documents.

84. *TsGADV*, f. 1154, o. 2, d. 27 (1883), l. 59o.

85. *TsGADV*, f. 702, o. 2. d. 516 (1913), l. 35.

86. *TsGADV*, f. 1154, o. 2. d. 27 (1893), l. 1o.

87. Forsyth, *A History of the Peoples of Siberia*, 219.

88. *TsGADV*, f. 702, o. 2. d. 516, l. 35.

89. Shternberg, *Giliaki*, 112; "Dnevnik puteshestviia L. Ia. Shternberga" (1891), *PF AAN RF* f. 282, o. 1, d. 190, l. 48.

90. Harrison, "*Kito Yezo Zusetsu*," 115.

91. *TsGADV*, f. 702, o. 1, d. 589 (1911).

92. *TsGADV*, f. 113, o. 1, d. 203 (1887), l. 8.

93. *TsGADV*, f. 702, o. 3, d. 317 (1909), l. 4.

94. *TsGADV*, f. 702, o. 3, d. 317 (1908), l. 331.

95. Vladimir Mikhailovich Latyshev and Mikhail Mikhailovich Prokof'ev," B. O. Pil'sudskii (1866–1918 gg.): Stranitsy biografii," in *Katalog etnograficheskikh kollektsii B. O. Pil'sudskogo v Sakhalinskom Oblastnom Kraevedcheskom Muzee* (Iuzhno-Sakhalinsk: SOKM, 1988), 11–12.

96. Ibid., 12.

97. Great Britain Foreign Office, *Sakhalin* (London: Her Majesty's Stationery

Office, 1920), 20. The Japanese schools may also have accommodated children of Nivkh families remaining in the southerly Korsakov Okrug. There were seventy-one Giliaks counted in the Korsakov Okrug in 1883 (*TsGADV*, f. 1154, o. 2, d. 27 [1883], l. 7o); only six were counted in the 1896 records (f. 1133, o. 1, d. 1428 [1896], l. 18).

98. P. Nikolaev maintains that although the tsarist administration did have five schools for Nivkhi, they were unknown to most and existed in name only. See "Natsional'nye shkoly na Sakhaline," *Prosveshchenie Natsional'nostei* 4 (1934): 43–46.

99. Quoted in Hawes, *In the Uttermost East*, 240–241.

100. *TsGADV*, f. R-3158, o. 1, d. 48 (1925), l. 30.

101. *TsGADV*, f. 702, o. 3, d. 310 (1909), ll. 293–294o.

102. *TsGADV*, f. 1164, o. 1, d. 11 (1887), ll. 2–5.

103. *TsGADV*, f. 1133, o. 1, d. 240 (1901), l. 270. For a broader survey of prerevolutionary missionary influence, see Chuner Mikhailovich Taksami, "Vliianie khristianstva na traditsionnye verovaniia nivkhov," in I. S. Vdovin, ed., *Khristianstvo i lamaizm u korennogo naseleniia Sibiri* (Leningrad: Nauka, 1979), 115–126; and Yuri Slezkine, "Savage Christians or Unorthodox Russians? The Missionary Dilemma in Siberia," in Galya Diment and Yuri Slezkine, eds., *Between Heaven and Hell: The Myth of Siberia in Russian Culture*, 15–32.

104. Slezkine, "Russia's Small Peoples," 87.

105. Shternberg, "Inorodtsy," in A. P. Kastelianskii, ed., *Formy natsional'nogo dvizheniia v sovremennykh gosudarstvakh* (St. Petersburg: Obshchestvennaia Pol'za, 1910), 532.

Chapter Four
1920s and the New Order

1. Lev Trotsky, *The Problems of Everyday Life* (New York: Monad, 1973), 140.

2. Ruvin Isaevich Fraerman, "Vas'ka Giliak," in *Izbrannoe* (Moscow: Sovetskii Pisatel', 1958), 156.

3. G. Lebedev, "Vymiraiushchie brat'ia," *Zhizn' Natsional'nostei* 19 (1920): 76.

4. Luks (1888–1932) spent much of his youth in and out of tsarist prisons since his first arrest in 1905 for his participation in the Social Democratic Party of his native Lithuania. In 1916 he was permanently exiled to eastern Siberia and worked for several years in a cement factory in Kamyshet in the Nizhneudinskii Uezd. He served on the Chita Revolutionary Committee from 1918 to 1920 and became the Minister of Nationalities Affairs in the Far East Republic from 1921 to 1922. He died in 1932 while on an expedition in the Far Northeast. For more on Luks, see the *Great Soviet Encyclopedia*, vol. 15 (New York: MacMillan, 1973), 175; A. P. Fetisov, *K. Ia. Luks* (Khabarovsk, 1966).

5. Karl Ia. Luks, "Vsem grazhdanam nerusskoi natsional'nosti DVR" [Brochure by Luks, dated 20 June 1921, Chita], *TsGADV* f. 623, o. 1, d. 11 (1921), l. 21.

6. Ibid.

7. *TsGADV*, f. R1468, o. 1, d. 120 (1921), "Zakony pravitel'stva DVR," ll. 1o–5o.

8. Waldemar Bogoras [Vladimir Bogoraz], *The Chukchee* (New York: Stechert, 1909), 732.

9. Vladimir Bogoraz, "O pervobytnykh plemenakh," *Zhizn' Natsional'nostei* 1 (1922): 130.

10. Vladimir Bogoraz, "Ob izuchenii i okhrane okrainnykh narodov," *Zhizn' Natsional'nostei* 3–4 (1923): 168–180.

11. Mikhail A. Sergeev, *Nekapitalisticheskii put' razvitiia malykh narodov Severa* [Trudy Instituta Etnografii, Novaia Seriia, vol. 27] (Moscow-Leningrad: Akademiia Nauk, 1955), 216. Other criticisms of Bogoraz's proposal can be found in Il'ia Samoilovich Gurvich, *Etnicheskoe razvitie narodnostei Severa v sovetskii period* (Moscow: Nauka, 1987) 15.

12. Stephan, *Sakhalin*, chap. 6, esp. p. 100.

13. TASS, 31 July 1992, reprinted in *RA Report* [Center for Russia in Asia, University of Hawaii at Manoa] 14 (1993): 44.

14. The decree is listed in *GASO*, f. 287, o. 2, d. 1 (1925), l. 39.

15. Teruyuki Hara, "Japanese Occupation of Northern Sakhalin: The Early 1920s," paper presented at the conference, "Siberia, the Far East, and the Northeast Asian Region," Princeton University, December 1993.

16. *GASO*, f. 267, o. 2, d. 10 (1926), "Po Rykovskomu Raionu" [Report by Abramenko], l. 56. For a Soviet assessment of the Japanese administration of North Sakhalin from 1920 to 1925, see Andrei Ivanovich Krushanov, ed., *Stranitsy istorii rybnoi promyshlennosti Sakhalinskoi Oblasti (1925–1987 gg.)* (Iuzhno-Sakhalinsk: Dal'nevostochnoe knizhnoe izdatel'stvo, 1989), 24.

17. *Sakhalinskii Tsentr Dokumentatsii Noveishei Istorii* (formerly the archive of the Communist Party of the Sakhalin Oblast', Iuzhno-Sakhalinsk) [hereafter *STsDNI*] f. 13, o. 1, d. 2 (1926), l. 52.

18. *STsDNI*, f. 2, o. 1, d. 1zh (1925).

19. The main source of information on the Committee of the North is *fond* 3977 at the Central State Archive of the October Revolution and Soviet Construction in Moscow. However, a number of the same points reviewed here are discussed at greater length in Sergeev, *Nekapitalisticheskii Put'*, pt. 2; Slezkine, "Russia's Small Peoples," 278–334; and Adele Weiser, *Die Völker Nordsibiriens: Unter Sowjetischef Herrschaft von 1917 bis 1936* (Munich: Klaus Renner, 1989).

20. *Tsentral'nyi gosudarstvennyi arkhiv oktiabr'skoi revoliutsii i sotsialisticheskogo stroitel'stva SSSR* [hereafter *TsGAOR*], f. 3977, o. 1, "Istoricheskaia spravka," l. 4

21. For more material on Culture Bases in general, see A. K. L'vov, "Kul'turnye bazy na Severe," *Sovetskaia Aziia* 3 (1926): 28–36; Petr Konstantinovich Ustiugov, "Zadachi natsional'noi raboty na krainem severe," *Revoliutsiia i Natsional'nosti* 1 (1931): 40–49, esp. 46.

22. *TsGAOR*, f. 3977, o. 1, d. 940, l. 7.

23. Ibid.

24. *TsGADV*, f. R4560, o. 1, d. 3 (1926–27), l. 69. For more information on the *Okhottovarishchestvo*, see the article "Pervye shagy," *Sovetskii Sakhalin* (26

August 1966), where the Sakhalin Congress of Hunters from 28 March 1926 is discussed. At the congress it was proposed that all game should go to the hunting union, administered through the local hunting cells and artels. In the interests of consolidating resources, it is relevant that several Nivkh villages north of Aleksandrovsk were relocated to Tyk, Viiakhta, Trambaus, and Vandy. "In this way, economic development prompted the necessity of the concentration of the local population." The union is also discussed in *GASO*, f. 287, o. 2, d. 1 (1925), l. 52.

25. An early planning meeting for *Sovetskii Rybak* is documented in "Protokoly s"ezda Sovetskogo Rybaka," *STsDNI*, f. 2, o. 2, d. 41 (1929), ll. 2–11o. For more on the early years of the Soviet fishing industry on Sakhalin, see Krushanov, *Stranitsy istorii*, 32; and Anna Vasil'evna Smoliak, "Osnovnye puti razvitiia ekonomiki, kul'tury i byta za gody sovetskoi vlasti u narodov basseina nizhnego Amura i Sakhalina," in I. S. Gurvich, ed., *Osushchestvlenie leninskoi natsional'noi politiki u narodov Krainego Severa* (Moscow: Nauka, 1971), 317. Some of the twenty-one fishing artels circa 1930 are listed in *TsGADV*, f. R4559, o. 1, d. 2 (1928–31).

26. *TsGAOR*, f. 3977, o. 1, d. 1117 (1928–31), ll. 22–24.

27. Ibid., ll. 153–154.

28. Shternberg, *Giliaki*, 2; *TsGAOR*, f. 3977, o. 1, d. 432 (1929).

29. *TsGADV*, f. R4560, o. 1, d. 3 (1926–27), "Vremennoe polozheniie ob upravlenii tuzemnykh plemen, prozhivaiushchikh na territorii Dal'nevostochnoi Oblasti."

30. "Vremennogo polozheniia ob upravlenii tuzemnykh plemen severnykh okrain RSFSR" (1926), in V. I. Mishchenko, "Proshloe nivkhov do oktiabria" (1957), *GASO, fond Ryzhkova*, ll. 20–23. In the 1936 document, the four tiers were referred to as *obshchee rodovoe sobranie, rodovye sovety, raionnye tuzemnye ispolkomy,* and *raionnye tuzemnye s"ezdy.*

31. *TsGADV*, f. R4559, o. 1, d. 5 (1931), l. 53.

32. *TsGAOR*, f. 3977, o. 1, d. 432 (1929).

33. *TsGADV*, f. R4559, o. 1, d. 4 (1929), l. 12.

34. *TsGADV*, f. R4559, o. 1, d. 4 (1931), l. 52.

35. Erukhim Kreinovich in *TsGAOR*, f. 3977, o. 1, d. 432 (1929).

36. Bogoraz in Slezkine, "Russia's Small Peoples," 294.

37. See, for example, Mikhail Dmitrievich Pechenkin, "Leninskii plan issledovaniia i osvoeniia Severa," in Vladimir Ivanovich Boiko et al., eds., *Problemy sovremennogo sotsial'nogo razvitiia narodnostei Severa* (Novosibirsk: Nauka, 1987), 16–28; and Il'ia Samoilovich Gurvich and Chuner Mikhailovich Taksami, "Vklad sovetskikh etnografov v osushchestvlenie leninskoi natsional'noi politiki na Severe," in Iulian Vladimirovich Bromlei, ed., *Leninizm i problemy etnografii* (Leningrad: Nauka, 1987), 181–197.

38. See Kreinovich, *Nivkhgu*, 9–21; also Slezkine, "Russia's Small People's," 298–299.

39. *Arkhiv Kreinovicha*, St. Petersburg. Emphases in the original.

40. Cf. also "Pis'ma E. A. Kreinovicha k L. Ia. Shternberg (1924–1930)," *PF AAN RF*, f. 282, o. 2, d. 154 (1927), l. 36.

41. Kreinovich's job with respect to credit was not only to arrange financial credit in the *faktorii* for Nivkhi, but to mete out livestock (cows and horses in the

main) to Nivkhi who showed the most promise of succeeding in agriculture. See *STsDNI*, f. 2, o. 1, d. 89 (1928) "Materialy po rabote sredi tuzemtsev," ll. 1–6.

42. *TsGADV*, f. R2413, o. 2, d. 394 (1927), l. 16.

43. *TsGADV*, f. R4560, o. 1, d. 3 (1926–27), ll. 76–76o.

44. Ibid., l. 79o. In a belletristic account of early work among the northern nationalities, Bogoraz cited the travails of the ethnographer "Prestovich" working on Sakhalin in conditions little better than those of the notorious tsarist labor camps (*Voskresshee Plemia* [Moscow: Khudozhestvennaia Literatura, 1935], 207–208). Kreinovich's troubles were consistent with those of many other early researchers; cf. Slezkine, "Russia's Small Peoples," 313–314.

45. *TsGADV*, l. 76o.

46. Ibid., ll. 17o–19o.

47. Il'ia Samoilovich Gurvich, "Osushchestvlenie leninskoi natsional'noi politiki u narodov Krainego Severa SSSR," *Sovetskaia Etnografiia* 1 (1970), 17–26. Writing in 1970, Gurvich described the late 1950s and 1960s as mainly improving on the state of affairs achieved in the final postwar period.

48. Petr Tuganov, "Giliaki sakhalinskoi taigi," *Tikhookeanskaia Zvezda* (28 April 1928), 3.

49. Anatolii Omel'chuk, "Institut narodov Severa," *Dal'nii Vostok* 2 (1981): 127–132.

50. "Protokol No. 18, Obshchego sobraniia tuzemtsev stoibishcha 'Kol'," *Dnevnik 1931 g. Arkhiva Kreinovicha.*

51. Credit goes to Natalya Sadomskaia for pointing out that while Dimanshtein's reference is to "Ezopovskii osel," the more traditional expression is "Buridanov osel."

52. S. I. Dimanshtein, "Sovetskaia vlast' i mel'kie natsional'nosti," *Zhizn' Natsional'nostei* 46 (1919): 17. Alcida Ramos writes of the Comtean strategy in Brazil in 1910 in "From Eden to Limbo: The Construction of Indigenism in Brazil," in George Bond and Angela Gilliam, eds., *The Social Construction of the Past: Representation as Power* (New York: Routledge, 1994).

53. M. Mel'nikov quoted in Sergeev, *Nekapitalisticheskii Put'*, 304. A second congress was held in Nogliki the following October but fewer natives attended because of the fishing season. Viskovo held its first district congress in December of the same year. For more on the congresses, see *TsGAOR*, f. 3977, o. 1, d. 1117 (1931), ll. 71–74.

54. Lev Alpatov, *Sakhalin (Putevye zapiski etnografa)* (Moscow: Federatsiia, 1930), 58.

55. "Stavka kulakov bita," *Za Bolshevistskuiu Putinu* (1 February 1931).

56. P. Ia. Skorik, "Kul'turnyi shturm taigi i tundry," *Prosveshchenie Natsional'nostei* 10 (1932), 32–39.

57. The long form for *kul'tarmeets* was *kul'turno-prosvetitel'nyi armeets* or Soldier of Cultural Enlightenment. For more on this and other related terms of the mass culture movement of the 1920s, see Barry Crowe, *Concise Dictionary of Soviet Terminology, Institutions and Abbreviations* (London: Pergamon, 1969). For the work of *kul'tarmeetsy* among Siberian indigenous peoples more broadly, see Slezkine, "Russia's Small Peoples," 388.

58. "The title of Shock Worker was awarded to workers who made outstand-

ing contributions to the raising of productivity and the most successful brigades were named Shock Brigades. The movement was at its height during the first Five Year Plan (1929–1932). By the end of 1929 some 300,000 workers had been awarded the title. Around 1935 the movement was replaced by the Stakhanovite movement" (from Crowe, *Concise Dictionary of Soviet Terminology*, 158).

59. Skorik, "Kul'turnyi shturm," 35.

60. Ibid., 33.

61. Ibid., 36.

62. The Black Hundreds movement was an umbrella organization for pro-tsarist activists in Russia in the early 1900s. The Kul'pin quotation is from *GASO*, f. 513, o. 1, d. 1 "Protokoly prezidiuma Zapadno-Sakhalinskogo natsional'nogo RIKa za 1931 g." (1931), l. 20. The same file documents the extensive assistance that Kul'pin extended to the Khabarovsk contingent, ll. 36–38.

63. Ibid., l. 37.

64. Further, by nationality, the 227 included 77 Nivkhi, 62 Tungusy, 44 Gol'dy, 31 Negidal'tsy, 9 Ul'chi and 4 Ainu (ibid., l. 38.

65. Ibid., l. 39.

66. *TsGADV*, f. R353, o. 1, d. 1 (1931–37), "Tsirkuliary i protokoly zasedanii prezidiuma Vsesoiuznogo Tsentral'nogo Komiteta Novogo Alfavita," l. 81. For a broader treatment of language politics in the USSR, see Michael Kirkwood, ed., *Language Planning in the Soviet Union* (London: Macmillan, 1990).

67. *GASO*, f. 513, o. 1, d. 1, l. 85.

68. Forsyth, *A History of the Peoples of Siberia*, 323.

69. *TsGADV*, f. R353, o. 1, d. 1 (1931), l. 31.

70. *TsGADV*, f. R353, o. 1, d. 1 (1931), l. 86.

71. Traditionally scholars have divided the Nivkh language into Amur, West Sakhalin, and East Sakhalin dialects. See, for example, Vladimir Zinevevich Panfilov, "Nivkhsko-altaiskie iazykovye sviazi," *Voprosy Iazykoznaniia* 5 (1973): 3–12. In the same article Panfilov challenges the presumption that the Nivkh language is a linguistic isolate. In the preparation of the first reader in 1932, Kreinovich relied on the Amur dialect.

72. For more on the work of the Far Eastern Committee of the New Alphabet, see *GASO*, f. 513, o. 1, d. 9 (1933) and d. 34 (1935–36).

73. *TsGAOR*, f. 3977, o. 1, d. 1117 (1931), l. 98.

74. P. N. Zhulev, *Kniga dlia chteniia (perevod s nivkhskogo iazyka E. A. Krei-novicha)* (Moscow-Leningrad: Gosudarstvennoe uchebno-pedagogicheskoe iz-datel'stvo, 1933), 73.

75. Cf. Slezkine, "Russia's Small Peoples," 400.

76. In the spirit of Pavel Morozov, the Russian boy folk hero who denounced his father to the courts, Siberian teachers, as in the rest of the Russian country-side, encouraged their native elementary school students to identify kulaks by polling students in class as to what various members of the community had inside their homes. For a Khant example, see Sergeev, "Nekapitalisticheskii Put'," 278.

77. Erukhim Abramovich Kreinovich, *Cuz Dif* [*Novoe Slovo*] (Leningrad: Gosudarstvennoe uchebno-pedagogicheskoe izdatel'stvo, 1932), 30, 44, 55, 63.

78. *TsGAOR*, f. 3977, o. 1, d. 19 (1925), l. 11.

79. Kreinovich, *Cuz Dif*, 20, 44, 55, 63.

Chapter Five
The Stalinist Period

1. On the transfer from artels to kolkhozes, see the "Rezoliutsiia o kollektivi-zatsii," in *STsDNI*, f. 13, o. 1, d. 5 (1930), ll. 42–44.

2. V. I. Mishchenko, "Proshloe nivkhov do oktiabria" (1957), in *GASO, fond Ryzhkova*, l. 67.

3. Nikolaev, "Natsional'nye shkoly," 44. The rate of 76 percent was slightly higher than the figure reported for Siberia and the Far East as a whole. By 1933 the Committee of the North had overseen the opening of a total of 338 schools, drawing 60.5 percent of the entire student-age population. See *TsGAOR*, f. 3977, o. 1, d. 144-2 (1926), l. 95.

4. Krames, "Iz doklada zaveduiushchego Sakhalinskoi kul'tbazoi Komitetu Sodeistviia Narodnostiiam Severa pri Prezidiume Dal'kraiispolkoma o rabote kul'tbazy za 1932–1934 gg." (1934), in N. I. Kolesnikov, ed., *Sotsialisticheskoe stroitel'stvo na Sakhaline (1925–1945 gg.)* (Iuzhno-Sakhalinsk: Sakhalinskaia oblastnaia tipografiia, 1967), 337–339. For a survey of changes over this period in the Siberian North as a whole see Smidovich's report, "Main points of the presentation on prospects for socialist construction in the Far North in the Second Five-Year Plan" (1935), *TsGAOR*, f. 3977, o. 1, d. 1048, as well as Anatolii Evgen'evich Skachko, "Desiat' let Komiteta Severa," *Sovetskii Sever* 2 (1934): 9–11.

5. See Nikolai Ssorin-Chaikov, "*Istoriia* and *Ulo*: A Critique of Sociological Reasoning with a Siberian Evenk Epistemology," M.A. thesis, Department of Anthropology, Stanford University, July 1991.

6. Pika, "Malye narody Severa," 320.

7. Slezkine, "Russia's Small Peoples," 373.

8. Erukhim Kreinovich, "Kolkhoznye zametki," *Sovetskii Sever* 3–4 (1934): 184–188.

9. *STsDNI*, f. 13, o. 1, d. 7 (1931), l. 98. [A separate system of pagination lists the same page as l. 13.]

10. *TsGADV*, f. R4559, o. 1, d. 5 (1931), "Doklady upolnomochennogo po tuzemnym delam pri prezidiume Sakhalinskogo okrrevkoma o kontsentratsii i kollektivizatsii korennogo naseleniia, 1928–1931 gg.," l. 51.

11. The experience of Siberian shamans throughout the Soviet period has been a turbulent one, and is a subject that I have left out of this project because of its magnitude. However, recent excellent examinations of the social dynamics of shamanism in the Soviet and post-Soviet periods include Marjorie Mandelstam Balzer's "Behind Shamanism: Changing Voices of Siberian Khanty Shamanism and Cosmology and Politics," *Social Science and Medicine* 24 (1987), 1085–1093, as well as "Two Urban Shamans: Unmasking Leadership in Fin-de-Soviet Siberia," in George Marcus, ed., *Perilous States: Conversations on Culture, Politics, and Nation* (Chicago: University of Chicago Press, 1993), and Caroline Humphrey, *The Karl Marx Collective: Economy, Society, and Religion in a Siberian Collective Farm* (Cambridge: Cambridge University Press, 1983), chap. 8.

12. *STsDNI*, f. 13, o. 1, d. 16 (1933), l. 1.

13. John J. Stephan, "'Cleansing' the Soviet Far East, 1937–1938," *Acta Slavica Iaponica* 10 (1992): 43. Alec Nove cites figures from the Russian scholar V. Popov on the *Ezhovshchina*, indicating how the number of people executed for counterrevolutionary offensives in the USSR as a whole shifted dramatically over the period, from 2,056 in 1934, 1,229 in 1935, and 1,118 in 1936 to 353,074 in 1937 and 328,618 in 1938 (Alec Nove, "The Soviet System in Retrospect: An Obituary Notice," The Fourth Annual W. Averell Harriman Lecture, Columbia University, 1993).

14. *STsDNI*, f. 13, o. 1, d. 7 (1931), l. 42.

15. Bronislaw Pil'sudskii, "The Gilyaks and their Songs," *Folk-Lore* 34 (1913), 483; Lev Shternberg, *Social Organization*, 10.

16. *TsGAOR*, f. 3977, o. 1, d. 1117 (1929–31), l. 98.

17. *STsDNI*, f. 13, o. 1, d. 16 (1933), l. 1.

18. See *GASO*, f. 856, o. 1, d. 1 (1931), l. 27; *TsGADV*, f. R4549, o. 1, d. 75 (1928–30), l. 77; and *STsDNI*, f. 4, o. 1, d. 3 (1931), ll. 72–79. For material on *raskulachivanie* on Sakhalin more generally, see Galina Ivanovna Dudarets and A. Strakhov, "Vtoraia voina 1929," *Molodaiia Gvardiia* (14 November 1989): 1–3; Aleksandr Kostanov, ed., *Istoriia bez belykh piaten'* (Iuzhno-Sakhalinsk: Ispolkom sakhalinskogo oblastnogo soveta narodnykh deputatov, 1989).

19. From the files of Vladimir L. Podpechnikov, *GASO*. Further material on the "Delo Ostrovnykh" is forthcoming in an article by the same name in the journal *Novaia Zhizn'*. A recent publication by the Iuzhno-Sakhalinsk Publishing House, *Kukhnia Diavola*, examines the career of V. M. Drekov.

20. *TsGAOR*, f. 3977, o. 1, d. 850 (1932), ll. 14–17.

21. Gurvich and Taksami, "Vklad sovetskikh etnografov," 187. For a broader treatment of the ideological turbulence in Soviet ethnography at the time, see also Yuri Slezkine, "The Fall of Soviet Ethnography, 1928–38," *Current Anthropology* 32, no. 4 (1991).

22. From interviews with Galina Aleksandrovna Razumikova, Voronezh, November 1990.

23. Slezkine, "Russia's Small Peoples," 477. For more on the role of industrialization among indigenous Siberians, see Gail Fondahl, "Native Economy and Northern Development: Reindeer Husbandry in Transbaykalia," Ph.D. dissertation, Department of Geography, University of California, Berkeley, 1989.

24. "Kreinovich, E. A. Pis'mo ego k S. A. Shternberg, 2 sent. 1930 g.," *PF AAN RF*, f. 282, o. 5, d. 27 (1930).

25. "Perekhod na novyi alfavit," *TsGADV*, f. R353, o. 1, d. 88 (1936), l. 16.

26. Ibid, l. 26.

27. Ibid., l. 18.

28. *GASO*, f. 509, o. 1, d. 34 (1936), l. 30.

29. *TsGADV*, f. R353, o. 1, d. 88 (1936), l. 20. See also *GASO*, f. 509, o. 1, d. 34 (1935–36), l. 26. Vasilii Nikolaevich Uvachan's insistence that latinization "artificially wrenched northern peoples away from the language of the brotherly Russian people, despite the Russian language having enriched the vocabularies of northern languages well before the October Revolution" is representative of the position taken at least on Sakhalin well until the 1980s. See Uvachan, *Perekhod k*

sotsializmu malykh narodov Severa (po materialam Evenkiiskogo i Taimyrskogo natsional'nykh okrugov) (Moscow: Politicheskaia Literatura, 1958), esp. 150–154. For a general review of the politics of the two alphabets, see Isabelle Kreindler, "The Changing Status of Russian in the Soviet Union," *International Journal of the Sociology of Language* 33 (1962): 5–135.

30. *Yarangas* were tents traditionally made from animal pelts, used in a number of Siberian indigenous communities.

31. Konstantin Dmitrievich Egorov, "*Protiv izvrashchenii i uproshchenstva (o bukvariakh dlia severnykh shkol)*" *Sovetskaia Arktika* 2 (1938), 31.

32. Ibid.

33. Stakhanovites were members of a movement that began in 1935 to raise labor productivity. Aleksei Stakhanov, the eponymous worker hero, set record production figures in coal mining, and became an icon for exemplary productivity in industry as a whole.

34. Egorov, "*Protiv izvrashchenii*," 31.

35. Ibid., 32.

36. *TsGADV*, f. R353, o. 1, d. 88 (1936), l. 7.

37. Nove, "The Soviet System," 24.

38. Robert Weinberg, "Purges and Politics in the Periphery: Birobidzhan in 1937," *Slavic Review* 52, no. 1 (1993): 13–27.

39. Churka had replaced Nikolai Akhmadeevich Akhmadeev, also a Nivkh, as head of the RIK in 1934 when Akhmadeev was arrested on April 7 of that year. Akhmadeev was charged under Article 58.2 of the constitution for inciting armed rebellion and participating in espionage.

40. The Sakhalin historian Vladimir Iakovlevich Kantorovich, who sat in the same prison as Churka, wrote that Churka died in prison in 1941. Others say he died in a camp in Magadan in 1947. The individuals who spoke against him for the prosecution disavowed their testimonies in 1958. The state rehabilitated him on 7 December 1959. From the files of Vladimir L. Podpechnikov, *GASO*.

41. See Skorik, "Kul'turnyi shturm," 37.

42. *STsDNI*, f. 13, o. 1, d. 29 (1937), l. 70. Orders for Kul'pin's arrest are listed on l. 93.

43. For the arrest of Kul'pin's son, see *STsDNI* f. 13, o. 1, d. 29 (1937), l. 93. The case of Kul'pin's coworker, Aleksei Ivanovich Alek, is documented in *STsDNI*, f. 13, o. 1, d. 38 (1938), l. 12.

44. Sergeev, *Nekapitalisticheskii Put'*, 383; Kolesnikov, *Sotsialisticheskoe stroitel'stvo*, 255.

45. Medvedev, "Politiko-ekonomicheskaia kharakteristika Rybnovskogo raiona sakhalinskoi oblasti," *GASO*, ll. 4o-5o.

46. Ibid., l. 6. The figures are comparable with those from Chukotka in Pika, "Malye narody Severa," 320.

47. Stephan, *Sakhalin*, 85.

48. On Japanese Karafuto, the Korean population reached 150,000 by 1941. Some 43,000 Koreans remained on the island when the Soviets reclaimed the South, from Stephan, *Sakhalin*, 151. Bok zi Kou's *Sakhalinskie koreitsy: problemy*

i perspektivy (Iuzhno-Sakhalinsk: SOKM, 1989) looks at the history of Sakhalin Koreans since their recruitment to the island.

49. *GASO*, f. 577, o. 1, dd. 111, 111a, 112 (1936–37). Most of these files are written in Korean. For material on the expulsion of Koreans elsewhere in the Far East, see Stephan, "'Cleansing' the Soviet Far East," 47.

50. Verkhovnyi Sovet SSSR, "Zhaloba v poriadke prokurorskogo nadzora ot ZK Kreinovicha Erukhima A., osuzhdennogo 1–8 ianvaria 1938 g. po delu 0016, st. 58(10–11), k 10 godam tiuremnogo zakliucheniia s porozheniem v pravakh na 5 let." *Arkhiv Kreinovicha*, St. Petersburg.

51. From conversations with Kreinovich's second wife, Galina Aleksandrovna Razumikova, Voronezh, November 1990.

52. *TsGAOR*, f. 3977, o. 1, d. 1139 (1934).

53. Ibid., ll. 2–8.

54. *STsDNI*, f. 16, o. 1, d. 17 (1936), ll. 121–122, 159–163.

55. *STsDNI*, f. 16, o. 1, d. 9 (1937–38), ll. 14–143.

56. *GASO*, f. 1071, o. 1, d. 2 (1934). The staff included a director, a chief accountant, a handyman, a janitor, a water carrier, two washerwomen, the director of the medical unit, a doctor, a nurse, a feldsher, four sanitation specialists, a stoker, the director of the school, five teachers, three day care workers (*vospitateli*), four cleaning women, two bakers, two additional kitchen staff, a metalworker, a joiner-carpenter, a shoemaker, a ploughman, a bathhouse attendant, a milkmaid, and a shepherd.

57. *GASO*, f. 1071, o. 1, d. 3 (1936–38), 4 (1939), 5 (1941–45).

58. *GASO*, f. 53, o. 2, d. 35 (1938), l. 8.

59. Krushanov, *Stranitsy istorii*, 109; *GASO*, f. 366, o. 1, d. 1 (1937–39), ll. 3–6.

60. See, for example, "Zveroboinyi zavod Liugi pered putinoi," *Sovetskii Sakhalin*, 28 March 1937, 4.

61. *GASO*, "Ekonomicheskoe polozhenie i rabota rybolovetsskikh kolkhozov Rybnovskogo raiona Sakhalinskoi oblasti" (1941).

62. Stephan, "'Cleansing' the Soviet Far East," 51.

63. A 1925 article on Rybnoe made note of a handsome young fisherman with suspiciously fine speech, "Evidently a fugitive White . . . Such 'fishermen' are most of the Rybnoe population . . . [with Rybnoe] a rare quiet haven for White Guard soldiers" ("Rybnyi Klondaik," *Sovetskii Sakhalin*, 27 September 1925, 3).

64. *GASO*, f. 509, o. 1, d. 35 (1938–39), ll. 33–34.

65. *GASO*, f. 1071, o. 1, d. 5 (1941–45), l. 2.

66. Pika, "Malye narody Severa," 321. See also Chichlo, "La collectivisation," 296.

67. *STsDNI*, f. 16, o. 1, d. 5 (1935), "Protokol No. 72 ot 26 dekabriia 1935 g."

68. *STsDNI*, f. 13, o. 1, d. 30 (1937), Postanovlenie Biuro Rybnovskogo RK VKP(b), "O sostoianii i podgotovke k putine kolkhoza 'Rybnoe'."

69. *STsDNI*, f. 13, o. 1, d. 26 (1936), "Protokoly zasedanii biuro Rybnovskogo raikoma," l. 178.

70. For the role of the *malye narody* more broadly during World War II, see Vasilii Nikolaevich Uvachan, *Gody, ravnye vekam (stroitel'stvo sotsializma na Krainem Severa)* (Moscow: Mysl', 1984), 155–157.

71. Kolesnikov, *Sotsialisticheskoe Stroitel'stvo*, 333–334, 348. For the role of the Sakhalin fishing industry during World War II more generally, see Krushanov, *Stranitsy istorii*, chap. 3.

72. Kolesnikov, *Sotsialisticheskoe stroitel'stvo*, 519.

73. A *tsentner* is a current unit of measurement denoting one hundred kilograms.

74. "Agitatsionno-propagandistskaia rabota sredi narodnostei Severa," *GASO, fond Ryzhkova* (1942), l. 21. The same file includes notes on model Nivkhi who served in the war.

75. *STsDNI*, f. 2, o. 2, d. 55 (1929), ll. 9–20.

76. *STsDNI*, f. 13, o. 1, d. 5a (1930–34), ll. 51–52, 67–69.

77. For more on Tamara Urziuk, see her application for party membership, in *STsDNI*, f. 17, o. 2, d. 911 (1942), l. 3; and P. Chernikov, "Doch' nivkhskogo naroda," *Sovetskii Sakhalin*, 10 December 1950.

78. Stephan, *Sakhalin*, 111, 125.

79. Stephan, "'Cleansing' the Soviet Far East," 43, 54.

80. P. M. Kalinin, "Sovetskii Sakhalin," *Sovetskii Sakhalin*, 10 September 1937, 4.

81. P. A. Burov, "Ostaius' rabotat' na Sakhaline," *Sovetskii Sakhalin*, 14 August 1937, 3.

82. From the film archives of *GASO*. In contrast, the first known footage of Soviet Sakhalin from the 1929 NKVD film, *Po Kamchatke i Sakhalinu*, focused on the overcoming of the island's dark past (*GASO*).

83. Slezkine, "Russia's Small Peoples," 338.

84. Anna Vasil'evna Smoliak, "Otrazhenie etnicheskikh protsessov v dukhovnoi kul'ture narodnostei Severa," in Gurvich, *Etnicheskoe razvitie*, 160.

85. *GASO*, f. 3. o. 1, d. 50 (1937), l. 19.

86. *STsDNI*, f. 13, o. 1, d. 70 (1943), l. 1.

87. *GASO*, f. 3, o. 1, d. 50 (1937), l. 22. The East Sakhalin district was eventually renamed as the Nogliki district.

88. *STsDNI*, f. 16, o. 1, d. 53a (1943), ll. 17–18.

89. *GASO*, f. 53, o. 25, d. 16 (1944), ll. 5o–6.

90. Chuner Mikhailovich Taksami, *Vozrozhdenie nivkhskoi narodnosti* (Iuzhno-Sakhalinsk: Sakhalinskoe knizhnoe izdatel'stvo, 1959), 47.

91. Ibid., 51.

92. Ibid., 60.

93. Documents from *GASO* suggest that labor camps existed throughout the 1930s, although the earliest verifiable sources are from 1947 (from S. Sakhtaganov, "Sakhlag," *Germes*, 1–15 July 1990.

94. Project Nos. 506 and 508, from Sakhtaganov, "Sakhlag"; Aleksandr Mikhailovich Pashkov and Galina Ivanovna Dudarets, "Ob"ekt No. 506," *Sakhalinskii Neftianik*, 23 December 1989, 6; "Materik, GULAG, Sakhalin," *Komsomol'skaia Pravda*, 2 March 1989, 4.

95. Frank J. Miller, *Folklore for Stalin* (Armonk, N.Y.: M. E. Sharpe, 1990), 81.

96. Kreinovich cited in Lydia Black, "Dogs, Bears and Killer Whales," 65. Shternberg makes the same observation in his field notes (*PF AAN RF*, f. 282, o. 1, d. 4 (1891), l. 360.

97. Stephan, *Sakhalin*, 186.

98. *STsDNI*, f. 4, o. 1, d. 23 (1940), "O rabote s narodnostiami Severa," l. 2

Chapter Six
1960s Resettlements and the Time of Stagnation

1. Ivan Pavlovich Miroliubov [Iuvachev], *Vosem' let na Sakhaline* (St. Petersburg: A. N. Suvorin, 1901), 152, in Konstantin Makarovich Braslavets, *Istoriia v nazvaniiakh na karte Sakhalinskoi Oblasti* (Iuzhno-Sakhalinsk: Dal'nevostochnoe knizhnoe izdatel'stvo, 1983), 86.

2. Harrison, "Kita Yezo Zusetsu," 93–117.

3. "Postanovlenie TsK KPSS i Soveta Ministrov SSSR 16 marta 1957 g.," *O merakh po dal'neishemu razvitiiu ekonomiki i kul'tury narodnostei Severa*," reprinted in Konstantin U. Chernenko and M. S. Smirtiukov, eds., *Resheniia partii i pravitel'stva po khoziastvennym voprosam. T. 4. 1953–61* (Moscow: Politicheskaia Literatura, 1968), 331–336. Early implementation of the decree on Sakhalin is discussed in *GASO*, f. 53, o. 25, d. 1991 (1960), ll. 41–45.

4. Stephen P. Dunn and Ethel Dunn, *Introduction to Soviet Ethnography* (Berkeley: Highgate Social Science Research Center, 1973), 90.

5. "Osnovnye etapy sotsial'no-ekonomicheskogo razvitiia rybnovskogo poberezh'ia," Archives of the Red Dawn kolkhoz, Nekrasovka.

6. Uvachan, *Gody, ravnye vekam*, 181.

7. Gurvich, *Etnicheskoe razvitie*, 92.

8. A. I. Gladyshev, ed., *Administrativno-territorial'noe delenie sakhalinskoi oblasti* (Iuzhno-Sakhalinsk: Dal'nevostochnoe knizhnoe izdatel'stvo, 1986), 79–106, 125. Gurvich estimated that as a result of the kolkhoz strengthening plan, the number of enterprises in northern regions was reduced by more than 60 percent. For example, on Chukotka, between 1953 and 1966, the government reduced the number of *selkhozarteli* (agricultural artels) from 1,444 to 300, and the number of fishing artels from 600 to 250. Inversely, the number of state farms in the area, considered by the state to be a more developed form of socialist industry, rose from 50 to 200 (from Gurvich, *Etnicheskoe razvitie*, 94; "Osushchestvlenie leninskoi natsional'noi politiki u narodov Krainego Severa SSSR," *Sovetskaia Etnografiia*, no. 1 (1970): 26). These figures are comparable to those on the Khanty-Mansiiskii okrug in Kuoljok's *Revolution in the North* (128).

9. *TsGAOR*, f. 53, o. 25, d. 2612 (1963), l. 53.

10. For favorable reports from 1959 to 1962 on Nivkh kolkhozes that were closed down thereafter, see *GASO*, f. 53, o. 25, d. 2612 (1963), ll. 9–12.; Krushanov, *Stranitsy istorii*, 213.

11. *Oblrybakkolkhozsoiuz* renamed Liugi's "Stalin" kolkhoz "Twenty-first Party Congress" after Khrushchev's "secret speech" criticizing Stalin.

12. *GASO*, f. 53, o. 25, d. 3897a (1968), ll. 101–104.

13. Ibid., l. 30.

14. *GASO*, f. 53, o. 25, d. 3897 (1969), ll. 4–6.

15. For discussions of this three-step process, see Yaroslav Bilinsky, "The Concept of the Soviet People and Its Implications for Soviet Nationality Policy," *Annals of the Ukrainian Academy of Arts and Science in the United States* 37–38 (1980): 87–133; Gail Lapidus, "Ethnonationalism and Political Stability: The Soviet Case," *World Politics* 36, no. 4 (1984): 355–380; and *Rastsvet i sblizhenie natsii v SSSR* (Moscow: Mysl', 1981). Lapidus is right to point out that by the "time of stagnation" most Soviets had long given up the idea of ethnic merger. What interests me here are the contradictions of a policy that continued to be advocated long after it lost its salience.

16. *GASO*, f. 53, o. 25, d. 3897a (1968), l. 73.

17. "Narodnosti Severa Ostrova Sakhalin," *GASO* (Unpublished report) (1989): 6.

18. Boiko, *Nivkhi Sakhalina*, 58.

19. Valentin Rasputin, "The Fire," in *Siberia on Fire* (DeKalb: Northern Illinois University Press, 1989), 109–110, 111.

20. *GASO*, f. 53, o. 25, d. 3897a (1968), ll. 26–34, 99–112; *GASO*, f. 53, o. 25, d. 3897ots (1968), ll. 128–136; "Uverennym shagom—k namechennym rubezham (s otchetnogo sobraniia upolnomochennykh rybkolkhoza 'Vostok'," *Znamiia Truda* (24 March 1967); *GASO*, f. 53, o. 25, d. 3897a-ots (1967), l. 183o.

21. *GASO*, f. 53, o. 25, d. 3897a (1968), l. 68.

22. Caroline Humphrey, "'Janus-faced signs'—the political language of a Soviet minority before *Glasnost'*," in Ralph Grillo, ed., *Social Anthropology and the Politics of Language* (London: Routledge, 1989), 158–160.

23. Gurvich, "Vvodnyi Ocherk: K sotsializmu, minuia kapitalizm," in *Etnicheskoe razvitie*, 28.

24. Uvachan, *Gody, ravnye vekam*, 4.

25. Cf. chapter 1, note 20.

26. *GASO*, f. 53, o. 25, d. 3584 (1968), l. 44.

27. *GASO*, f. 53, o. 25, d. 3897a (1968), ll. 72–78.

28. Derevianko and Boiko, "Puti kul'turnogo razvitiia," 11.

29. Shternberg, *Giliaki*, 78.

30. Humphrey, *The Karl Marx Collective*, 141.

31. Frances Yates, *The Art of Memory* (London: Ark, 1984); Renato Rosaldo, *Ilongot Headhunting, 1883–1974* (Stanford: Stanford University Press, 1980).

32. Todorov in Debbora Battaglia, *On the Bones of the Serpent* (Chicago: University of Chicago Press, 1990), 70.

33. Igor Krupnik and Anna Vasil'evna Smoliak, "Sovremennoe polozhenie korennogo naseleniia Severa sakhalinskoi oblasti" [Dokladnaia zapiska, po materialam poezdki s sentiabria 1982 g.] (Unpublished manuscript, 1982), 7.

34. Zoia Petrovna Sokolova, "Narody Severa SSSR: Proshloe, nastoiashchee i budushchee," *Sovetskaia Etnografiia*, no. 6 (1990): 19.

35. Aleksandr Ivanovich Pika and Boris Borisovich Prokhorov, "Bol'shie problemy malykh narodov," *Kommunist* 16 (1988): 81.

36. Pika, "Malye narody Severa," 306.

37. Pika and Prokhorov, "Bol'shie problemy," 80.

38. Ibid.

39. Nikolai Ivanovich Solov'ev, Presentation to the Congress of Northern Peoples, Moscow, March 1990.

40. Ssorin-Chaikov, "*Istoriia* and *Ulo*," 30.

41. Derevianko and Boiko, "Puti kul'turnogo razvitiia," 11 [italics added].

42. Taksami in Kuoljok, *Revolution in the North*, 142–143.

43. Anderson, "Turning Hunters into Herders," 12–22.

44. Boiko, *Nivkhi Sakhalina*, 38.

45. Eric Hobsbawm and Terence Ranger, eds., *The Invention of Tradition* (New York: Cambridge University Press, 1983); Michael Taussig, *The Devil and Commodity Fetishism* (Chapel Hill: University of North Carolina Press, 1980).

46. Mikhail Stanislavovich Vysokov, "Sovremennaia iazykovaia situatsiia v raionakh prozhivaniia sakhalinskikh nivkhov," in Valerii O. Shubin, ed., *Etnograficheskoe issledovanie Sakhalinskogo Oblastnogo Kraevedcheskogo Muzeiia* (Iuzhno-Sakhalinsk: Sakhalinskoe knizhnoe izdatel'stvo, 1985); and Tjeerd de Graaf, "The Small Languages of Sakhalin," *International Journal of the Sociology of Language* 94 (1992): 185–200.

47. Boris Borisovich Prokhorov, Aleksandr Ivanovich Pika et al., *Metodicheskie osnovy kontseptsii gosudarstvennoi politiki optimizatsii uslovii zhiznedeiatel'nosti malochislennykh narodov Severa* (Moscow: Institut Problem Zaniatosti AN RF i Mintruda RF, 1992).

Chapter Seven
Perestroika Revisited: On Dissolution and Disillusion

1. *Moscow News* 11 (1989): 16.

2. The North Sakhalin newspaper *Svobodnyi Sakhalin* listed the average monthly income on the island as 3,172 rubles for the start of May 1992; an average family's minimum monthly expenses for survival was 4,937.7 rubles; and the average combined household income was 6,028 rubles (from *RA Report* 13 [1992]: 33).

3. Presidential Decree No. 397, 22 April 1992, "O neotlozhnykh merakh po zashchite mest prozhivaniia i khoziaistvennoi deiatel'nosti malochislennykh narodov Severa," stipulated that free land be allotted on a permanent basis to northern native peoples for traditional land use. Peoples of the North would have a voting role in the distribution of licenses issued on this land for fishing, hunting, and other resource-related pursuits.

4. Andrei Vladimirov, "Rodovye khoziaistva: vozvrashchenie k istokam," *Svobodnyi Sakhalin*, 9 July 1992, 7.

5. For a look at the role of barter in Siberia during the same period, see Caroline Humphrey, " 'Icebergs,' barter, and the mafia in provincial Russia," *Anthropology Today* 7, no. 2 (1991): 8–14.

Chapter Eight
Conclusions: The Subjects Presumed to Know

1. Hawes, *In the Uttermost East*, 240.

2. Don DeLillo, *White Noise* (New York: Penguin, 1985), 317–318.

3. A similar project among Evenki is discussed in David A. Anderson, "Property Rights and Civil Society in Siberia: An Examination of the Social Movements of the Zabaikal'skie Evenki," *Praxis International* 12, no. 1 (1992): 83–105.

4. Sigmund Freud, *Civilization and Its Discontents* (New York: Norton, 1989); Friedrich Nietzsche, *On the Genealogy of Morals* (New York: Vintage, 1989), 57–58.

5. Chingiz Aitmatov, "Spotted Dog Running along the Seashore," in *Mother Earth and Other Stories* (London: Faber and Faber, 1989), 229–309.

Appendix
"A Recently Discovered Case of Group Marriage,"
by Frederick Engels

1. This article by Frederick Engels was published in *Die Neue Zeit* in 1892 (vol. 11, no. 12, Band 2, 373–375). Reprinted here from Engels, *The Origin of the Family, Private Property and the State* (New York: International Publishers, 1972), 238–241, with the kind permission of the publisher.

Bibliography

Afanas'ev, G. A.
1928   Zaniatiia i zhizn' sakhalinskikh evenkov. Taiga i tundra 1: 38–42.
Aipin, Yeremei
1989   Not by Oil Alone. Moscow News 39: 20(12).
Aitmatov, Chingiz
1989   Spotted Dog Running along the Seashore. *In* Mother Earth and Other Stories. London: Faber and Faber. [Published in Russian as "Pegii pes begushchii kraem moria." *In* Povesti. Moscow: Khudozhestvennaia Literatura, 1989.]
Alekseev, A. E.
1986   Vtoraia Rodina. Iuzhno-Sakhalinsk.
Alekseev, Veniamin
1989   Siberia in the Twentieth Century. Moscow: Novosti.
Allison, Anthony P.
1990   Siberian Regionalism in Revolution and Civil War, 1917–1920. Siberica 1 (1): 78–97.
Alpatov, Lev
1930   Sakhalin: Putevye zapiski etnografa. Moscow: Federatsiia.
Amalrik, Andrei
1970   Involuntary Journey to Siberia. New York: Harcourt, Brace, Jovanovich.
Anderson, David A.
1991   Turning Hunters into Herders: A Critical Examination of Soviet Development Policy among the Evenki of Southeastern Siberia. Arctic 44 (1): 12–22.
1992   Property Rights and Civil Society in Siberia: An Examination of the Social Movements of the Zabaikal'skie Evenki. Praxis International 12 (1): 83–105.
Anderson, Madelyn Klein
1987   Siberia. New York: Dodd, Mead.
Andreev, I. L.
1974   The Ethnic Minorities of the North and Their Road to Socialism. *In* National Relations in the USSR: Theory and Practice. Moscow.
Antropova, Valentina Vasil'evna
1972   Uchastie etnografov v prakticheskom osushchestvlenii leninskoi natsional'noi politiki na Krainem Severe (1920–1930 gg.). Sovetskaia Etnografiia 6: 19–27.
Aristov, F. F.
1922   Znachenie Sakhalina v strategicheskom otnoshenii. Novyi Vostok 2: 396–399.

Armstrong, Terence
  1986   Soviet Government Policy toward Northern Peoples of the USSR. *In* Arctic Policy [paper presented at the Arctic Policy Conference, 1985, Centre for Northern Studies and Research, McGill University].
  1958   The Russians in the Arctic: Aspects of Soviet Exploration and Exploitation, 1937–1957. London: Methuen.
  1975   Yermak's Campaign in Siberia. London: Hakluyt Society.
  1978   Northern USSR: The North in a Socialist Economy. *In* The Circumpolar North. London: Methuen.
Armstrong, William Jackson
  1890   Siberia and the Nihilists: Why Kennan Went to Siberia. Oakland: Pacific Press.
Arutiunov, Sergei Aleksandrovich
  1984   U beregov Ledovitogo Okeana. Moscow: Russkii Iazyk.
Austerlitz, Robert
  1956   Gilyak Nursery Words. Word 12: 260–279.
  1957   A Linguistic Approach to the Ethnobotany of South Sakhalin. Ninth Pacific Science Congress of the Pacific Science Association. Bangkok.
  1959   Gilyak Religious Terminology in the Light of Linguistic Analysis. The Transactions of the Asiatic Society of Japan 7: 207–223.
  1961   The Identification of Folkloristic Genres (Based on Gilyak Materials). Poetics—Poetyka—-Poetika. Donald Davie et al., eds. Warsaw: Panstwowe Wydawnictwo Naukow and The Hague: Mouton.
  1967   Two Gilyak Song Texts. *In* To Honor Roman Jakobson: Essays on the Occasion of His Seventieth Birthday, 11 October 1966, 1: 99–113. The Hague: Mouton.
  1968   Native Seal Nomenclatures in South Sakhalin. *In* Papers of the C.I.C. Far Eastern Language Institute. Joseph K. Yamagiwa, ed. Ann Arbor.
  1974   Paleosiberian Languages. *In* Encyclopaedia Britannica, 15th ed. Pp. 914–916.
  1977   The Study of Paleosiberian Languages. *In* Roman Jakobson: Echoes of His Scholarship. Lisse: The Peter de Ridder Press.
  1978   Folklore, Nationality, and the Twentieth Century in Siberia and the Soviet Far East. *In* Folklore, Nationalism, and Politics. Felix Oinas, ed. Columbus, Ohio: Slavica.
  1981   Gilyak Internal Reconstruction, 1: Seven Etyma. Folia Slavica 5 (1–3).
  1983   Studies of Paleosiberian Languages. *In* Roman Jakobson: What He Taught Us. Morris Halle, ed. Columbus: Slavica.
  1984a   Ten Nivkh Erotic Poems. Acta Ethnographica of the Academy of Sciences of Hungary 33 (1–4): 33–44.
  1984b   Gilyak Internal Reconstruction, 2: Iron and Questions Related to Metallurgy. Folia Slavica 7 (1–2): 38–48.
  1984c   On the Vocabulary of Nivkh Shamanism: The Etymon of *qas* ("Drum") and Related Questions. *In* Shamanism in Eurasia. Mihaly Hoppal, ed. Pp. 231–241. Gottingen: Herodot.
  1985a   Etymological Frustration (Gilyak). International Journal of American Linguistics 51: 336–338.

1985b Gilyak Verse and Music. *In* Proceedings of the International Symposium on Bronislaw Pil'sudskii's Phonographic Records and the Ainu Culture. Hokkaido University.

1986a Shaman [on the Gilyak origins of the word]. Ural-Altaic Yearbook 58: 143–144.

1986b Gilyak Internal Reconstruction, 3: Ligneous Matter. Folia Slavica.

1988 Lexicography of the Paleosiberian Languages. *In* Dictionaries, an International Encylopaedia. Berlin: Walter de Gruyter.

Avgustinovich, F. M.
1872 Zhizn' russkikh i inorodtsev na Ostrove Sakhalin—Vsemirnyi puteshestvennik. Vol. 2. St. Petersburg.

1880 Zametki ob Ostrove Sakhaline. St. Petersburg.

Azhaev, Vasilii
1985 Daleko ot Moskvy. Moscow: Sovremennik.

Babbage, Ross, ed.
1989 The Soviets in the Pacific in the 1990s. New York: Elsevier.

Babkin, Evgenii Nikolaevich, and Iurii Vasil'evich Shashkov
1980 Na samykh dal'nikh rubezhakh. Iuzhno-Sakhalinsk. Dal'nevostochnoe knizhnoe izdatel'stvo.

Baddeley, John F.
1983 (1919) Russia, Mongolia, and China. 2 vols. New York: Benjamin Franklin.

Bagrov, Viktor Nikolaevich
1985 Pobeda na ostrovakh. Iuzhno-Sakhalinsk: Dal'nevostochnoe knizhnoe izdatel'stvo.

Balitskii, V. G.
1969 Ot patriarkhalno-obshchinnogo stroia k sotsializmu. Moscow: Mysl'.

1984 Velikii oktiabr' v sud'bakh malykh narodov Dal'nevostochnogo Severa SSSR. Vladivostok.

Balzer, Marjorie Mandelstam
1978 Strategies of Ethnic Survival: Interaction of Russians and Khanty (Ostiak) in Twentieth-Century Siberia. Ph.D. dissertation, Department of Anthropology, Bryn Mawr College.

1980 The Route to Eternity: Cultural Persistence and Change in Khanty Burial Ritual. Arctic Anthropology 17 (1): 77–89.

1981 Rituals of Gender Identity: Markers of Siberian Khanty Ethnicity, Status, and Belief. American Anthropologist 83 (4): 850–867.

1982 Peoples of Siberia. *In* Guide to the Study of Soviet Nationalities: The Non-Russian Peoples of the USSR. Stephen M. Horak, ed. Pp. 239–252. Littleton, Colorado: Libraries Unlimited.

1983a Ethnicity without Power: The Siberian Khanty in Soviet Society. Slavic Review 42 (4): 633–648.

1983b Doctors or Deceivers? The Siberian Khanty Shaman and Soviet Medicine. *In* The Anthropology of Medicine. Lola Romanucci-Ross, ed. Pp. 54–76. New York: Praeger.

1987 Behind Shamanism: Changing Voices of Siberian Khanty Shamanism and Cosmology and Politics. Social Science and Medicine 24: 1085–1093.

1992 Dilemmas of the Spirit: Religious Atheism in the Yakut-Sakha Republic. *In* Religious Policy in the Soviet Union. Sabrina Ramet, ed. Pp. 231–251. New York: Cambridge University Press.

1993 Two Urban Shamans: Unmasking Leadership in Fin-de-Soviet Siberia. *In* Perilous States: Conversations on Culture, Politics, and Nation. George Marcus, ed. Pp. 131–164. Chicago: University of Chicago Press.

Bartels, Dennis

1983 Cultural Relativism, Marxism, and Soviet Policy toward the Khanty. Culture 3 (2): 25–30.

1985 Shamanism, Christianity, and Marxism: Comparisons and Contrasts between the Impact of Soviet Teachers on Eskimos, Chukchis, and Koryaks of Northeastern Siberia, and the Impact of an Early Anglican Missionary on Baffin Island Inuit. Canadian Journal of Education 12 (3): 1–7.

Bartels, Dennis, and Alice Bartels

1988 Are Siberian native peoples part of a "Fourth World"? Dialectical Anthropology 12: 245–252.

Bassin, Mark

1983 The Russian Geographical Society, the Amur Epoch, and the Great Siberian Expedition, 1855–1863. The Annals of the Association of American Geographers 73: 240–256.

1988 Expansion and colonialism on the eastern frontier: Views of Siberia and the Far East in pre-Petrine Russia. Journal of Historical Geography 14: 3–21.

1991a Russia between Europe and Asia. Slavic Review 50 (1): 1–17.

1991b Inventing Siberia: Visions of the Russian East in the Early Nineteenth Century. American Historical Review (June): 763–794.

Battaglia, Debbora

1990 On the Bones of the Serpent. Chicago: University of Chicago Press.

1993 At Play in the Fields (and Borders) of the Imaginary: Melanesian Transformations of Forgetting. Cultural Anthropology 8 (4): 430–442.

Bawden, C. R.

1985 Shamans, lamas and evangelicals: The English missionaries in Siberia. London: Routledge, Kegan, Paul.

Bazanov, A. G.

1936 Ocherki po istorii missionerskikh shkol na Krainem Severe (Tobol'skii Sever). Leningrad: Institut Narodov Severa im. P. G. Smidovicha Glavsevmorputi.

Belousov, I. E.

1977 Eto nasha zemlia. Iuzhno-Sakhalinsk: Dal'nevostochnoe knizhnoe izdatel'stvo.

Belousov, I. E., ed.

1963 Pesni Sakhalina. Iuzhno Sakhalinsk: Sakhalinskoe knizhnoe izdatel'stvo.

Benjamin, Walter

1990 The Origin of German Tragic Drama. London: Verso.

Berman, Marshall

1988 All That Is Solid Melts into Air. New York: Penguin.

Bichurin, N. Ia.
1950(1981)   Sobranie svedenii o narodakh obitavshikh v Srednei Azii v drevnie vremena. Vols. 1–3. Moscow-Leningrad: Academy of Sciences.

Bilinsky, Yaroslav
1980   The Concept of the Soviet People and Its Implications for Soviet Nationality Policy. Annals of the Ukrainian Academy of Arts and Sciences in the United States 37–38: 87–133.

Black, Lydia
1972   Relative Status of Wife Givers and Wife Takers in Gilyak Society. American Anthropologist 74 (5): 1244–1248.
1973a   The Nivkh (Gilyak) of Sakhalin and the Lower Amur. Arctic Anthropology 10 (1): 1–110.
1973b   Dogs, Bears, and Killer Whales: An Analysis of the Nivkh Symbolic System. Ph.D. dissertation, Department of Anthropology, University of Massachusetts, Amherst.

Bobrick, Benson
1992   East of the Sun. New York: Poseidon.

Bogoraz [Bogoras], Vladimir Germanovich
1909   The Chukchee. Franz Boas, ed. [Memoirs of the American Museum of Natural History, vol. 11, pts. 1–3.] Leiden: E. J. Brill; New York: Stechert.
1922   O pervobytnykh plemenakh. Zhizn' Natsional'nostei 1: 130.
1923   Ob izuchenii i okhrane okrainnykh narodov. Zhizn' Natsional'nostei 3–4: 168–180.
1927   Severnyi rabfak. Sovetskaia Aziia 2: 52–63.
1932   Religiia kak tormoz sotsstroitel'stva sredi malykh narodnostei Severa. Sovetskii Sever 1–2: 142–157.
1935   Voskresshee Plemia. Moscow: Khudozhestvennaia Literatura.
1936   Osnovnye tipy fol'klora severnoi Evrazii i Severnoi Ameriki. Sovetskii Fol'klor 4–5: 29–50.

Bogoraz, Vladimir Germanovich, and N. J. Leonov
1928   Cultural Work among the Lesser Nationalities of the North in the USSR. In Proceedings of the Twenty-third International Congress of Americanists.

Boiko, Vladimir Ivanovich, ed.
1986   Kul'tura narodnostei Severa: traditsii i sovremennost'. Nauka: Novosibirsk.
1988   Nivkhi Sakhalina. Sovremennoe sotsial'no-ekonomicheskoe razvitie. Novosibirsk. Nauka.
1989   Kul'tura narodov Severa: filosofsko-sotsiologicheskii analiz. Novosibirsk: Nauka.

Boiko, Vladimir Ivanovich, P. Nikitin, and Aleksei Ivanovich Solomakha, eds.
1987   Problemy sovremennogo sotsial'nogo razvitiia narodnostei Severa. Novosibirsk: Nauka.

Boiko, Vladimir Ivanovich, and Iurii Vladimirovich Popkov
1987   Razvitiie otnosheniia k trudu u narodnostei Severa pri sotsializme. Nauka: Novosibirsk.

Boshniak, N. K.
1858   Puteshestviia v Priamurskom Krae. *In* Morskoi Sbornik 12.
1859   Puteshestviia v Priamurskom Krae. *In* Morskoi Sbornik 1–3.
Braslavets, Konstantin Makarovich
1983   Istoriia v nazvaniiakh na karte sakhalinskoi oblasti. Iuzhno-Sakhalinsk: Dal'nevostochnoe knizhnoe izdatel'stvo.
Bromlei, Iulian Vladimirovich
1975   The Main Tendencies in the Cultural Development of the Indigenous Population of the Soviet Far East [Manuscript held in the Lenin Library, Moscow].
Budarin, Mikhail Efimovich
1968   Put' malykh narodov krainego Severa k kommunizmu: KPSS—organizator sotsialisticheskikh preobrazovanii v natsional'nykh raionakh Severo-Zapadnoi Sibiri. Omsk: Zapadno-Sibirskoe knizhnoe izdatel'stvo.
Bugaeva, A. L., and Aleksandra A. Kudria
1983   Prosveshchenie na krainem Severe. Leningrad: Prosveshchenie.
Burov, P. A.
1937   Ostaius' rabotat' na Sakhaline. Sovetskii Sakhalin (14 August): 3.
Bush, Richard James
1970   (1871) Reindeer, Dogs, and Snowshoes: A Journal of Siberian Travel and Explorations Made in the Years 1865, 1866, and 1867. New York: Arno.
Busse, Nikolai Vasil'evich
1872   Ostrov Sakhalin i ekspeditsiia 1853–1854: Dnevnik 25 avgusta 1853 g.–19 maia 1854 g. St. Petersburg: F. S. Sushchinskii.
Butkovskii, Ia.
1874   Sakhalin i ego znachenie. Morskoi Sbornik 2 (April): 131–139.
1882   Ostrov Sakhalin. Istoricheskii Vestnik 10: 175–186.
Cardin, Elis, and Arlette Fraysse, eds.
1983   Siberiana. Paris: CNRS.
Chang, Sung-Hwan
1974   Russian Designs on the Far East. *In* Russian Imperialism from Ivan the Great to the Revolution. Taras Hunczak, ed. Pp. 299–321. New Brunswick: Rutgers University Press.
Chard, Chester
1961   Sternberg's Materials on the Sexual Life of the Gilyak. Anthropological Papers of the University of Alaska 10 (1): 13–23.
Chekhov, Anton
1967   The Island: A Journey to Sakhalin. Translated by Luba and Michael Terpak. New York: Washington Square Press.
1993   A Journey to Sakhalin. Translated by Brian Reeve. Cambridge: Ian Faulkner.
Chernenko, Konstantin U., and M. S. Smirtiukov, eds.
1968   Resheniia partii i pravitel'stva po khoziaistvennym voprosam. Vol. 4. 1953–1961. Moscow: Politicheskaia Literatura.
Chernikov, P.
1950   Doch' nivkhskogo naroda. Sovetskii Sakhalin (10 December).

Chesalin, V.
    1981   Otvazhnyi ymkhi. *In* Nivkhskie legendy. Iuzhno-Sakhalinsk: Sakha-
linskii Oblastnoi Kraevedcheskii Muzei (SOKM).
Chichlo, Boris
    1978   La collectivisation en Sibérie: un problème de nationalités. *In*
L'expérience soviétique et le problème national dans le monde. 1920–1939.
Vol. 1. Pp. 279–307. Paris: CNRS.
    1981   Les Nevuqaghmiit ou la fin d'une ethnie. Études/Inuit/Studies 5 (2).
    1985   Cult of the Bear in Soviet Ideology in Siberia. Religion in Communist
Lands 13 (2): 166–183.
    1990   Les "Petits Peuples" de Sibérie. Pourquoi? 253: 10–15.
Collins, David N., and Jan Smele
    1988   Kolchak and Siberia: Documents and Studies, 1919–1926, 2 vols.
White Plains, New York: Kraus International.
Colson, Elizabeth
    1953   The Makah Indians: A Study of an Indian Tribe in Modern American
Society. Manchester: University Press.
Comaroff, John
    1991   Humanity, Ethnicity, Nationality: Conceptual and Comparative Per-
spectives on the USSR. Theory and Society 20 (5): 661–687.
Comrie, Bernard
    1981   The Languages of the Soviet Union. New York: Cambridge University
Press.
Connoly, Violet
    1967   Beyond the Urals. London: Oxford University Press.
    1976   Siberia Today and Tomorrow. New York: Taplinger.
Conrad, Joseph L.
    1990   Anton Chekhov's Views of the Ainu and Giljak Minorities on Sakhalin
Island. *In* Anton P. Cechov: Werk und Wirkung. Rolf-Dieter Kluge, ed. Pp.
433–443. Wiesbaden: Otto Harrassowitz.
Crowe, Barry
    1969   Concise Dictionary of Soviet Terminology: Institutions and Abbrevia-
tions. London: Pergamon.
Czaplicka, Marie A.
    1969 (1914)   Aboriginal Siberia. Oxford: Oxford University Press.
    n.d.   My Siberian Year. London: Mills and Boon.
Dallin, David, and Boris Nicolaevsky
    1947   Forced Labour in Soviet Russia. New Haven: Yale.
De Graaf, Tjeerd
    1991   Dutch Encounters with Sakhalin and the Ainu People [unpublished
paper given to the Pil'sudskii Conference, Iuzhno-Sakhalinsk, November
1991].
    1992   The Small Languages of Sakhalin. International Journal of the Sociol-
ogy of Language 94: 185–200.
Delaby, Laurence
    1989   De l'autocannibalisme différé chez les Nivx. Cahiers de Sociologie
Économique et Culturelle 12: 167–170.

DeLillo, Don
1985   White Noise. New York: Penguin.
Demin, Lev Mikhailovich
1965   Za Tatarskim Prolivom. Moscow: Mysl'.
1983   Sakhalinskie zapiski. Moscow: Sovetskaia Rossiia.
Derevianko, Anatolii Panteleevich, and Vladimir Ivanovich Boiko.
1986   Puti kul'turnogo razvitiia Sibiri. *In* Kul'tura narodnostei Severa: traditsii i sovremennost'. Vladimir Ivanovich Boiko, ed. Novosibirsk: Nauka.
Detienne, Marcel
1986   The Creation of Mythology. Chicago: University of Chicago Press.
DeWindt, Harry
1896   The New Siberia: Being an Account of a Visit to the Penal Island of Sakhalin, and Political Prison and Mines of the Trans-Baikal District, Eastern Siberia. London: Chapman and Hall.
Dienes, Leslie
1987   Soviet Asia. Boulder: Westview.
Dimanshtein, S. I.
1919   Sovetskaia vlast' i mel'kie natsional'nosti. Zhizn' Natsional'nostei 46: 17.
Diment, Galya, and Yuri Slezkine, eds.
1993   Between Heaven and Hell: The Myth of Siberia in Russian Culture. New York: St. Martin's.
Dmytryshyn, Basil
1990   Russian Expansion to the Pacific, 1580–1700: A Historiographical Overview. Siberica 1 (1): 4–37.
Dmytryshyn, Basil, E.A.P. Crownhart-Vaughan, and Thomas Vaughan
1985   Russia's Conquest of Siberia, 1558–1700, a Documentary Record. Vol. 1. Portland: Western Imprints.
Dolgikh, Boris Osipovich
1958   Etnicheskii sostav i rasselenie narodov Amura v XVII v. po russkim istochnikam. *In* Sbornik statei po istorii Dal'nego Vostoka. Moscow.
1967   Obrazovanie sovremennykh narodnostei Severa SSSR. Sovetskaia Etnografiia 3: 3–15.
Dominguez, Virginia
1989   People as Subject, People as Object: Selfhood and Peoplehood in Contemporary Israel. Madison: University of Wisconsin Press.
Donner, Kai
1946   La Sibérie. La vie en Sibérie, les temps anciens. Paris: Gallimard.
Doroshevich, Vlas Mikhailovich
1903   Sakhalin: Katorga. Moscow: I. D. Shchukin.
Dostoevskii, Fedor
1939   The House of the Dead. London: Dent.
Dremova, L. I.
1982   Sotsialno-ekonomicheskoe razvitie Sibirskoi kolkhoznoi derevni v period razvitogo sotsializma: uchebnoe posobie k spetskursu dlia studentov istoricheskogo fakul'teta. Novosibirsk: Novosibirskii Gosudarstvennyi Pedagogicheskii Institut.

Dudarets, Galina Ivanovna, and A. Strakhov
1989   Vtoraia voina 1929. Molodaia Gvardiia (14 November 1989): 1–3.

Dunn, Stephen P., and Ethel Dunn
1972   The Peoples of Siberia and the Far East. In Russia and Asia. Wayne C. Vucinich, ed. Stanford: Hoover.
1973   Introduction to Soviet Ethnography. Berkeley: Highgate Social Science Research Center.

Egorov, Konstantin Dmitrievich
1938   Protiv izvrashchenii i uproshchenstva (o bukvariakh dlia severnykh shkol). Sovetskaia Arktika 2: 30–32.

Engels, Frederick
1972   The Origin of the Family, Private Property, and the State. New York: International.

Ermolinskii, Leonid Leont'evich
1985   Sibirskie gazety 70–80kh godov XIX v. Irkutsk: Irkutskii Universitet.

Fabian, Johannes
1983   Time and the Other: How Anthropology Makes Its Object. New York: Columbia University Press.

Fedorov, Valentin Petrovich
1990   Revoliutsionnyi eksperiment na Sakhaline [unpublished manuscript].
1991   Sakhalin i rynok. Dal'nii Vostok 1: 120–128.
1992   Let's Make a Deal. International Economy 6 (2): 39.

Feoktistov, S.
1956   Nivkhskie skazki. Khabarovsk.

Fetisov, A. P.
1966   K. Ia. Luks. Khabarovsk.

Fisher, Raymond
1943   The Russian Fur Trade, 1500–1700. Berkeley: University of California.

Fondahl, Gail
1989   Native Economy and Northern Development: Reindeer Husbandry in Transbaykalia. Ph.D. dissertation, Department of Geography, University of California, Berkeley.

Forsyth, James
1989   The Indigenous Peoples of Siberia in the Twentieth Century. In The Development of Siberia. Alan Wood, ed. Pp. 72–95. New York: St. Martin's.
1991   The Siberian Native Peoples before and after the Russian Conquest. In The History of Siberia: From Russian Conquest to Revolution. Alan Wood, ed. Pp. 69–91. London: Routledge.
1992   A History of the Peoples of Siberia: Russia's North Asian Colony, 1581–1990. Cambridge: Cambridge University Press.

Fraerman, Ruvin Isaevich
1958   Vas'ka Giliak. In Izbrannoe. Moscow: Sovetskii Pisatel'.

Freed, Stanley A., et al.
1988   Capitalist Philanthropy and Russian Revolutionaries: The Jesup North Pacific Expedition (1897–1902). American Anthropologist 90: 7–24.

French, R. A., and James Bater, eds.
1983   Studies in Russian Historical Geography, 2 vols. London: Academic Press.

Freud, Sigmund
1989   Civilization and Its Discontents. New York: Norton.

Fries, Hans J.
1974   A Siberian Journey, 1774–1776. London: Frank Cass.

Gagen-Torn, Nina Ivanovna
1975   Lev Iakovlevich Shternberg. Moscow: Nauka.

Gellner, Ernest
1976   The Soviet and the Savage. Current Anthropology 16 (4): 595–616.
1988   State and Society in Soviet Thought. London: Basil Blackwell.

Gellner, Ernest, ed.
1980   Soviet and Western Anthropology. New York: Cambridge University Press.

Gemuev, Izmail Nukhovich, and Andrei Markovich Sagalaev
1987   Traditsionnye verovaniia i byt narodov Sibiri XIX-nachal XX v. Novosibirsk: Nauka.

Gladyshev, A. I., ed.
1986   Administrativno-territorial'noe delenie Sakhalinskoi Oblasti. Iuzhno-Sakhalinsk: Dal'nevostochnoe knizhnoe izdatel'stvo.

Gleason, Abbott
1980   Young Russia: The Genesis of Russian Radicalism in the 1860s. New York: Viking.

Gleason, Abbott, et al., eds.
1985   Bolshevik Culture: Experiment and Order in the Russian Revolution. Bloomington: Indiana University Press.

Goldberg-Gurevich, Tamara Serafimovna
1981   Obshchee i osobennoe v dukhovnoi zhizni malykh narodov razvitogo sotsialisticheskogo obshchestva (Yamal/Nentsy) [unpublished manuscript in Lenin Library, Moscow].

Gontmakher, Petr Iakovlevich
1973   O natsional'nom svoeobrazii narodnogo iskusstva nivkhov. *In* Istoriia i kul'tura narodov Dal'nego Vostoka. Pp. 281–289. Iuzhno-Sakhalinsk: Akademiia Nauk.
1974a Istoriia kul'tury nivkhov. [Dissertation, Vladivostok State University, held in Institut Nauchnykh Informatsii po Obshchestvennym Naukam (INION), Moscow.]
1974b Istoriografiia narodnogo dekorativno-prikladnogo iskusstva nivkhov. *In* Voprosy istorii i kul'tury narodov Dal'nego Vostoka. Issue 2 [book series]. Pp. 139–152. Vladivostok: Akademiia Nauk.
1974c Narodnye istoki zhivopisi nivkhskogo khudozhnika S. Gurka. *In* Materialy po istorii Dal'nego Vostoka. Pp. 288–294. Vladivostok: Akademiia Nauk.
1978   Khudozhestvennaia obrabotka metalla u nivkhov. *In* Kul'tura narodov Dal'nego Vostoka SSSR [XIX–XX vv.]. Pp. 71–74. Vladivostok: Akademiia Nauk.

1981   K probleme khudozhestvennogo stilia v dekorativnom iskusstve nivkhov. *In* Etnografiia i fol'klor narodov Dal'nego Vostoka. Pp. 93–96. Vladivostok: Akademiia Nauk.

1988   Zolotye niti na rybei kozhe (Nivkhi). Khabarovsk.

Gor, Gennadi Samoilovich
1949   Sakhalin. Moscow: V pomoshch'shkol'niku.
1968   Bol'shie pikhtovye lesa. Leningrad: Sovetskii pisatel'.

Goriushkin, Leonid Mikhailovich
1988   Politicheskaia ssylka i revoliutsionnoe dvizhenie v Rossii, konets XIX—nachalo XX v.: Sbornik nauchnykh trudov. Novosibirsk: Nauka.
1989   Istochniki po istorii osvoeniia Sibiri v period kapitalizma: Sbornik nauchnykh trudov. Novosibirsk: Nauka.

Goskomstat SSSR
1990   Raspredelenie naseleniia po natsional'nosti, rodnomu iazyku i vtoromu iazyku narodov SSSR po Sakhalinskoi Oblasti. Vol. 1. Iuzhno-Sakhalinsk: Izdatel'stvo Sakhalinskogo Oblispolkoma.

Great Britain Foreign Office
1920   Sakhalin. London: Her Majesty's Stationery Office.

Great Soviet Encyclopedia
1973   New York: Macmillan.

Gribov, Iu.
1972   U nivkhov. *In* Druzhbe naviki verny: Dokumental'noe khudozhestvennoe sobranie. Pp. 104–107. Magadan: Magadanskoe knizhnoe izdatel'stvo.

Gurvich, Il'ia Samoilovich
1966   Etnicheskaia istoriia severo-vostoka Sibiri. Moscow: Nauka.
1970   Osushchestvlenie leninskoi natsional'noi politiki u narodov Krainego Severa SSSR. Sovetskaia Etnografiia 1: 15–34.
1977   Etnokul'turnoe sblizhenie narodov SSSR. Sovetskaia Etnografiia 5: 23–35.
1980   Polveka avtonomii narodnostei Severa SSSR. Sovetskaia Etnografiia 6: 13–17.
1982   Osobennosti sovremennogo etapa etnokul'turnogo razvitiia narodov Sovetskogo Soiuza. Sovetskaia Etnografiia 6: 15–27.

Gurvich, Il'ia Samoilovich, ed.
1971   Osushchestvlenie leninskoi natsional'noi politiki u narodov Krainego Severa. Moscow: Nauka.
1974   Sotsial'naia organizatsiia i kul'tura narodov Severa. Moskva: Nauka.
1979   "Nekotorye voprosy istoriografii natsional'nogo razvitiia narodov Krainego Severa v sovetskii period. *In* Osnovnye napravleniia izucheniia natsional'nykh otnoshenii v SSSR. Pp. 277–302. Moscow: Nauka.
1980   Etnogenez narodov Severa. Moscow: Nauka.
1982   Etnicheskaia istoriia narodov Severa. Moscow: Nauka.
1987   Etnicheskoe razvitie narodnostei Severa v sovetskii period. Moscow: Nauka.

Gurvich, Il'ia Samoilovich, and Boris Osipovich Dolgikh, eds.
1970   Preobrazovaniia v khoziaistve i kul'ture i etnicheskie protsessy u narodov Severa. Moscow: Nauka.

Gurvich, Il'ia Samoilovich, and Chuner Mikhailovich Taksami
1985   Sotsial'nye funktsii iazykov narodnostei Severa i Dal'nego Vostoka SSSR v sovetskii period. Sovetskaia Etnografiia 2: 54–63.
1987   Vklad sovetskikh etnografov v osushchestvlenie leninskoi natsional'noi politiki na Severe. In Leninizm i problemy etnografii. Iulian Vladimirovich Bromlei, ed. Pp. 181–197. Leningrad: Nauka.

Gushchin, Nikolai Iakovlevich
1987   Kritika burzhuaznykh kontseptsii istorii sovetskoi Sibirskoi derevni. Novosibirsk: Nauka.

Handler, Richard
1988   Nationalism and the Politics of Culture in Quebec. Madison: University of Wisconsin Press.

Harrison, John A., trans.
1955   Kita Yezo Zusetsu or a Description of the Island of Northern Yezo by Mamiya Rinsō. Proceedings of the American Philosophical Society 99 (2): 93–117.

Hawes, Charles H.
1904   In the Uttermost East. London: Harper.

Hiroshi, Kimura
1989   The Soviet-Japanese Territorial Dispute. Harriman Institute Forum 2 (6).

Hobsbawm, Eric, and Terence Ranger, eds.
1983   The Invention of Tradition. New York: Cambridge University Press.

Howard, B. Douglas
1893   Life with Trans-Siberian Savages. London: Longmans, Green.

Howe, Jovan E.
1976   Pre-Agricultural Society in Soviet Theory and Method. Arctic Anthropology 13 (1): 84–115.

Humphrey, Caroline
1980   Theories of North Asian Shamanism. In Soviet and Western Anthropology. Ernest Gellner, ed. Pp. 243–254. New York: Cambridge University Press.
1983   The Karl Marx Collective: Economy, Society, and Religion in a Siberian Collective Farm. Cambridge: Cambridge University Press.
1984   Some Recent Developments in Ethnography in the USSR. Man 19: 310–320.
1986   Rural Society in the Soviet Union. In Understanding Soviet Society. Michael Sacks and Jerry Pankhurst, eds. Pp. 53–70. Boston: Unwin Hyman.
1989   "Janus-faced signs"—the political language of a Soviet minority before Glasnost'. In Social Anthropology and the Politics of Language. Ralph Grillo, ed. Pp. 145–175. New York: Routledge.
1991   "Icebergs," barter, and the mafia in provincial Russia. Anthropology Today 7 (2): 8–14.

Iadrintsev, Nikolai Mikhailovich
1891   Sibirskie inorodtsy, ikh byt i sovremennoe polozhenie. St. Petersburg: N. M. Sibiriakov.

1892   Sibir' kak koloniia v geograficheskom, etnograficheskom, i istori-cheskom otnosheniiakh. St. Petersburg: M. M. Stasiulevich.

International Committee for Political Prisoners
1925   Letters from Russian (Soviet) Prisons. New York: A & C Boni.

Ispolkom Sakhalinskoi Oblasti
1971   Sel'skie i poselkovye sovety Sakhalinskoi Oblasti v sovremennykh usloviiakh. Iuzhno-Sakhalinsk: Sakhoblispolkom.

Ivanov, P. N.
1966   Pervye meropriatiia partiinykh i sovetskikh organitsatsii Sibiri po likvidatsii ekonomicheskoi otstalosti nerusskikh narodov (1920–1925). *In* Sibir' v period stroitel'stva sotsializma i perekhod k kapitalizmu. Issue 6 [book series]. Novosibirsk: Nauka.

Ivanov, Sergei Vasil'evich, Maksim Grigor'evich Levin, and Anna Vasil'evna Smoliak
1956   Nivkhi. *In* Narody Sibiri. Maksim Grigor'evich Levin and Leonid Pavlovich Potapov, eds. Moscow-Leningrad: Akademiia Nauk.

Ivashchenko, Lev Iakovlevich
1985   Voprosy izucheniia narodov Dal'nego Vostoka SSSR v otechestvennoi i zarubezhnoi literature. Khabarovsk: Akademiia Nauk.

Jakobson, Roman
1957a   Notes on Gilyak. Studies presented to Yuen Rin Choo. Academia Sinica. Bulletin of the Institute of History and Philosophy 29 (pt. 1): 255–281.
1957b   Paleosiberian Peoples and Languages: A Bibliographic Guide. New Haven: Human Relations Area Files Press.

Janhunen, Juha
1989   Siberian Studies in Japan. Journal de la Société Finno-Ougrienne 82: 271–277.
1991   Ethnic Death and Survival in the Soviet North. Journal de la Société Finno-ougrienne 83: 111–122.

Jochelson, Waldemar
1928   The Gilyak. *In* Peoples of Asiatic Russia. Pp. 57–60. New York: AMNH.

Joyce, Walter
1989   Problems of the Cultural and Social Infrastructure of Siberia. Sibirica 4: 6–10.

Kalinin, P. M.
1937   Sovetskii Sakhalin. Sovetskii Sakhalin (10 September): 4.

Kantorovich, Vladimir Iakovlevich
1934   Sakhalinskie Ocherki. Iuzhno-Sakhalinsk: Biblioteka ekspeditsii i puteshestvii.

Kantor, E.
1935   Liudi i fakty: staroe i novoe. Sovetskii Sever 3–4: 189–193.

Karklins, Rasma
1986   Ethnic Relations in the USSR. Boston: Allen and Unwin.

Kataev, Valentin Petrovich
1933   Time, Forward! Translated by Charles Malamuth. New York: Farrar and Rinehart.

Kennan, George
1871   Tent life in Siberia, and adventures among the Koryaks and other tribes in Kamchatka and Northern Asia. London: Low and Marston.
1981   Siberia and the Exile System. New York: Century.
Kertulla, Anna
1991   The Chukchi Reindeer Herders of Sireniki: Social and Cultural Change among Native People under Soviet Ideology. [Series: One Man's Heritage Project of the Shared Beringian Heritage Program: Ethnohistory.] U. S. National Parks Service.
Khazanovich, Amaliia M.
1939   Krasnyi chum v Khatangskoi tundre. Leningrad: Glavsevmorput'.
Kiesner, W. F.
1990   The Sakhalin Island Experiment. International Economy 4: 54–6.
Kirby, Stuart
1971   The Soviet Far East. New York: St. Martin's.
Kirkwood, Michael
1990   Language Planning in the Soviet Union. London: Macmillan.
Kleshchenok, Ivan Pavlovich
1968   Narody Severa: Leninskaia natsional'naia politika v deistvii. Moscow: Vyshaia shkola.
Kniazev, N. I., ed.
1959   Pobeda sovetskoi vlasti na Severnom Sakhaline (1917–1925 gg.). Iuzhno-Sakhalinsk: Sakhalinskoe knizhnoe izdatel'stvo.
Kolesnikov, N. I., ed.
1967   Sotsialisticheskoe stroitel'stvo na Sakhaline (1925–1945 gg.). Iuzhno-Sakhalinsk: Dal'nevostochnoe knizhnoe izdatel'stvo.
Kolosovskii, Aleksei, and Iu. Denisova
1987   Lekarstvennye rasteniia rybnovskikh nivkhov [brochure]. Okha: Okhinskaia tipografiia.
Komarov, Boris (pseudonym)
1980   Will Siberia be a wasteland? New Scientist (13 November): 444–446.
Komsomol'skii, G. V., ed.
1967   Atlas sakhalinskoi oblasti. Iuzhno-Sakhalinsk: Akademiia Nauk.
Kosarev, Valerii Dmitrievich
1989   Etnicheskie aspekty traditsionnogo prirodopol'zovaniia narodov Sakhalina. Leningrad.
Kostanov, Aleksandr
1989   Istoriia bez belykh piaten'. Iuzhno-Sakhalinsk: Ispolkom sakhalinskogo oblastnogo soveta narodnykh deputatov.
1991   Osvoenie Sakhalina russkimi liudmi. Iuzhno-Sakhalinsk: Dal'nevostochnoe knizhnoe izdatel'stvo.
Kou, Bok Zi
1989   Sakhalinskie koreitsy: problemy i perspektivy. Iuzhno-Sakhalinsk: SOKM.
Kozlov, Viktor Ivanovich
1982   Natsional'nosti SSSR. Moscow: Finansy i Statistika.
1988   The Peoples of the Soviet Union. London: Hutchison.

Kozyreva, Rimma Vasil'evna
1967 Drevnii Sakhalin. Leningrad: Nauka.
Krasnov, A.
1894 Na Sakhaline [iz vospominanii puteshestvennika po vostoku Azii]. Istoricheskii Sbornik 55: 383–410, 713–737.
Kreindler, Isabelle
1962 The Changing Status of Russian in the Soviet Union. International Journal of the Sociology of Language 33: 5–135.
Kreinovich, Erukhim Abramovich
1928 Rasselenie tuzemnogo naseleniia v sovetskoi chasti strany. Dal'nevostochnoe Statisticheskoe Obozrenie 12 (51): 1–9.
1929 Ocherk kosmogenicheskikh predstavlenii giliakov. Etnografiia 7 (1): 78–102.
1930a Rozhdenie i smert' cheloveka po vozzreniam giliakov. Etnografiia 9 (1–2): 89–113.
1930b Sobakovodstvo u nivkhov i ego otrazhenie v religioznoi ideologii. Etnografiia 12 (4): 29–54.
1932a Giliatskie chislitel'nye. Trudy Instituta Narodov Severa 1 (3): 1–26.
1932b Cuz Dif [Novoe Slovo] Nachal'naia uchebnaia kniga. Leningrad: Gosudarstvennoe uchebno-pedagogicheskoe izdatel'stvo.
1934a Morskoi promysel giliakov derevni Kul'. Sovetskaia Etnografiia 5: 78–96.
1934b Nivkhskii iazyk. Institut Narodov Severa, Trudy po lingvistike 3 (3): 181–222.
1934c Kolkhoznye zametki. Sovetskii Sever 3–4: 184–188.
1935a Okhota na belugu giliakov derevni Puir. Sovetskaia Etnografiia 2: 108–115.
1935b Kniga dlia chteniia. Moscow-Leningrad.
1936 Perezhitki rodovoi sobstvennosti i gruppovogo braka u giliakov. Trudy Instituta Antropologii, Arkheologii i Etnografii 4: 711–754.
1937 Fonetika nivkhskogo (giliakskogo) iazyka. Institut Narodov Severa, Trudy po lingvistike 5.
1955 Giliaksko-tunguso-manchurskie iazykovye paralleli. AN SSSR, Institut Iazykoznaniia, Doklady i Soobshcheniia 8: 135–167.
1973a Nivkhgu. Zagadochnye obitateli Sakhalina i Amura. Moscow: Nauka.
1973b O perezhitkakh gruppovogo braka u nivkhov. In Strany i narody Vostoka. Issue 15 [book series]. Moscow.
1974 Medvezhii prazdnik u nivkhov. In Drevniaia Sibir'. Pp. 339–348. Novosibirsk.
1977 La fête de l'ours chez les Nivkh. Ethnographie 74–75: 195–208.
1980 O shmidtovskom dialekte nivkhskogo iazyka. In Diakhroniia i Tipologiia Iazykov. Moscow: Akademiia Nauk.
1982 O kul'te medvedia u nivkhov. In Strany i Narody Vostoka 24: 244–283. Moscow.
1987 Etnograficheskie nabliudeniia u nivkhov, 1927–1928 gg. In Strany i Narody Vostoka 25: 107–123. Moscow.

Kristof, Ladis
1968 The Russian Image of Russia. *In* Essays in Political Geography. Charles Fisher, ed. London: Methuen.

Kruglov, A.
1933 O revoliutsionnoi zakonnosti na mestakh. Sovetskii Sever 1: 97–102.

Krupnik, Igor, and Anna Vasil'evna Smoliak
1982 Sovremennoe polozhenie korennogo naseleniia Severa Sakhalinskoi Oblasti [Dokladnaia zapiska, po materialam poezdki s sentiabria 1982 g.]. Moscow: Institute of Ethnography.

Krushanov, Andrei Ivanovich
1981 Opyt nekapitalisticheskogo puti malykh narodov Severa. Vladivostok: Akademiia Nauk.

Krushanov, Andrei Ivanovich, ed.
1989 Stranitsy istorii rybnoi promyshlennosti Sakhalinskoi Oblasti (1925–1987 gg.). Iuzhno-Sakhalinsk: Dal'nevostochnoe knizhnoe izdatel'stvo.

Kukutin, V. E.
1985 Kraevedy vedut poisk. Iuzhno-Sakhalinsk: Dal'nevostochnoe knizhnoe izdatel'stvo.

Kuoljok, Kerstin Eidlitz
1985 The Revolution in the North: Soviet Ethnography and Nationality Policy. Stockholm: Almqvist and Wiksell.

Kuzakov, Kuz'ma Grigor'evich
1973 Ozhivshaia tundra. Sotsializm i sud'by narodov Severa Dal'nego Vostoka. Vladivostok.
1978 Kul'tura narodov Dal'nego Vostoka SSSR. Moscow.
1981 Sotsializm i sud'by malykh narodov. Magadan: Magadanskoe knizhnoe izdatel'stvo.

Kuzin, A. T., ed.
1982 Sotsialisticheskoe stroitel'stvo na Sakhaline i Kuril'skikh Ostrovakh (1946–1975 gg.). Iuzhno-Sakhalinsk: Dal'nevostochnoe knizhnoe izdatel'stvo.

Kvanskaia, I. I.
1979 Kul'turnoe stroitel'stvo v Sibiri, 1917–1941. Novosibirsk: Zapadno-Sibirskoe knizhnoe izdatel'stvo.

Kwon, Heonik
1993 Maps and Actions: Nomadic and Sedentary Space in a Siberian Reindeer Farm. Ph.D. dissertation, Department of Social Anthropology, University of Cambridge.

Labbé, Paul
1903 Ostrov Sakhalin: putevye vpechatleniia [Translated from the French]. Moscow: M. V. Kliukin.

Lantzeff, George
1943 Siberia in the Seventeenth Century: A Study of the Colonial Administration. Berkeley: University of California Press.

Lapidus, Gail
1984 Ethnonationalism and Political Stability: The Soviet Case. World Politics 36 (4): 355–380.

Latyshev, Vladimir Mikhailovich, and Mikhail Mikhailovich Prokof'ev
  1988   Katalog etnograficheskikh kollektsii B. O. Pil'sudskogo v Sakhalinskom
  Oblastnom Kraevedcheskom Muzee. Iuzhno-Sakhalinsk: Upravlenie Kul'tury
  Sakhoblispolkoma.

Lavrov, Igor Petrovich
  1949   Ob izobrazitel'nom isskustve nivkhov i ainov. Kratkie Soobshcheniia
  Instituta Etnografii 5: 32–39.

Lawton, Lancelot
  1912   Empires of the Far East: A Study of Japan and the Colonial Possessions
  of China and Manchuria and of the Political Questions of East Asia and the
  Pacific, 2 vols. Boston: Small, Maynard.

Lebedev, G.
  1920   Vymiraiushchie brat'ia. Zhizn' Natsional'nostei 19: 76.

Lemke, M.
  1904   Nikolai Mikhailovich Iadrintsev. Biograficheskii ocherk. St. Petersburg:
  Gerol'd.

Leonov, Nikolai Ivanovich
  1929   Tuzemnye sovety v taige i tundrakh. In Sovetskii Sever. Pervyi sbornik
  statei. Moscow: Komitet Severa.
  1930   Kul'tbaza v taige. Prosveshchenie Natsional'nostei 9–10: 86–91.

Leonov, Pavel Artemovich
  1974   Oblast' na ostrovakh. Iuzhno-Sakhalinsk.
  1975   Ocherk istorii Sakhalinskoi organizatsii KPSS. Iuzhno-Sakhalinsk.

Leont'ev, Vladilen Viacheslavovich
  1973   Khoziaistvo i kul'tura narodov Chukotki 1958–70 gg. Novosibirsk:
  Nauka.

Leshkevich, Viacheslav V.
  1947   Sakhalin. Khabarovsk: OGIZ.

Levin, Maksim Grigor'evich, and Leonid Pavlovich Potapov
  1964   The Peoples of Siberia. Chicago: University of Chicago Press.

Levi-Strauss, Claude
  1969   The Elementary Structures of Kinship. Boston: Beacon.

Lineton, Philip
  1978   Soviet Nationality Policy in North Western Siberia: A Historical Perspective. Development and Change 9: 87–102.

Losev, Aleksei
  1978   Pis'ma. Kontinent 16: 241–246.

Lutz, Catherine, and Jane L. Collins
  1993   Reading National Geographic. Chicago: University of Chicago Press.

L'vov, A. K.
  1926   Kul'turnye bazy na Severe. Sovetskaia Aziia 3: 28–36.

Maack, Richard Karlovich
  1859   Puteshestvie na Amur. St. Petersburg: S. F. Solov'ev.

Majewicz, Alfred E.
  1992   Collected Works of Bronislaw Pil'sudskii. Vol. 1: The Aborigines of
  Sakhalin. Compiled and translated, with an introduction, by Alfred Majewicz.

Steszew, Poland: International Institute of Ethnolinguistic and Oriental
Studies.

Markov, Il'ia
1933   Kul'tpokhod v deistvii. Sovetskii Sever 4: 88–91.

Martin, Robert P.
1981   Siberia: Land of Riches but a Soviet Headache. U.S. News and World
Report (30 March): 68–69.

McConkey, James
1971   A Journey to Sakhalin. New York: Coward, McCann, and Geohagen.
1986   To a Distant Island. New York: Dutton.

McGill, Peter
1989   Dreams of a Soviet Paradise at the Ends of the World. The Observer (3
September).

Miakinenkov, Valerii Mikhailovich, ed.
1977   Problemy rasseleniia v raionakh Severa. Leningrad.

Miller, Frank J.
1990   Folklore for Stalin. Armonk, N.Y.: M. E. Sharpe.

Miroliubov [Iuvachev], Ivan Pavlovich
1901   Vosem' let na Sakhaline. St. Petersburg: A. N. Suvorin.

Mishchenko, V. I.
1955   Perekhod sakhalinskikh nivkhov ot patriarkhal'nogo uklada k sotsializmu. [Dissertation, Economics, held in INION, Moscow.]

Mitsulia, M. S.
1873   Ocherk ostrova Sakhalina. St. Petersburg.

Nazariants, T. M.
1971   K kharakteristike prosvetitel'skikh vzgliadov N. M. Iadrintseva (60-e-
nachala 70-kh godov XIX v.). In Voprosy russkoi i sovetskoi literatury Sibiri.
Novosibirsk: Nauka.

Nerhood, Harry W.
1968   To Russia and Return, An Annotated Bibliography of Travelers' English-language Accounts of Russia from the Ninth Century to the Present.
Columbus: Ohio State University Press.

Nevel'skoi, Gennadi I.
1878   Podvigi russkikh morskikh ofitserov na Krainem Vostoke Rossii, 1849–
1855. St. Petersburg: Russkaia Skoropechat'.

Nielsen, Paul
1972   An Appraisal of the Importance of the National Languages among the
North Siberian Peoples. Folk 14–15: 205–253.

Nietzsche, Friedrich
1989   On the Genealogy of Morals. New York: Vintage.

Nikitin, Nikolai Ivanovich
1987   Sibirskaia epopeia XVII veka (nachalo osvoeniia Sibiri russkimi
liud'mi). Moscow: Nauka.

Nikolaev, P.
1934   Natsional'nye shkoly na Sakhaline. Prosveshchenie Natsional'nostei 4:
43–46.

Norton, Henry K.
1982 (1923) The Far Eastern Republic of Siberia. Westport, Connecticut: Hyperion.

Nove, Alec
1993 The Soviet System in Retrospect: An Obituary Notice. New York: Harriman Institute.

Novembergskii, Nikolai Iakovlevich
1903 Ostrov Sakhalin. St. Petersburg: Dom Prizreniia Maloletnykh Bednykh.

Okladnikov, Aleksei Pavlovich
1956 Istoriia Sibiri. Leningrad: Nauka.

Omel'chuk, Anatolii
1981 Institut narodov Severa. Dal'nii Vostok 2: 127–132.

Orlova, E. P.
1964 Nozhi giliakov, amulety giliakov. *In* Arkheologiia i etnografiia Dal'nego Vostoka 1: 215–222, 223–240. Novosibirsk.
1971 Religioznye perezhitki u nivkhov sokhranivshiesia v obriadakh pogrebeniia [po materialism ekspeditsii 1955–1957 gg.]. *In* Etnografiia narodov SSSR. Pp. 146–152. Leningrad.

Osipova, L.
1933 Ogon'ki sovetskoi kul'tury na Severe. Sovetskii Sever 2: 77–79.

Otaina, Galina Aleksandrovna
1971 O nazvaniiakh tsveta v nivkhskom iazyke. Trudy Instituta Istorii, Arkheologii i Etnografii Dal'nego Vostoka 8: 106–109. Vladivostok.
1977 Nivkhskie toponimy; Lichnye imena nivkhov. *In* Filologiia narodov Dal'nego Vostoka [Onomastika]. Pp. 67–75, 86–93. Vladivostok: Akademiia Nauk.
1979 Sovremennost' i izmeneniia v soznanii nivkhov. *In* XIV Tikhookeanskii Nauchnyi Kongress—Sotsial'nye i Gumanitarnye Nauki 2: 29–31. Khabarovsk.
1981 Nivkhskie narodnye pesni. *In* Etnografiia i fol'klor narodov Dal'nego Vostoka. Nadezhda Konstantinovna Starkova, ed. Pp. 110–123. Vladivostok: Akademiia Nauk.
1978 Kachestvennye glagoly v nivkhskom iazyke. Moscow: Nauka.
1983a Otrazhenie etnokul'turnykh protsessov v nivkhskom iazyke. *In* Traditsii i sovremennost' v kul'ture narodov Dal'nego Vostoka. Pp. 53–56. Vladivostok: Akademiia Nauk.
1983b Fol'klornye motivy v romane V. Sangi "Zhenit'ba Kevongov." *In* Vzaimodeistvie literatur narodov Sibiri i Dal'nego Vostoka. Pp. 252–256. Novosibirsk: Nauka.
1984 Otrazhenie mifologicheskikh i religioznykh predstavlenii v nivkhskom iazyke. *In* Kul'tura narodov Dal'nego Vostoka: traditsii i sovremennost'. Pp. 157–164. Vladivostok: Akademiia Nauk.
1985 Istoriia sobraniia i izucheniia nivkhskogo fol'klora. *In* Voprosy izucheniia narodov Dal'nego Vostoka SSSR v otechestvennoi i zarubezhnoi literature. Pp. 110–119. Khabarovsk: Akademiia Nauk.

Pallas, Peter Simon
1794 Voyages du Pallas dans plusiers provinces de l'empire de Russe. Vol. 5. Translated by C. Gautheir de la Peyronie. Paris: Maradan. [Original: Reise durch Verschiedene Provinzen des Russischen Reichs in den Jahren 1768–1773, Vol. 2, St. Petersburg, 1773.]
Panfilov, Vladimir Zinov'evich
1973 Nivkhsko-altaiskie iazykovye sviazi. Voprosy Iazykoznaniia 5: 3–12.
1976 Kategorii myshleniia i iazyka, stanovlenie i razvitie kategorii kachestva. Voprosy Iazykoznaniia 6: 3–18.
Panov, A. A.
1905 Sakhalin kak koloniia. Moscow: I. D. Sykin.
Pashkov, Aleksandr Mikhailovich
1975 Stranitsy geroicheskoi letopisi. Iuzhno-Sakhalinsk.
Pashkov, Aleksandr Mikhailovich, and Galina Ivanovna Dudarets
1989 Ob"ekt No. 506. Sakhalinskii Neftianik (23 December): 6.
Payne, Robert
1967 Introduction. In The Island: A Journey to Sakhalin. Translated by Luba and Michael Terpak. Pp. xi–xxxvii. New York: Washington Square Press.
Pechenkin, Mikhail Dmitrievich
1987 Leninskii plan issledovaniia i osvoeniia Severa. In Problemy sovremennogo sotsial'nogo razvitiia narodnostei Severa. V. I. Boiko, ed. Pp. 16–28. Novosibirsk: Nauka.
Pereira, Norman
1988 The "Democratic Counterrevolution" of 1918 in Siberia. Nationalities Papers 16 (1): 71–94.
Pestkovskii, S.
1919 Natsional'naia kul'tura. Zhizn' Natsional'nostei 21: 29.
Petri, Berngard Eduardovich
1928 Proekt kul'tbazy dlia malykh narodov Sibiri. In Pervyi Sibirskii kraevoi nauchno-issledovatel'skii s"ezd. Vol. 4. Pp. 118–127. Tomsk: Krasnoe Znanie.
Pika, Aleksandr Ivanovich
1989 Malye narody Severa: iz pervobytnogo kommunizma v real'nyi sotsializm. In Perestroika, Glasnost', Demokratiia, Sotsializm: v chelovecheskom izmerenii. Moscow: Progress.
Pika, Aleksandr Ivanovich, and Boris Borisovich Prokhorov
1988 Bol'shie problemy malykh narodov. Kommunist 16: 76–83.
Pikul', Valentin S.
1989 Katorga. Vladivostok: Dal'nevostochnoe knizhnoe izdatel'stvo.
Pil'sudskii, Bronislaw
1905 Pis'mo komandirovannogo na O. Sakhalin B. O. Pil'sudskogo (na imia sekretaria Komiteta) IRKISVA 5: 24–30.
1907(1898) Nuzhdi i potrebnosti sakhalinskikh giliakov. Zapiski izucheniia amurskogo kraiia IV (IV): 1–38. Vladivostok. [First published in ZPOIRGO (20 April 1898) 4 (4): 1–38.]
1909a Aborigeny Ostrova Sakhalina. Zhivaia Starina 2–3: 3–16.

1909b L'accouchement, la grossesse et l'avortement chez les indigènes de l'île Sakhaline. Bulletins et Mémoires de la Société d'Anthropologie de Paris 10: 692–699.

1910 Rody, beremennost', vykidyshi, bliznetsy, urody, bezplodie i plodovitost' u tuzemtsev ostrova Sakhalina. Zhivaia Starina 73–74.

1913 The Gilyaks and Their Songs. Folk-lore 34: 477–490.

1964 The Aborigines of Sakhalin. Human Relations Area Files 10: 1–16. Translated by A. Holborn.

1989 (1904) Iz poezdki k orokam ostrova Sakhalina v 1904 g. Iuzhno-Sakhalinsk: Akademiia Nauk.

1990 (1911) Poeziia giliakov. Kraevedcheskii Biulleten' 1: 76–111. Translated from Polish by V. M. Drakunov.

Polevoi, Boris Petrovich
1959 Pervootkryvateli Sakhalina. Iuzhno-Sakhalinsk: Dal'nevostochnoe knizhnoe izdatel'stvo.

Poliakov, I. S.
1883 Puteshestvie na Ostrov Sakhalin v 1881–1882. St. Petersburg: A. S. Suvorin.

Pomeroy, William J.
1983a Affirmative action: a case study of Soviet Siberia. New World Review 51: 20–24.

1983b The Siberian Epic. New World Review 51: 8–11.

Popkin, Cathy
1992 Chekhov as Ethnographer: Epistemological Crisis on Sakhalin Island. Slavic Review 51 (1): 36–51.

Popov, V. L.
1929 Istoricheskaia piatiletka Severnoi Azii. Sovetskaia Aziia 4: 5–24.

Potapov, Leonid Pavlovich
1955 O natsional'noi konsolidatsii narodov Sibiri. Voprosy Istorii 10.

Potapov, Leonid Pavlovich, and Sergei Vasil'evich Ivanov, eds.
1971 Religioznye predstavleniia i obriady narodov Sibiri v 19–20 veka. Leningrad: Nauka.

Prokhorov, A. M., ed.
1973 Luks, K. Ia. In Great Soviet Encyclopedia 15: 175. New York: Macmillan.

Prokhorov, Boris Borisovich, Aleksandr Ivanovich Pika, et al.
1992 Metodicheskie osnovy kontseptsii gosudarstvennoi politiki optimizatsii uslovii zhiznedeiatel'nosti malochislennykh narodov Severa. Moscow: Institut Problem Zaniatosti AN RF i Mintruda RF.

Prokopenko, V. I.
1988a Ispol'zovanie nivkhskikh igr v rezhime shkol'nogo dnia. Sverdlovsk: Ministerstvo Prosveshcheniia.

1988b Igry i natsional'nye vidy sporta narodnostei severa-nivkhov. Moscow: Gosudarstvennyi komitet RSFSR po fizicheskoi kul'ture i sportu.

Pushkar', Arnol'd
1987 Ostrov sokrovishch. Moscow. Sovetskaia Rossiia.

Pystina, L. I.

1987 Obshchestvennye organizatsii nauchno-tekhnicheskoi intelligentsii Sibiri, 20–30-e gg. Novosibirsk: Nauka.

Raeff, Marc

1956 Siberia and the Reforms of 1822. Seattle: University of Washington Press.

Rakowska-Harmstone, Teresa

1986 Minority Nationalism Today: An Overview. *In* The Last Empire: Nationality and the Soviet Future. Robert Conquest, ed. Pp. 235–264. Stanford: Hoover.

Ramos, Alcida

1994 From Eden to Limbo: The Construction of Indigenism in Brazil. *In* The Social Construction of the Past: Representation as Power. George Bond and Angela Gilliam, eds. New York: Routledge.

Rasputin, Valentin

1979 Live and Remember. New York: Macmillan.

1989 Siberia on Fire. DeKalb: Northern Illinois University Press.

Razgon, I. M.

1959 Pobeda sovetskoi vlasti na severnom sakhaline (1917–1925). Iuzhno-Sakhalinsk: Sakhalinskoe knizhnoe izdatel'stvo.

Resnick, Abraham

1983 Siberia and the Soviet Far East: Endless Frontiers. Moscow: Novosti.

Riasanovsky, Nicholas

1972 Asia through Russian Eyes. *In* Russia and Asia. Wayne C. Vucinich, ed. Stanford: Hoover.

Rinsi-Fai [Rinsifee, of Sendai]

1832 San kokf, Tsou Ran, To Sets (Apercu general des trois royaumes). Translated into French from Japanese and Chinese by Jules Heinrich Klaproth. Paris: Oriental Translation Fund of Great Britain and Ireland.

Rinchenko, E. D.

1922 Inorodcheskii vopros v Sibiri. Zhizn' Natsional'nostei 9 (6): 104.

Roon, Tatiana Petrovna

1991 Odezhda nivkhov sakhalina v sobraniiakh Sakhalinskogo Oblastnogo Kraevedcheskogo Muzeia. Kraevedcheskii Biulleten' 4: 29–46.

Rosaldo, Renato

1980 Ilongot Headhunting, 1883–1974. Stanford: Stanford University Press.

Rusakova, Lidiia Mikhailovna

1987 Traditsionnye obriady i iskusstvo russkogo i korennykh narodov Sibiri. Novosibirsk: Nauka.

Rytkheu, Iurii Sergeevich

1988 The Shaping of Identity. Soviet Weekly (3 September).

Rywkin, Michael, ed.

1989 Russian Colonial Expansion to 1917. London and New York: Mansell.

Safronov, Fedor Grigor'evich

1977 Zapiski Genrikha Fika o iakutakh i tungusakh pervoi poloviny XVIII v. *In* Istochnikovedenie i arkheografiia Sibiri. Nikolai Nikolaevich Pokrovskii and Elena Konstantinovna Romodanovskaia, eds. Novosibirsk: Akademiia Nauk.

Sakhtaganov, S.
1990   Sakhlag. Germes (1–15 July): 1.
Sangi, Vladimir Mikhailovich
1967   Legendy Ykh-Mifa. Moscow: Sovetskaia Rossiia.
1969   Izgin. Moscow: Detskaia literatura.
1971   "Mudraia" nerpa. Moscow: Sovetskaia Rossiia.
1973   V tsarstve vladyk. Moscow: Sovremennik.
1975   Zhenit'ba Kevongov. Moscow: Sovetskii Pisatel'.
1981   U istoka: romany, povesti, rasskazy. Moscow: Sovremennik.
1983   Izbrannoe. Leningrad: Khudozhestvennaia literatura.
1985a   Puteshchestvie v stoibishche Lunvo. Moscow: Sovremennik.
1985b   Mesiats runnogo khoda: romany, povesti, rasskazy, skazki. Moscow:
Sovetskii Pisatel'.
1988a   Otchuzhdenie. Sovetskaia Rossiia (11 September).
1988b   Bez Umileniia. Literaturnaia Gazeta (1 April).
1989a   Pesn' o nivkhakh. Moscow: Sovremennik.
1989b   Shtoby krona ne ogolilas'. Literaturnaia Gazeta (15 February):
1, 7.
1989c   Polozhenie o gosudarstvenno-kooperativnoi agrofirme "Aborigen
Sakhalina" [Unpubished bulletin].
1989d   Protokol konferentsii "Aborigen Sakhalina" Nogliki (4 October
1989) [unpublished bulletin].
Sangi, Vladimir Mikhailovich, ed.
1983   Vtoroe rozhdenie. Moscow: Sovremennik.
1985   Legendy i mify Severa. Moscow: Sovremennik.
1986   A Stride across a Thousand Years: Works by Writers of the Soviet North
and Far East. Moscow: Progress.
1987   Spolokhi: sbornik stikhotvorenii i poem poetov narodnostei Severa i
Dal'nego Vostoka. Moscow: Sovremennik.
1989   Antologiia fol'klora narodnostei Sibiri, Severa i Dal'nego Vostoka.
Krasnoiarsk: Krasnoiarskoe knizhnoe izdatel'stvo.
Sangi, Vladimir Mikhailovich, and Galina Aleksandrovna Otaina
1981   Nivkhskii iazyk. Uchebnik i kniga dlia chteniia dlia pervogo klassa
(sakhalinskii dialekt). Leningrad: Prosveshchenie.
Sansone, Vito
1980   Siberia—Epic of the Century. Moscow: Progress.
Sanzhiev, G. L.
1980   Perekhod narodov Sibiri k sotsializmu minuia kapitalizm. Novosibirsk:
Nauka.
Sarkisyanz, E.
1954   Russian Attitudes toward Asia. Russian Review 13 (4): 245–254.
Savel'eva, Karina
1989   Narody Severa: problemy i resheniia. [Interview with Vladimir Sangi.]
Okhota 8: 28–31.
Savel'eva, Valentina Nikolaevna, and Chuner Mikhailovich Taksami
1965   Russko-nivkhskii slovar'. Moscow: Sovetskaia Entsiklopediia.
1970   Nivkhsko-russkii slovar'. Moscow: Sovetskaia Entsiklopediia.

Schindler, Debra L.
1991   Theory, Policy, and the Narody Severa. Anthropological Quarterly 64 (2): 68–79.
Seed, Patricia
1993   Poststructuralism in Postcolonial History. Maryland Historian 24 (1): 9–28.
Segal, Gerald
1990   The Soviet Union and the Pacific. Boston: Unwin Hyman.
Semenov, Iu. N.
1963   Siberia: Its Conquest and Development. Translated from the German by J. R. Foster. London: Hollis and Carter.
Senchenko, Ivan Andreevich
1957   Ocherki istorii Sakhalina (vtoraia polovina XIX v. do nachala XX v.).
1961   Issledovateli Sakhalina i Kurilskikh ostrovov.
1963   Revoliutsionery Rossii na Sakhalinskoi katorge. Iuzhno-Sakhalinsk: Sakhalinskoe knizhnoe izdatel'stvo.
1974   Adres Podviga-Dal'nii Vostok-Zovut kraia dalekii. Khabarovsk.
Sergeeva, K.
1935   V Ureliksom natssovete. Sovetskii Sever 1: 95–101.
Sergeev, Mikhail A.
1934a   Desiat' let raboty komiteta Severa. Sovetskoe Stroitel'stvo 7.
1934b   Rekonstruktsia byta narodov Severa. Revoliutsiia i Natsional'nosti 3: 90–95.
1955   Nekapitalisticheskii put' razvitiia malykh narodov Severa. Moscow-Leningrad: Academy of Sciences USSR.
Sesiunina, Marina Georgievna
1974   G. N. Potanin i N. M. Iadrintsev—ideologi sibirskogo oblastnichestva: k voprosu o klassovoi sushchnosti sibirskogo oblastnichestva vtoroi poloviny XIX v. Tomsk: Izdatel'stvo Tomskogo Universiteta.
Shanin, Teodor
1986   Soviet Theories of Ethnicity: The Case of a Missing Term. New Left Review 158: 113–122.
Sharov, Valerii
1988   Mala li zemlia dlia malykh narodov? Novoe Russkoe Slovo (11 October): 9.
1990   Posledniaia gran'. [Interview with E. A. Gaer.] Trezvost' i Kul'tura 3: 4–10.
Shifrin, A.
1980   The First Guidebook to Prisons and Concentration Camps of the Soviet Union. Uhldingen-Seewis (Suisse).
Shinkarev, L.
1990   Land should regain its genuine owners. [Interview with Vladimir Sangi.] International Work Group for Indigenous Affairs (IWGIA) Newsletter (December).
Shmakov, V. S., ed.
1989   Narody sibiri na sovremennom etape. Natsional'nye i regional'nye osobennosti razvitiia. Novosibirsk: Nauka.

Shternberg, Lev Iakovlevich
1893 Sakhalinskie Giliaki. Etnograficheskoe Obozrenie 17 (2): 1–46.
1896 Puteshestvie na krainyi Sever Ostrova Sakhalina. Sakhalinskii Kalendar'. Pp.16–52.
1900 Obraztsy materialov po izucheniiu giliakskogo iazyka i fol'klora. Imperatorskaia Akademiia Nauk. Izvestiia 13 (4): 387–434.
1904 Giliaki. Etnograficheskoe Obozrenie 1: 1–42; 2: 19–55; 4: 66–119.
1908 Materialy po izucheniiu giliakskogo iazyka i fol'klora, sobrannye i obrabotannye.
1910 Inorodtsy. In Formy natsional'nogo dvizheniia v sovremennykh gosudarstvakh. A. P. Kastelianskii, ed. St. Petersburg: Obshchestvennaia Pol'za.
1933a Giliaki, orochi, gol'dy, negidal'tsy, ainy. Khabarovsk: Dal'nevostochnoe knizhnoe izdatel'stvo.
1933b Sem'ia i rod u narodov Severo-Vostochnoi Azii. Leningrad: Institut Narodov Severa.
n.d. The Social Organization of the Gilyak [unpublished translation manuscript]. Archives of the Department of Anthropology, AMNH.
Shtromas, Alexander
1987 Dissent, Nationalism, and the Soviet Future. Studies in Comparative Communism 20: 280.
Shubina, Ol'ga Alekseevna
1990 Sovremennoe sostoianie arkheologicheskoi izuchennosti sakhalina i zadachi sakhalinskoi arkheologii. Kraevedcheskii Biulleten' 4: 106–119.
1992 K voprosu o drevnem naselenii Ostrova Sakhalina [unpublished manuscript]. SOKM.
Shubin, Valerii Orionovich
1985 Etnograficheskoe issledovanie Sakhalinskogo Oblastnogo Kraevedcheskogo Muzeia. Iuzhno-Sakhalinsk: Sakhalinskoe knizhnoe izdatel'stvo.
Shuling, T. S.
1989 Russkie issledovateli kul'tury i byta malykh narodov Amura i Sakhalina (konets 19–nachala 20 v.). Vladivostok.
Sis'kogo, Alla Viktorovna
1983 Zhanry traditsionnogo fol'klora sakhalinskikh nivkhov na sovremennom etape. In Traditsii i sovremennost' v kul'ture narodov Dal'nego Vostoka. Pp.117–124. Vladivostok: Akademiia Nauk.
Skachko, Anatolii Evgen'evich
1930 Problemy Severa. Sovetskii Sever 1: 15–37.
1934 Desiat' let Komiteta Severa. Sovetskii Sever 2: 9–21.
Skachkov, I.
1934 Ob antireligioznoi rabote na Severe. Revoliutsiia i Natsional'nosti 7: 50–54.
Skorik, P. Ia.
1932 Kul'turnyi shturm taigi i tundry. Prosveshchenie Natsional'nostei 10: 32–39.
Sletov, Petr Vladimirovich
1933 Na Sakhaline-Ocherki.

Slezkine, Yuri

1989   Russia's Small Peoples: The Policies and Attitudes toward the Native Northerners, 17th c.–1938. Ph. D. dissertation, Department of History, University of Texas at Austin.

1991   The Fall of Soviet Ethnography, 1928–1938. Current Anthropology 32 (4):476–484.

1992   The Soviet Far North: 1928–1938. Slavic Review 51 (1): 52–76.

1993   Savage Christians or Unorthodox Russians? The Missionary Dilemma in Siberia. *In* Between Heaven and Hell: The Myth of Siberia in Russian Culture. Galya Diment and Yuri Slezkine, eds. Pp. 15–32. New York: St. Martin's.

1994   Arctic Mirrors: Russia and the Small Peoples of the North. Ithaca: Cornell University Press.

Slobodskii, M.

1925   Literatura po etnografii Sibiri v etnologichesko-geograficheskikh izdaniiakh, 1901–1917 gg. Irkutsk: Vostochno-Sibirskoe Otdelenie Russkogo Geograficheskogo Obshchestva.

Smidovich, P. G.

1930   Sovetizatsiia Severa. Sovetskii Sever 1: 5–14.

Smoliak, Anna Vasil'evna

1953   Ekspeditsiia G. I. Nevel'skogo i pervye russkie etnograficheskie issledovaniia v Priamur'e, Primor'e i na Sakhaline. Sovetskaia Etnografiia 3.

1960   Zametki po etnografii nivkhov Amurskogo Limana. Trudy Instituta Etnografii 56: 92–147.

1963   O nekotorykh etnicheskikh protsessakh u narodov Nizhnego i Srednego Amura. Sovetskaia Etnografiia 3.

1967   O sovremennom etnicheskom razvitii narodov Nizhnego Amura i Sakhalina. Sovetskaia Etnografiia 3: 95–103.

1970   Sotsial'naia organizatsiia narodov Nizhnego Amura i Sakhalina (novye materialy o nivkhakh). *In* Obshchestvennyi stroi narodov Severnoi Sibiri. Moscow.

1971   Osnovnye puti razvitiia ekonomiki, kul'tury i byta za gody Sovetskoi vlasti u narodov basseina nizhnego Amura i Sakhalina. *In* Osushchestvlenie leninskoi natsional'noi politiki u narodov Krainego Severa. Il'ia Samoilovich Gurvich, ed. Pp. 314–341. Moscow: Akademiia Nauk.

1974   Rodovoi sostav nivkhov v XIX–nachale XX v. *In* Sotsial'naia organizatsiia i kul'tura narodov Severa. Pp. 176–217. Moscow: Akademiia Nauk.

1975a   [Review of Kreinovich 1973a.] Sovetskaia Etnografiia 2: 171–173.

1975b   Etnicheskie protsessy u narodov Nizhnego Amura i Sakhalina. Moscow: Nauka.

1977   [Review of Taksami 1975.] Sovetskaia Etnografiia 6: 130–134.

1978   O starinnykh promyslakh materinovikh nivkhov. *In* Polevye issledovaniia Instituta Etnografii za 1976 g. Moscow.

1979a   Rodovoi sostav nivkhov v XIX–nachala XXv. Moscow.

1979b   O vzaimnykh kul'turnykh vliianiiakh narodov Sakhalina. *In* Etnogenez i etnicheskaia istoriia narodov Severa. Il'ia Samoilovich Gurvich, ed. Moscow: Akademiia Nauk.

1982   Narody nizhnego Amura i Sakhalina. *In* Etnicheskaia istoriia narodov Severa. Il'ia Samoilovich Gurvich, ed. Moscow: Akademiia Nauk.

1992   Spisok osnovnykh trudov. Etnograficheskoe Obozrenie 3.

Sokolova, Zoia Petrovna
1990   Narody Severa SSSR: Proshloe, nastoiashchee i budushchee. Sovetskaia Etnografiia 6: 17–32.

Solov'ev, Nikolai Ivanovich
1990   Presentation to the Congress of Northern Peoples, Moscow [unpublished manuscript]. March.

Spasskii, Grigorii
1825   Aziatskii Vestnik. St. Petersburg: Meditsinskii Departament Ministerstva Vnutrennikh Del.

Ssorin-Chaikov, Nikolai
1991   Istoriia and Ulo: A Critique of Sociological Reasoning with a Siberian Evenk Epistemology. M.A. thesis, Department of Anthropology, Stanford University.

Stajner, Karlos
1988   Seven Thousand Days in Siberia. New York: Farrar Strauss Giroux.

Starkova, Nadezhda Konstantinovna
1984   Kul'tura narodov Dal'nego Vostoka: Traditsii i sovremennost'. Vladivostok: Akademiia Nauk.

Starkova, Nadezhda Konstantinovna, ed.
1983   Traditsii i sovremennost' v kul'ture narodov Dal'nego Vostoka. Vladivostok: Dal'nevostochnoe knizhnoe izdatel'stvo.

Starr, S. Frederick
1985   Red and Hot: The Fate of Jazz in the Soviet Union. New York: Limelight.

Stephan, John J.
1971   Sakhalin: A History. Oxford: Clarendon.
1990   Far Eastern Conspiracies: Russian Separatism on the Pacific. Australian Slavonic and Eastern European Studies 4(1/2): 135–152.
1992   "Cleansing" the Soviet Far East, 1937–1938. Acta Slavica Iaponica 10: 43–64.

Stephan, John J., and V. P. Chichkanov, eds.
1986   Soviet-American Horizons on the Pacific. Honolulu: University of Hawaii Press.

St. George, George
1969   Siberia: The New Frontier. New York: David McKay.

Stites, Richard
1989   Revolutionary Dreams: Utopian Vision and Experimental Life in the Russian Revolution. New York: Oxford University Press.

Strathern, Marilyn
1988   The Gender of the Gift. Berkeley: University of California Press.

Svatikov, Sergei Grigor'evich
1929   Rossiia i Sibir' (K istorii sibirskogo oblastnichestva v XIX v.). Pp. 40–53. Prague: Izdatel'stvo obshchestva sibiriakov v ChSR.

Swearingen, Rodger, ed.
1987   Siberia and the Soviet Far East. Stanford: Hoover.
Taksami, Chuner Mikhailovich
1959a   Vozrozhdenie nivkhskoi narodnosti. Iuzhno-Sakhalinsk: Sakhalinskoe knizhnoe izdatel'stvo.
1959b   Zhilye i khoziaistvennye postroiki nivkhov Amura i Amurskogo limana. Avtoreferat. Leningrad.
1960a   Sovremennaia kul'tura i byt narodov Severa. In Doklady i soobshcheniia nauchnoi konferentsii po istorii Sibiri i Dal'nego Vostoka: Sektsii istorii i etnografii sovetskogo perioda. Pp. 104–105. Tomsk.
1960b   Sovremennye nivkhskie seleniia i zhilishcha. Sovetskaia Etnografiia 1: 23–37.
1961   Seleniia, zhil'e i khoziastvennye postroiki nivkhov Amura i zapadnogo poberezh'ia Ostrova Sakhalina. In Trudy Instituta Etnografii 64: 98–166.
1964   Dar nivkhov Muzeiu antropologii i etnografii. In Sbornik Muzeiia antropologii i etnografii 22: 191–199. Moscow: Institut Etnografii.
1967a   Nivkhi (Sovremennoe khoziaistvo, kul'tura i byt). Leningrad: Nauka.
1967b   Ustanovlenie sovetskoi vlasti i organizatsii sovetov sredi nivkhov. In Velikii oktiabr' i malye narody Severa. Leningrad: Institut im. Gertsena.
1969a   Geograficheskie predstavleniia nivkhov i ikh ispol'zovanie russkimi issledovateliami Sakhalina i nizov'ev Amura. Izvestiia Vladisvostokskogo Geograficheskogo Obshchestva 101 (1): 41–48.
1969b   Nekotorye voprosy fol'klora i iskusstva nivkhov [Iz istorii sobraniia i izucheniia fol'klora]. In Uchenye Zapiski 383: 138–151. Leningrad: Institut im. Gertsena.
1969c   Pervobytnye otnosheniia i religioznye verovaniia u nivkhov. Strany i Narody Vostoka 8: 53–69.
1970   Odezhda nivkhov. In Odezhda narodov Sibiri. Leningrad: Akademiia Nauk.
1971   K voprosu o kul'te predkov i kul'te prirody u nivkhov. In Muzei Antropologii i Etnografii, Trudy 21: 201–210. Moscow.
1972   Nivkhi. Voprosy Istorii 10: 212–217.
1974   Problemy istorii nivkhskogo etnosa i ego kul'tury. In Kratkoe soderzhanie dokladov godichnoi nauchnoi sessii Instituta Etnografii AN SSSR (23–26 July 1974): 85–88. Leningrad.
1975   Osnovnye problemy etnografii i istorii Nivkhov. Leningrad: Nauka.
1976   Predstavleniia o prirode i cheloveke u nivkhov. In Priroda i chelovek v religioznykh predstavleniiakh narodov Sibiri i Severa. Pp. 203–216. Leningrad: Nauka.
1977a   Nivkhi. Problemy khoziaistva, obshchestvennogo stroiia i etnicheskoi istorii. Doktorskoi avtoreferat. Moscow.
1977b   Sistema kul'tov u nivkhov. Sbornik Muzeiia Antropologii i Etnografii 33: 90–116.
1978a   Problèmes de l'ethnogenèse des Nivkhes. Inter-Nord 15: 65–78.
1978b   Dve sud'by narodov ostrovnoi zemli [O nivkhakh i ainakh Sakhalina i nizhnego Amura]. In Dva Mira—Dve Sud'by. Pp. 65–72. Magadan: Magadanskoe knizhnoe izdatel'stvo.

1979   Vliianie khristianstva na traditsionnye verovaniia nivkhov. *In* Khristianstvo i lamaizm u korennogo naseleniia Sibiri. I. S. Vdovin, ed. Pp. 115–126. Leningrad: Nauka.
1980   Problemy etnogeneza nivkhov. *In* Etnogenez narodov Severa. Il'ia Samoilovich Gurvich, ed. Pp. 196–211. Moscow: Nauka.
1981a   Shamanstvo u nivkhov. *In* Problemy istorii (po materialam vtoroi poloviny XIX-nachala XX v.). Pp. 165–177. Leningrad: Nauka.
1981b   Nivkhi. *In* Rasy i Narody. Vol. 2. Moscow: Institut Etnografii.
1982   K vershinam znanii [o razvitii kul'tury i prosveshcheniia u nivkhov za gody Sovetskoi vlasti]. *In* Porodilis' na Amure: Ocherki. Pp. 145–159. Khabarovsk.
1984   Nivkhskoe pis'mo. *In* Sakhalinskii Literaturno-Khudozhestvennyi Sbornik. Pp. 178–187. Iuzhno-Sakhalinsk: Dal'nevostochnoe knizhnoe izdatel'stvo.
1987   Sootnosheniia traditsionnogo i novogo v kul'ture narodnostei Severa. *In* Problemy sovremennogo sotsial'nogo razvitiia narodnostei Severa. V. I. Boiko, ed. Novosibirsk: Nauka.
1989   Liudi u kromki zemli. Pravda (3 March): 3.
Taracouzio, T. A.
1938   Soviets in the Arctic. New York: Macmillan.
Tarasov, I. A.
1967   KPSS. Organizator sotsialisticheskogo preobrazovaniia khoziaistva malykh narodnostei Severa. Yakutsk.
Taussig, Michael
1980   The Devil and Commodity Fetishism. Chapel Hill: University of North Carolina Press.
Teplinskii, Mark
1990   A. P. Chekhov na Sakhaline. Iuzhno-Sakhalinsk: Dal'nevostochnoe knizhnoe izdatel'stvo.
Terekov, Evgenii
1981   Eshche ne razgadannyi ostrov. Iuzhno-Sakhalinsk: Dal'nevostochnoe knizhnoe izdatel'stvo.
Terletskii, Petr Evgen'evich
1935   Kul'tbazy Komiteta Severa. Sovetskii Sever 1: 36–47.
Terzani, Tiziano
1989   Perestroika am Ende der Welt. Der Spiegel 39: 182–197.
Tikhmenev, Petr Aleksandrovich
1863   Istoricheskoe obozrenie obrazovaniia rossiisko-amerikanskoi kompanii i deistvii ee do nastoishchego vremeni. Vol. 2. St. Petersburg: Eduard Veimar.
Tikhmirov, N. E.
1953   Greipfrut na Severnom Sakhaline. Priroda 42: 119.
Troitskaia, N. A.
1991   Russkaia burzhuaziia na Ostrove Sakhalin, materialy k biografiiam. Kraevedcheskii Biulleten' 1: 10.
Trotsky, Lev
1973   The Problems of Everyday Life. New York: Monad.

Tsilin, Aleksandr Pavlovich
 1962 Stepka-Sakhalinets (Povest'). Iuzhno-Sakhalinsk.
 1967 Znamia sovetov na Sakhaline (Istoricheskii ocherk). Iuzhno-Sakhalinsk: Dal'nevostochnoe knizhnoe izdatel'stvo.
 1974 Znamia sovetov na ostrovnom krae. Iuzhno-Sakhalinsk: Dal'nevostochnoe knizhnoe izdatel'stvo.
Tuganov, Petr
 1928 Giliaki sakhalinskoi taigi. Tikhookeanskaia Zvezda (28 April): 3.
Ustiugov, Petr Konstantinovich
 1931 Zadachi natsional'noi raboty na Krainem Severe. Revoliutsiia i Natsional'nosti 1: 40–49.
Uvachan, Vasilii Nikolaevich
 1958 Perekhod k sotsializmu malykh narodov Severa (po materialam Evenkiiskogo i Taimyrskogo natsional'nykh okrugov). Moscow: Politicheskaia Literatura.
 1963 Leninskaia natsional'naia politika i malye narody Severa. Sovetskaia Etnografiia 3.
 1975 The Peoples of the North and Their Road to Socialism. Moscow: Progress.
 1984 Gody, ravnye vekam (stroitel'stvo sotsializma na Krainem Severa). Moscow: Mysl'.
Uvarov, Petr Konstantinovich
 1905 Tipy i nravy Sakhalina. Moscow: D. P. Efimov.
Van Stone, James
 1985 An ethnographic collection [North Sakhalin Island]. In Fieldiana (1361). New York: AMNH.
Vasil'ev, V. I., et al., eds.
 1967 Novaia zhizn' narodov Severa. Moscow: Nauka.
Vazhdaev, Viktor
 1934 Po stoibishchiam naroda Nibakh. Moscow: Molodaiia Gvardiia.
Vdovin, I. S.
 1976 Priroda i chelovek v religioznykh predstavleniiakh narodov Sibiri i Severa. Leningrad: Akademiia Nauk.
Vdovin, I. S., ed.
 1981 Problemy istorii obshchestvennogo soznaniia aborigenov Sibiri. Leningrad: Nauka.
Vegman, V.
 1923 Oblastnicheskie illiuzii, rasseiannye revoliutsiei. Sibirskie Ogni 3: 89–116
Verdery, Katherine
 1988 Ethnicity as Culture: Some Soviet-American Contrasts. Canadian Review of Studies in Nationalism 15 (2): 107–110.
Vinokurov, I., and F. Florich
 1950 Po Iuzhnomu Sakhalinu (detskaia literatura). Iuzhno-Sakhalinsk.
Vitebsky, Piers
 1989 The Reindeer Herders of Northern Yakutia. Polar Record 25, no. 154: 213–218.

1990   Centralized Decentralization: The Ethnography of Remote Reindeer Herders under Perestroika. Cahiers du Monde Russe et Sovietique 31 (2–3): 345–356.

Vladimirov, Andrei
1992   Rodovye khoziaistva: vozvrashchenie k istokam. Svobodnyi Sakhalin (9 July): 7.

Von Schrenk, Leopold
1855   Voyages [Lettres de M. Léopold Schrenk a l'Académicien Middendorf (Lu le 13 avril 1855)]. *In* Bulletin de la Classe Physico-Mathematique de l'Academie Imperiale des Sciences de St.-Petersbourg 14: 40–46, 184–192, 217–222 [in German]. Leipzig: L. Voss.
1883   Ob inorodtsakh Amurskago kraiia. Vol. 1. St. Petersburg: Izdanie Imperatorskoi Akademii Nauk.
1899   Ob inorodtsakh Amurskago kraiia. Vol. 2. St. Petersburg: Izdanie Imperatorskoi Akademii Nauk.
1903   Ob inorodtsakh Amurskago kraiia. Vol. 3. St. Petersburg: Izdanie Imperatorskoi Akademii Nauk.

Vysokov, Mikhail Stanislavovich
1985   Sovremennaia iazykovaia situatsiia v raionakh prozhivaniia sakhalinskikh nivkhov. *In* Etnograficheskie issledovaniia Sakhalinskogo Oblastnogo Kraevedcheskogo Muzeiia. Valerii O. Shubin, ed. Iuzhno-Sakhalinsk: SOKM.

Wasson, Valentina P., and R. Gordon
1957   Mushrooms, Russia, and History. New York: Pantheon.

Wasson, R. Gordon
1971   Soma: Divine Mushroom of Immortality. New York: Harcourt Brace Jovanovich.

Wasson, R. Gordon, et al.
1986   Persephone's Quest: Entheogens and the Origins of Religion. New Haven: Yale University Press.

Watrous, Stephen Digby
1970   Russia's "Land of the Future": Regionalism and the Awakening of Siberia, 1819–1894. Ph.D. dissertation, Department of History, University of Washington.

Weinberg, Robert
1993   Purges and Politics in the Periphery: Birobidzhan in 1937. Slavic Review 52 (1): 13–127.

Weiser, Adele
1989   Die Völker Nordsibieriens: Unter Sowjetischef Herrschaft von 1917 bis 1936. Munich: Klaus Renner.

Williams, Brackette
1989   A Class Act: Anthropology and the Race to Nation across Ethnic Terrain. Annual Review of Anthropology 18: 401–444.

Wixman, Ronald
1988   The Peoples of the USSR, an Ethnographic Handbook. Armonk, N.Y.: M. E. Sharpe.

Wood, Alan
1989   Crime and Punishment in the House of the Dead. *In* Civil Rights in

Imperial Russia. Olga Crisp and Linda Edmondson, eds. Pp. 215–233. Oxford: Clarendon.

1990   Siberian Exile in the Eighteenth Century. Siberica 1 (1): 38–63.

Wood, Alan, ed.

1987   Siberia: Problems and Prospects for Regional Development. London: Croom Helm.

1991   The History of Siberia: From Russian Conquest to Revolution. London: Routledge.

Wood, Alan, and R. A. French

1987   Siberia: Problems and Prospects for Regional Development. London: Croon Helm.

1989   The Development of Siberia: People and Resources. London: Macmillan.

Yates, Frances

1984   The Art of Memory. London: Ark.

Zaslavsky, Victor, and Yuri Luryi

1979   The Passport System in the USSR and Changes in Soviet Society. Soviet Union/Union Sovietique, pt. 2: 137–153.

Zeitlin, Morris

1982   Urban Growth in Siberia. New World Review 50: 12–15.

Zeland, N.

1886   Izvestiia imperialisticheskogo obshchestva liubitelei estestvoznaniia, antropologii i etnografii 49 (3). Moscow.

1887   Protokoly antropologicheskogo otdela obshchestva liubitelei estestvoznaniia i etnografii. Kazan'.

Zenzinov, Vladimir

1931   The Road to Oblivion. New York: Robert McBride.

Zhulev, P. N.

1933   Kniga dlia chteniia. Chast' pervaia. Pervyi god obucheniia. Translated by E. A. Kreinovich. Moscow-Leningrad: Gosudarstvennoe uchebno-pedagogicheskoe izdatel'stvo.

Zibarev, Viktor Andreevich

1969   Sovetskoe stroitel'stvo u malykh narodnostei Severa. Tomsk: Tomskii Gosudarstvennyi Universitet.

1971   Ukazatel' gazetnykh statei. Tomsk: Tomskii Gosudarstvennyi Universitet.

Zolatarev, A. M.

1933a   K voprosu o genezise klassoobrazovaniia u giliakov. Za Industrializatsiiu Sovetskogo Vostoka 3.

1933b   O perezhitkakh rodovogo stroia u giliakov raiona Chome. Sovetskii Sever 2: 52–66.

Zuev, V. F.

1947   Materialy po etnografii Sibiri (1771–1772). In Trudy Instituta Etnografii im. N. N. Miklukho-Maklaia. Moscow-Leningrad: Akademiia Nauk.

Index

About the Author

BRUCE GRANT is Assistant Professor of Anthropology at Swarthmore College.

DATE DUE